World University Library

The World University Library is an international
series of books, each of which has been specially
commissioned. The authors are leading scientists
and scholars from all over the world who, in an age
of increasing specialisation, see the need for a
broad, up-to-date presentation of their subject.
The aim is to provide authoritative introductory
books for university students which will be of
interest also to the general reader.
The series is published in Britain, France, Germany,
Holland, Italy, Spain, Sweden and the United States.

Frontispiece Low-relief sculpture of a male figure, from Laussel. (Ht. 38 cm).

Peter J. Ucko

Andrée Rosenfeld

Palaeolithic Cave Art

World University Library

McGraw-Hill Book Company
New York   Toronto

© Peter J. Ucko and Andrée Rosenfeld 1967
Library of Congress Catalog Card Number: 66-16481
Phototypeset from computed copy by BAS Printers Limited,
Wallop, Hampshire, England
Printed by Officine Grafiche Arnoldo Mondadori, Verona, Italy

Contents

Addendum

Since this book went to press a re-analysis of the cave of Nancy has appeared (A. Roussot, C. Andrieux, A. Chauffriasse 1966. La Grotte Nancy, Commune de Sireuil (Dordogne), *l'Anthropologie*, 70) which confirms our suggestions:

p.114   that suitable rock surfaces often remain undecorated, for at Nancy engravings are confined to entrance and terminal regions.

p.198   that Leroi-Gourhan accepts associations between widely separated representations, for at Nancy he takes a horse to be associated with bison-ibex which are separated by 30m (even with the new identification of a horse, any such association is still separated by 3m).

p.52   that there is a close connection between engraving and low relief, for at Nancy Laming describes a sculpted horse, where Roussot sees an engraving.

Furthermore these authors point out that Laming's indentification of a bison at Nancy is wrong (as also Chaire à Calvin [D. de Sonne-ville-Bordes 1963, Étude de la frise sculptée de la Chaire à Calvin, *Annales de Paléontologie*, 49]).

Notes on the illustrations

The following drawings have been done specially for this book: figures 1, 2, 5, 6, 17, 26, 34, 42, 65, 67, 70, 71, 72, 77, 78, 79, 81, 86, 89 *overleaf right*, 90, 91, 92, 93, 104, 105, 106. For those of cave art (except the chart, figure 6, and the comparison of horses' heads, figure 72) the following conventions have been adopted: for engravings, white lines or stippled lines on brown or blue; for low-relief, black lines or stippled lines on brown or blue; for painting, coloured or black lines on white; for painting and engraving combined, black, coloured and white lines on brown.

Introduction

There are many books on Palaeolithic art. Most of those aimed at the non-specialist are picture books designed to attract the buyer as a souvenir to help recall the wonders which he has seen for himself in the caves accessible to the casual visitor. This book has an additional aim.

In the following pages the·intention is to show that the reasons why Stone Age hunters went to considerable lengths to decorate rock shelters and caves is in itself a fascinating problem. There is no reason why the tourist who has heard of Palaeolithic art should confine his interest to admiration for the vivacity with which some of the animals have been represented or to astonishment at the excellent state of preservation of colours in certain caves. His understanding will be deeper if he examines these Palaeolithic works while also speculating on their function. Since this book is intended for the university student, as well as for the specialist in prehistoric art, some readers may well wish to omit reading some sections of this book, particularly the detailed discussions in chapter 4. To facilitate selective reading, as many subheadings as possible have been used throughout and the main findings and problems are summarised in chapter 5. The views of early workers on prehistoric art are presented in their historical contexts (chapter 3). By doing this it is hoped to show how the approaches to Palaeolithic art have changed with changing attitudes to prehistoric archaeology and to 'primitive' peoples. With these changes, theories about the function of Palaeolithic art have had to be modified, culminating in the rejection by modern authors of the comparative approach of the classic workers, and their replacement by a more analytical method.

Many of the individual points brought forward by those who have sought to explain the phenomenon of Palaeolithic art are interesting and pertinent. The common denominator of nearly all the interpretations is the assumption that all Palaeolithic parietal (see below) art can be explained by one comprehensive hypothesis. Throughout, this assumption has been found unsatisfactory: there may as well be one hundred reasons why Palaeolithic men decorated caves. If the following pages do anything to bring together for the reader the positive suggestions put forward by many workers who have devoted much thought to the study and understanding of

7

Palaeolithic art, and at the same time persuade the reader that much is still left in doubt and obscurity, they will have fulfilled their purpose.

An historical perspective is essential for the understanding of the various interpretative hypotheses discussed (chapter 3), as are also the facts known about other, non-artistic, activities of the people who lived in Europe at this remote period (chapter 1). Interpretations of Palaeolithic art have often been based on the totemic practices of modern non-literate peoples in Australia. This, however, is a very narrow approach and it is a further range of artistic activities of modern non-literates from Australia and elsewhere which is, therefore, examined in this book (chapter 4).

In the space available it is impossible to deal adequately with all the kinds of artistic activity undertaken by Palaeolithic man; this book is devoted predominantly to Palaeolithic *parietal* art (art on walls) while Palaeolithic *mobile* art (art which is not fixed to any one place) is only occasionally referred to for comparative purposes. In practice the term 'parietal' art is extended to include all Palaeolithic works of art executed on permanent features: ceilings and floors, as well as the walls of rock shelters and caves. This term is also used to refer to art on large blocks of limestone placed around inhabited rock shelters. Although mobile art is the mainstay of much of the relative dating of Palaeolithic art this is not the primary concern of this book. For interpretation it is essential to consider the contexts of the various pieces of art. Parietal art is in the position intended by the Palaeolithic artists, whereas for mobile art this is not necessarily so. Interpretation of the functions of much Palaeolithic art, therefore, depends almost entirely on parietal and not mobile art.

Some of the Palaeolithic parietal art is truly great art. Despite the physical difficulties of access into many of the Palaeolithic caves, the considerable time wasted and annoyance incurred in gaining admission to some privately-owned ones, and repeated visits to the same caves, both authors remain greatly impressed with the superlative technical achievements of many of the artists and the artistic sensitivity of our remote Palaeolithic ancestors. In the following pages, silence about the artistic qualities of the Palaeolithic representations reflects the interpretative intention and bias of this book.

1 The Palaeolithic period

The Old Stone Age, or Palaeolithic period of man's history lasted for roughly one million years until the end of the Ice Age, about 10,000 years BC. The Lower Palaeolithic lasted for the greater part of the Ice Age while the Upper Palaeolithic only started during the last of four major periods of glaciation in the Ice Age or Pleistocene. The cultures, or sub-divisions, of the Palaeolithic recognised by archaeologists are based solely on the techniques of stone working employed and on the principal types and shapes of stone tools.

The Upper Palaeolithic

The Upper Palaeolithic is normally distinguished from the earlier periods of the Palaeolithic by the appearance of a new and distinctive technique of stone working, the use of bone to make tools, a greater specialisation of tools, and by the appearance of a new type of man, *Homo sapiens*[1]. The divisions of the Upper Palaeolithic are primarily defined by technological considerations. The Upper Palaeolithic began earlier in the Near East and eastern Europe than in western Europe, while in many parts of the world no Upper Palaeolithic stage existed at all. The distribution of the Upper Palaeolithic cultures was restricted to Europe, North Africa and Asia Minor. The problem of the origin of both Homo sapiens and of the Upper Palaeolithic cultures is still among the unsolved questions of Palaeolithic archaeology. Both are believed to have originated somewhere in the region of south west Asia[2], and from there to have spread principally westwards into Europe and North Africa. Elsewhere, throughout Asia and sub-Saharan Africa, the Lower Palaeolithic cultures continued to develop into various localised 'late Palaeolithic' cultures and, except for an isolated pocket in Kenya, apparently remained free from any influence from Upper Palaeolithic traditions.

The new distinctive technique of stoneworking in the Upper Palaeolithic was the manufacture of long narrow flakes with more or less parallel sides, 'blades', from which tools were fashioned (figure 1). The range of tool types made was greater and more varied than ever before. The most important new tool type found in the Upper Palaeolithic is the burin, or graver (figure 1b, h). Burins were

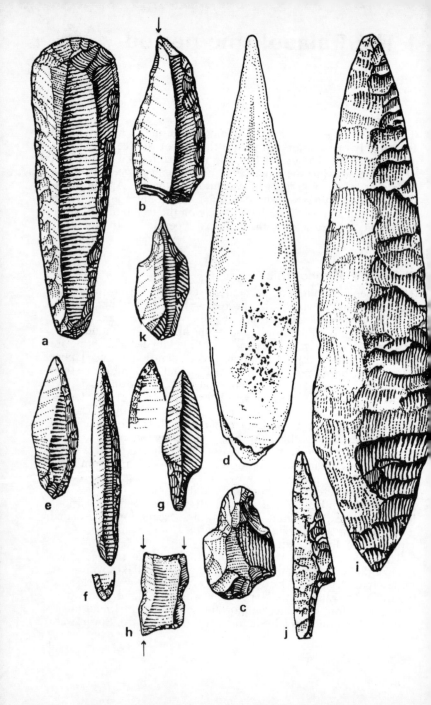

1 *Flint and bone implements:* **a** Aurignacian scraper on end of blade, from La Ferrassie, with characteristic retouch along both edges. **b** Aurignacian burin on a blade, from La Ferrassie. **c** Aurignacian scraper on a thick flake, from La Ferrassie. **d** Aurignacian lozenge-shaped bone point, from Isturitz. **e** Chatelperron point, from La Ferrassie, with the curved side blunted by abrupt retouch. **f** Gravette point, from Roque St Cristophe, with one of the straight sides blunted by abrupt retouch. **g** Font Robert point of the Late Perigordian from Le Fourneau du Diable, with base narrowed for hafting. **h** Noailles burin of the Late Perigordian, from Oreille d'Enfer, with notches to prevent the burin spall from extending the whole length of the blade. **i** Solutrean laurel leaf point, from Pech de la Boissière. **j** Solutrean shouldered point, from Pech de la Boissière. **k** Solutrean awl on a short blade, from Laugerie Haute.

also made on flakes before the Upper Palaeolithic, but they were never common. Another new flint tool type is the awl (figure 1k). Flints with narrow points may have been used to pierce skins which were then tied or sown into bags, clothing etc., and they were certainly used to drill holes in objects such as shell, pebbles, teeth and small bone carvings used as beads and pendants. The principal bone working tool, however, was the burin. Burins were made by removing narrow long flakes from the edges of a flint blade, to form a narrow but strong chisel edge across the thickness of the blade or flake. Burins are characteristic of Upper Palaeolithic tool assemblages, and both their numbers and variety increased with the exploitation of bone and antler as raw materials. This use of antler, bone and ivory for the manufacture of tools and other objects is also one of the major differences between the Lower and Upper Palaeolithic cultures. As in previous times it is not known to what extent wood and other organic materials were used since these materials are not preserved in the archaeological record.

Perhaps one of the most striking achievements of the Upper Palaeolithic people was their art. It has been claimed that the very regular geometric forms of some finely worked handaxes are evidence of an aesthetic sensibility already in the later stages of the Lower Palaeolithic[3], and there is little doubt that these objects were finished with more care and refinement than was necessary for purely functional purposes. However, it is only in the Upper Palaeolithic cultures of Europe that the arts of carving, engraving and painting are known to have developed. Besides rock painting, colorants, and particularly ochre, were used very extensively in some Palaeolithic sites, possibly for body paint and for use on perishable objects. Occasionally, as at Arcy sur Cure, objects such as flint tools have been found embedded in a kneaded lump of ochre.

During the Upper Palaeolithic, as in the earlier Mousterian period, people continued to bury their dead in shallow graves in caves or in their camps. The bodies were inhumed in pits and accompanied with grave goods and ochre. In several such burials, as at the cave of Grimaldi on the Mediterranean coast, skeletons were partially covered in small pierced shells and teeth, which had formed either necklaces or the decoration of leather skull caps and aprons worn as clothing.

Most of the early work on the Upper Palaeolithic period was carried out in France, and the first major divisions of this period were recognised in, and named after, French sites. The French terminology has subsequently been applied widely also outside France to other Upper Palaeolithic cultures which appear to be similar, and to fill the same stage of an evolutionary development which was believed to be universally applicable to man. This application of the French terminology outside France has greatly confused the picture of the Upper Palaeolithic in the rest of Europe. In the last two decades, however, several central European archaeologists[4] have contributed much to a re-examination of the Upper Palaeolithic in countries such as Yugoslavia, Hungary, Czechoslovakia, Poland and Germany. Farther east, in southern Russia, in Turkestan and in the Near East, several Upper Palaeolithic cultures flourished, which it was believed were the direct sources of the more westerly cultures. But, although the general spread of Upper Palaeolithic traditions does appear to have reached western Europe from the east, the relationship between the various cultures is probably less close than was previously thought. Despite their many features in common, adaptations to various habitats and climates, as well as the isolation of groups, has resulted in diversification of the minutiae of their material culture and economy.

The Abbé Breuil recognised[5] the three main stages of the French Upper Palaeolithic: Aurignacian, Solutrean and Magdalenian, and identified evolutionary substages in each of these: Early, Middle and Late Aurignacian, primarily on the basis of flint tools; a three stage development of the Solutrean on the basis of the development and refinement of beautifully flaked spear heads; and a six stage development of the Magdalenian based on the development of bone working, and particularly on the manufacture of increasingly elaborate bone or antler spear points and harpoon heads.

Breuil's subdivisions of the Solutrean and Magdalenian still form the basis of modern French Palaeolithic classification.

An alternative view of Breuil's Aurignacian sequence was first put forward by the French archaeologist D. Peyrony[6]. This scheme was adopted by Breuil and is still accepted by the majority of workers in France. Peyrony considered the Early and Late Aurignacian of Breuil to represent the developmental stages of a single culture, the Perigordian, which is more or less contemporary with, but distinct from, the Aurignacian in its strict sense (Breuil's Middle Aurignacian) and which only became widespread in its later phases when it largely replaced the Aurignacian[7].

The Perigordian (figure 1). The early Perigordian, or Chatelperronian, is known from comparatively few sites and is restricted in its distribution to south west France (west of the Rhone), north as far as the limestone regions of Vienne and Saone et Loire, and south as far as northern Spain. It is found directly above late Mousterian levels, and is succeeded by early Aurignacian (in its strict sense)[8] levels. Its chronological position between final Mousterian and early Aurignacian is therefore well established.

The early Perigordian is characterised by the Chatelperron point (figure 1e). Other blade tools which characterise it as an Upper Palaeolithic culture are burins and scrapers on the end of blades. Few bone tools are known. Many of the flint tools are made on flakes as in the preceding Mousterian cultures, and many tool types are in fact indistinguishable from a late and specialised type of Mousterian in France. In certain sites, as at Arcy sur Cure in the Yonne, it is possible to see a developmental sequence in stone tools from this late Mousterian to a true early Perigordian. In fact the Chatelperron point itself can be derived typologically from a broad knife blade with curved blunted back of the Mousterian, known as the Audi point. On typological grounds, therefore, the early Perigordian can be considered as a development of the Mousterian, possibly with some cultural influence from other Upper Palaeolithic groups.

The distribution of the late Perigordian is not much greater than that of the early phase, but sites are more numerous and richer in material. The late Perigordian is characterised by narrow, abruptly blunted 'Gravette blades' and other tools which show the same type of blunting, such as points in which the tip is shaped and thinned by inverse retouch (figure 1f).[9] A distinctive point was made with the base assymetrically narrowed for hafting by abrupt retouch (figure 1g). Some finely made Chatelperron points also occur. Scrapers are mostly simple end scrapers on broad blades or flakes and a variety of burins are made on blades or flakes. The bone industry of the late Perigordian is poor and does not include very characteristic forms. Bone was used for the manufacture of awls, punches, spatulate shaped implements and simple points, and teeth, shell etc. were pierced as beads or pendants for personal adornment. Lumps of ochre and of the white clay, kaolin, found in Perigordian levels attest the use of paints, and a few small figurines carved in soft rock such as calcite, can be dated to the late Perigordian, as are also bas-reliefs of male and female figures at Laussel (e.g. figure 3 and frontispiece).

At Laugerie Haute Peyrony found a Perigordian level which he considered to be a middle Perigordian. Since then the same assemblage of tools has been found at very few sites, but at the Abri Pataud it occurs in a distinct level *above* the late Perigordian levels. It is clear, therefore, that instead of being an intermediate stage this phase of the Perigordian is in fact a very late stage.

The intermediate stages between the Chatelperronian and the late Perigordian are therefore rather elusive. The indeterminate nature of the middle Perigordian has led some archaeologists to emphasise the similarities between the late Perigordian and the central European backed blade cultures[10], and to see in the French late Perigordian a new influx from the east, but with a distinctive local development. It is, at this stage, difficult to be certain of the cultural affinities of the French late Perigordian. Some diffusion of culture from eastern Europe cannot be ruled out, but the existence of the Chatelperron point in Late Perigordian assemblages, shows that the archaeological material does not reflect one sudden full scale invasion of people from the east.

The Aurignacian (figure 1). The Aurignacian differs from the Perigordian culture in the absence of abruptly backed blades, the greater importance and variety of scraper forms and the greater standardisation of burin forms. There is more emphasis on bone and antler for the manufacture of tools and weapons which also distinguishes the Aurignacian from the Perigordian. Aurignacian sites in France are both more frequent and often larger than in the Perigordian, suggesting that these people lived in bigger groups. The subdivisions of the Aurignacian sequence were first formulated by Peyrony for the four separate levels at the cave of La Ferrassie[11] and the late Aurignacian at Laugerie Haute[12] which he called Aurignacian v. Peyrony's subdivisions are still generally accepted as they form a convenient way of assessing the developmental stage of any new Aurignacian site. The divisions are, however, simply stages of what appears to be a continuous development, and they cannot necessarily be matched exactly in different sites. Some recently found sites which are earlier than the lowest level at la Ferrassie have been referred to as Aurignacian o.

In the early Aurignacian scrapers (figures 1a, 1c) are by far the most common tool type, and they are generally made on rather broad blades which were blunted by characteristic Aurignacian retouch which invades the upper surface of the blade. Notched and 'strangulated' blades (with a notch on each side) are characteristic. Many scrapers were also made on thick chunky flakes or on the cores of flint when these became too small to detach any more useful blades. Burins (figure 1b) occur regularly as do also knife blades which may or may not be retouched in characteristic Aurignacian manner.

Stages I and II are primarily distinguished by their characteristic bone spear points. The earlier ones are more or less conical in shape with a split base for hafting on a tapered shaft. In the second stage the hafting method is the same, but the points are very flat and lozenge shaped in outline (figure 1d). Other bone tools include awls, spatulae, pins and pendants cut out of flat bone (such as shoulder blades) and sometimes decorated with scratched design. Pierced teeth, shells, pebbles etc. were used as beads or ornamentation. In the Aurignacian ii-iv levels at La Ferrassie large limestone blocks were found which had been deeply engraved in broad lines with animal outlines and with representations frequently interpreted as sexual symbols (e.g. figure 34).

With the development of the Aurignacian comes the thickening

2 *Flint and bone implements* (*Magdalenian*): **a** Magdalenian
compound tool on a blade consisting of a burin at one end
and a scraper at the other, from La Madeleine. **b** Late
Magdalenian 'parrot-beak' burin with characteristic
'nibbled' retouch, from Les Eyzies. **c** Magdalenian pick,
from Abri Reverdit, used for rock carving. **d** Early Magdalenian

of the bone points which develop oval cross-sections, and finally in
Aurignacian IV assume biconical shapes. The flint tools remain
basically the same, but the characteristic Aurignacian retouch is
used less and less and the appearance of the tools becomes generally
finer. Steep scrapers remain characteristic of the culture. Flint awls
become more frequent and a characteristic stout burin is made with
a wide chisel edge formed by the intersection of several parallel
narrow burin facets and one broad facet. Among the objects of
mobile art small stone slabs have been found with animal paintings
and engravings on them.

Bone was used not only for the manufacture of points, pins etc.,
but also for a multitude of objects, sometimes decorated, the use of
which remains enigmatic. Very characteristic amongst these is the
so-called *bâton de commandement* generally made out of antler
and consisting essentially of a T-shaped piece with a circular hole
pierced at the T junction.

Several female figurines have been assigned to this culture, but
the actual circumstances of discovery of many of them are obscure
and their exact dates are unknown.

The Early Perigordian started during a period of comparatively
mild climate during the last glaciation. In early Perigordian levels,
at La Ferrassie, the kitchen debris contains many remains of
aurochs and also other woodland animals such as deer, but horse
and reindeer, which require more open country, were also hunted.
The main development of the Perigordian and Aurignacian cultures
takes place during a return of glacial conditions when, even in the
sheltered regions of south west France, most woodland disappeared
and was replaced by open shrubland. Farther north and east, in the
region between the Scandinavian ice sheets and the Alpine glaciers,
the climate was intensely cold and the vegetation was that of present day arctic tundra. In the Dordogne certain non-arctic steppe
animals survived, such as horse and bison. Reindeer were abundant
and the mammoth and woolly rhinoceros though not consistently
hunted, were certainly known and exploited when the opportunity
arose. At Arcy sur Cure, for instance, the remains of a small crude
hut structure were found consisting of upright posts of mammoth
tusks built at the entrance of the large cave mouth[13]. Smaller game
such as arctic hare and arctic fowl were also hunted. Ibex and

antler point, from Laugerie Haute. **e** Middle Magdalenian
antler harpoon with small barbs on one side only, from
La Madeleine. **f** Late Magdalenian antler harpoon
with strong barbs on both sides, from La Madeleine.
g Middle Magdalenian antler tool decorated with
a carved horse, from Bruniquel.

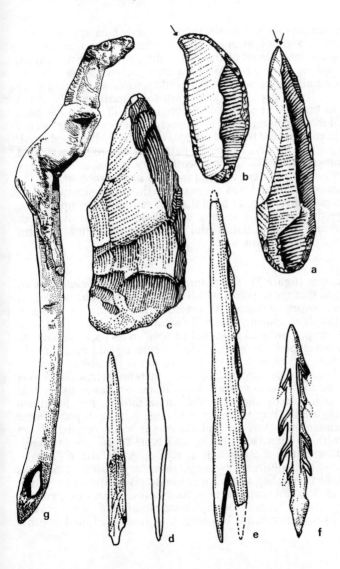

3 Female representation, from Laussel, with
one arm outstretched and legs broken off.
4 *Far right* Black painted bison, standing on
its hind legs, from El Castillo; the
shape of its back is indicated by a
natural stalagmite boss.

musk-ox remains are sometimes found, but musk-ox appears not to
have been as common as in the more northerly tundra regions.

During the later stages of the Perigordian some deer were again
hunted, and the climate became, for a time, somewhat less extreme.
At the open air site of Solutré, Perigordian tools were found in an
exceptional 'bone deposit' which consisted almost entirely of the
remains of horse[14]. The site is at the foot of a cliff, and it has been
suggested that the horses were driven across the gently rising slopes
to the cliff edge, where they fell off, and could be easily slaughtered.
The Perigordian hunters of Solutré have been said to be specialised
horse hunters. There is no evidence for any specialisation at any
other Perigordian site known, and it seems more probable that the
specialisation at Solutré was restricted to this site which would be
re-visited periodically, or at most that one particular group or tribe
of Perigordians adopted such a specialised form of livelihood.
Other cultures found at Solutré did not exploit the natural features
of the countryside in this way.

The Solutrean (figure 1). The Solutrean culture is characterised by
leaf-shaped flint spear points which are shaped by excellent flaking
over their entire surfaces. At several sites, including Laugerie
Haute, the development of the Solutrean may be clearly traced
from the simple unifacial point flaked only on its upper surface, to
the fully developed 'laurel leaf point' (figure 1i) and finally to the
delicate narrow 'willow leaf points'. The rest of the Solutrean stone
industry is not exceptional; indeed except in its final phases it appears
archaic. It contains numerous tools made on flakes as well as
various points retouched by the characteristic flat Solutrean
retouch (figure 1j). Burins are few, and bone working is poor. In the
late Solutrean, however, the flint industry is based very largely on
blades, with an increase in burins and bone tools, simple points,
awls and pins, and for the first time, needles. At the site of Parpallo
in Spain the late Solutrean levels contained very characteristic tools
and weapons including small barbed and tanged arrowheads, of a
type which does not reappear until the Neolithic. It is also from the
late Solutrean of Parpallo that evidence of painting and engraving
on pebbles is known, while bas-relief sculptures are found in other

late Solutrean sites (see chapter 2). Recent excavations in the Rhone valley suggest that the Solutrean may be a local development from rather archaic cultures which survived in this region.[15]

Most of the Solutrean period was one of intensely cold climatic conditions, and reindeer formed one of the main food sources at the site of Laugerie Haute. Horse, aurochs, ibex and other large animals of the late Pleistocene were hunted and in Spanish sites, where the climatic conditions were less severe, reindeer was absent. During the final stages of the Solutrean the climate became less severe, and habitations of this stage are generally smaller suggesting a higher mobility of smaller groups. The climatic improvement was of short duration, and it is during this stage that the Solutrean culture disappears and a different culture, the Magdalenian, appears in western Europe.

The Magdalenian (figure 2). The earliest phase of the Magdalenian culture existed during a short-lived mild phase, but the greater part of its development took place during the last major ice advance of the Pleistocene. This caused severe, cold and arid conditions with a more distinctly arctic flora and fauna than during previous glacial periods. Large mammals which required a certain amount of woodland, such as ox, pig or deer, became very scarce and reindeer appear to have roamed in large herds in most parts of western Europe, as well as mammoth, woolly rhinoceros, horse, ibex and also bison. The late Magdalenian phases saw a return to less severe conditions with a corresponding change in fauna, particularly the partial replacement of reindeer by deer, and an increase in animals such as bison, horse and ox, whereas the mammoth and woolly rhinoceros decreased in numbers.

This last of the Ice Age cultures, the Magdalenian, is known from a great number of sites in France, Spain, western Germany and probably as far east as Poland. Cave sites are very numerous, but recent discoveries have included a few open air camps, both in northern France and in the Dordogne. In these open air sites the Magdalenians built shelters of light construction held down by large stones and probably used them as summer camps; however, studies of the reindeer remains in caves has shown[16] that caves were inhabited all the year round and were not just winter camps. The occurrence of reindeer all the year round also suggests that these animals were not as distinctly migratory during the Late Palaeolithic in western Europe as their modern North American counterparts, the caribou.

The most characteristic feature of Magdalenian culture is the extensive use of antler and bone for a variety of tools, weapons and other objects, and the quality of their artistic achievements in these materials (figure 2g).

The early Magdalenian is less widespread than later phases of the Magdalenian and is best known from south west France. It has been subdivided into three stages by Breuil on the basis of bone tools, and a similar division can be recognised from statistical analyses of the stone tools.[17]

A variety of bone points were made with bevelled base (figure 2d), often striated, some with single bevel in the earlier phases, and double rectangular bevel by Magdalenian III. Some points are long and pointed, others quite short and stout. From Magdalenian II come points which were sometimes grooved, and it has been suggested that this was for the attachment of poison. Other bone and antler tools include pins, needles, spatulate objects, punches, semicylindrical rods (often decorated), simple *bâtons de commandement*, pendants and beads. Bone objects only become really abundant in Magdalenian III.

The stone tools include the usual Upper Palaeolithic tool types (figure 2a) but in the early phases many tools were also made on thin flakes. There is a higher percentage of burins than scrapers, contrary to the previous Aurignacian and Perigordian practice. The retouch is abrupt and frequently very fine and delicate and is sometimes known as 'nibbled' retouch (figure 2b). Small thin round scrapers are characteristic of Magdalenian I, and a distinct tendency to manufacture small geometric tools, rectangles and triangles is characteristic in Magdalenian II. This latter tendency returns in the final stages of the Magdalenian. The technique of manufacturing long parallel-sided blades was then perfected and many of the burins, scrapers and knives, particularly in the later stages of the Magdalenian, are made on very elegant flint blades.

A variety of bone points were made with bevelled base (figure 2d), such as limestone, schist or slate are found, and these pebbles frequently contain innumerable superimposed drawings, some apparently unfinished. It is difficult or even impossible to disentangle all the lines, but some of these engravings are extremely fine and skilfully executed. The Magdalenian engraving technique differs from that of the Aurignacian in that the lines are finer and shallower, and the drawings are much more detailed.

The Upper Magdalenian is also divided into three phases which reflect the development of the barbed point from a 'proto-harpoon' with a single row of incipient notched barbs (Magdalenian IV) to uniserial harpoons (figure 2e) in Magdalenian V and biserial harpoons (figure 2f) in Magdalenian VI. The number and size of barbs varies considerably on Magdalenian V and VI harpoons; they may be small and closely spaced forming a serrated edge, or large and curved, widely spaced. Frequently there is a lateral projection at the base of these unpierced harpoons for attachment to the shaft. Associated with these harpoons are a great variety of different points, short forked projectile heads (possibly for fish) and also the usual pins, needles, awls, spatulae etc.

In Magdalenian IV and V the art of bone carving reaches its peak and objects such as *bâtons de commandement* are often richly decorated with animal engravings or 'bas-relief' and geometric designs. A new weapon, the spear thrower, was invented at this stage in man's history and these spear throwers were often very finely engraved or sculpted with animal representations. Pendants in the shape of horses' heads were common on Pyrenean sites, and pendants cut out of flat bone (often shoulder blade) were engraved with animal, human or geometric designs. In Magdalenian v, carvings in the round and accurate animal representations become less frequent, and much of the decoration consisted of finely engraved geometric or 'abstract' designs. Magdalenian burials do not differ notably from earlier Aurignacian ones.

The Mediterranean region. The Upper Palaeolithic of the Mediterranean zone is less well known. In Spain Upper Palaeolithic cultures with close affinities to those recognised in France developed some local variants, particularly during the Solutrean when very distinctive tanged and barbed arrowheads were made. The four major cultural divisions recognised in France are, however, also valid for Spain. Italy and the French Mediterranean coast east of the Rhone appear to have remained largely isolated from the later Upper Palaeolithic cultures in France. A distinctive Upper Palaeolithic culture, the Grimaldian, has its roots in an early Aurignacian on the Mediterranean coast. The later Italian Upper Palaeolithic also contains backed blades and other elements which are presumably derived from central Europe, but the industries usually are very poor in bone tools. A few figurines carved in soft rock and animal engravings on flat stones are known, and late Palaeolithic cultures, characterised by very small tools are found throughout Italy and Sicily, for example in the decorated caves and shelters of Romanelli and Levanzo.

Central and eastern Europe. It used to be thought that the Upper Palaeolithic cultural sequence was more or less uniform throughout Europe. The Upper Palaeolithic of Europe, therefore, was interpreted on French lines by emphasising the similarities between the French and other cultures. These similarities include a hunting and gathering economy, the manufacture of tools on blades, tool forms (some of which are closely similar or identical), the use of bone, antler and ivory and the development of art, both decorative design on objects of various types and the carving of figurines.

More recent and detailed research has however, tended to emphasise the differences which exist between these and other cultures, thus stressing local groupings and developments. One such major difference is the complete absence of parietal art in many regions, even where caves were available and inhabited. In mobile art also, there are important differences: whereas in western Europe decorative art on tools and weapons consisted, to a great extent, of carefully executed animal representations, much of the central and eastern European mobile art consisted of geometric designs, sometimes of great complexity. Although both animal and human figurines were carved throughout Europe out of ivory or soft stones, they were vastly more common and more varied in the eastern cultures.

The modern view of the Upper Palaeolithic as consisting of numerous geographically distinct groups, all with a similar stone age hunting economy and similar basic technical traditions, but with distinctive local characteristics is undoubtedly the result of more and more detailed analyses of the material remains of these various groups. Earlier workers had been concerned with establishing the broad lines of man's development and the main trends of evolution and migration of new ideas and techniques, and they had therefore, naturally, emphasised resemblances between widely separated cultures. In this way they attempted to locate the origins of different cultures and to determine their routes of migration. This emphasis on the 'evolution' of man obscured the separate identities of local cultures and resulted in a picture of an apparently unified Upper Palaeolithic province which stretched over a vast distance.

Environment of the Upper Palaeolithic. The Upper Palaeolithic people lived during the last of the main ice sheet advances of the Pleistocene. During this period there was at least one short-lived retreat of the glaciers during which climatic conditions became less extreme, although they were still considerably colder than now. Large ice sheets spread southwards from the Scandinavian highlands as far as the Elbe in northern Germany and across the

5 *Distribution map of Palaeolithic parietal art.*

6 Time chart of the Upper Palaeolithic period in western Europe, based on archaeological data and carbon-14 determinations and showing some typical dated examples of parietal art: **a** Engraved bull from Teyjat. **b** Low-relief horse from Cap Blanc. **c** Low-relief bison with boar's head from Roc de Sers. **d** Low-relief Venus from Laussel. **e** Low-relief fish from Le Poisson. **f** Engraved head from Le Ferrassie. **g** Deeply incised sign from Le Ferrassie.

Years BC	Culture	
10,000		
		Late
15,000	MAGDALENIAN	Middle
		Early
20,000	SOLUTREAN PROTO-MAGDALENIAN PERIGORDIAN IV-VI	Late
25,000		
	AURIGNACIAN	Middle
		Early
30,000	CHATELPERRONIAN	

North Sea, reaching the Midlands in England and covering northern Ireland. A separate ice sheet formed over the Alps and smaller ice sheets formed over the highest parts of the Pyrenees, but the eastern and western extremeties of the Pyrenean chain remained unglaciated. The existence of such large ice sheets had far reaching effects on the geography and climate of Europe. They caused a lowering of the sea level by approximately 100 metres, thus exposing areas of coastal land which are now submerged, particularly in the North Sea and the Channel. The Mediterranean coast

Tools and weapons	Parietal art

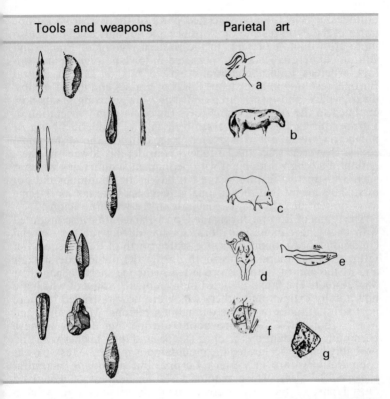

line, which is particularly steep, was not considerably different from today. A more significant effect of the existence of large ice sheets, and the depression of sea level, was the diversion of depressions from the Atlantic farther south across the Mediterranean, so that countries such as Spain and Italy enjoyed heavier rainfalls than at present. The conditions in the western Mediterranean were comparable to those of the temperate forest zones of the present day, with extensive woodland of deciduous trees merging into coniferous forest on higher ground, and Alpine flora at high altitudes, e.g. in the non-glaciated parts of the Pyrenees. Europe north of the Pyrenees and the Alps became not only colder, but also more arid, than at present. In the western regions of France and Britain coniferous woodland persisted in lowland regions and valleys, whereas tundra conditions existed farther east in central Europe, resulting in arid steppe floras of grasses and dwarf shrubs, dwarf willow and dwarf birch and many low growing plants now confined to the Alps. In many ways the climate and vegetation of Europe during this period resembled that of modern Siberia or northern Canada, but with greater precipitation in the westernmost zones. However, since the latitude is considerably lower, the alternation of a long winter night with permanent summer day which is such a distinctive feature of present day arctic conditions did not exist. This meant that the seasonal differences were not as extreme as in present day Siberia, particularly in the western regions.

The fauna of Europe during the Upper Palaeolithic also migrated with changing climate and flora, so that during the fully glacial conditions forest animals became scarce north of the Pyrenees but returned to southern France both during the milder interstadials and at the end of the Pleistocene when the ice sheets began their final retreat. The fauna included many animals, some of which are now totally extinct, and others which are now restricted to more northerly latitudes or sparsely inhabited regions. Mammoths and woolly rhinoceros lived throughout Europe, but appear to have been more abundant on the open steppe land than farther west and probably hardly penetrated the mountainous regions. Musk-ox was comparatively rare in western Europe, but abundant in central Europe. Reindeer, which require a certain amount of woodland during part of the year, were particularly abundant in western Europe and largely replaced the fallow deer during the peak of glacial conditions, whereas the deer largely replaced the reindeer during the milder interstadials. Both animals existed throughout the Upper Palaeolithic of south west France, for deer do not necessarily require extensive woodland for survival. Wild horses and bison which can live in woodland or steppes formed an important part of the diet of Upper Palaeolithic hunters, and in more wooded regions the wild ox or aurochs and wild boar were also hunted. The principal carnivore remains include cave lion, wolf, arctic fox, glutton and brown bear, and smaller animal remains include particularly the arctic hare and arctic birds such as ptarmigan. Fishing was certainly practised and in western Europe seals were caught, but since fish remains are less well preserved than the bones of larger mammals the extent to which fishing was practised is difficult to assess.

Some animals which are nowadays considered to require a very specialised ecology like the ibex as a mountain animal, or the lion as a hot semi-desert animal, were much more widely distributed in the Pleistocene. The ibex appears to have been relatively common in Pleistocene western Europe, but did not spread into the fully open steppe land. The lion, and also other animals such as brown bear and wolf, is tolerant of a very wide range of climate, and its present-day restricted occurrence is largely the result of human interference.

Dating the Upper Palaeolithic

The dating of the various Upper Palaeolithic cultures (figure 6) to interstadial or to glacial periods is based to a large extent on the relative amounts of animal remains found among the food debris and their correlation with climatic conditions. The Chatelperronian and earliest Aurignacian levels are found with fauna which indicate interstadial conditions when the climate was approximately as today, and the vegetation included deciduous forests. These early Upper Palaeolithic cultures began at the close of this interstadial, when deciduous forest had begun to give way to pine and birch forests, and arctic animals such as reindeer were hunted. However, horse, bison, aurochs, deer and wild boar still formed the major part of the game hunted. As the glaciation proceeded and the Aurignacian and Perigordian cultures developed, the emphasis on reindeer, mammoth and horse increased while aurochs, deer, etc. became considerably scarcer in the kitchen debris, though they did not become extinct. The late Solutrean/early Magdalenian interstadial was considerably less marked than the preceding one and only resulted in an increase in the spread of pine and birch forests, and a few deciduous trees. The final phase of the last glaciation was more arid than previous phases with concomittant extensive

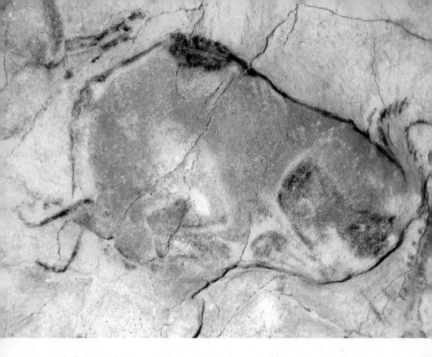

deforestation. This, in turn, resulted in the complete disappearance of those animals which required a woodland habitat, such as wild boar and aurochs, and in the marked dominance of reindeer, horse and other steppe animals such as woolly rhinoceros, mammoth and also bison. There were also other minor climatic oscillations, which can be detected from pollen studies, and these also caused changes in the relative extent of forest, shrub and grassland vegetations. Their effect on the larger mammals is difficult to ascertain.

Estimates of the duration of the Upper Palaeolithic vary widely. Early estimates[18] were based on geological criteria, such as the formation of soils and the rate of river erosion, and these suggested an approximate duration of the last glacial phase of around 100,000 years, and of the Upper Palaeolithic around 50,000 years. Similar estimates (120,000 years) were obtained on the basis of a theory about the shape of the earth's orbit around the sun, which relates the successive advances and retreats of Ice Age glaciers to changes of solar radiation received from the sun at various latitudes.[19]

The development of radioactive dating techniques[20], particularly of the radiocarbon dating of charcoal and charred bone, gave the possibility of dating actual archaeological deposits, or objects closely associated with archaeological material. The chronology for

7 Painted and engraved polychrome
bison on natural boss of the
ceiling at Altamira.

31

the Upper Palaeolithic derived from radiocarbon estimates is considerably shorter than that of earlier estimates. The accuracy of radiocarbon dating decreases sharply with increasing age, and although a statistical error is normally quoted with any given date, these only give a sixty per cent probability of the age range. Thus, unless a large number of dates are available for any particular event, radiocarbon dates cannot provide absolutely reliable estimates and the application of this dating method to a period as remote as the Palaeolithic has been much criticised. However, the increasing number of radiocarbon dates now available have begun to reveal a fairly consistent pattern and an outline chronology can be ascertained.

There are only a few early Aurignacian dates and these vary between 30,000 and 31,000 years BP.[21] At Arcy sur Cure, the Chatelperronian is dated to about 33,500 years BP. Late Perigordian dates are known from Abri Pataud ranging from 24,000 to 19,000 years BP, whereas the succeeding Protomagdalenian at the same site has been dated quite consistently to around 21,000 years BP. This latter industry is dated to 22,000 years BP at Laugerie Haute and there the early Solutrean is dated to 21,000 years BP. There are no early Magdalenian dates, but Magdalenian III has been dated at a number of sites around 15,000–13,000 years BP[22], whereas the Final Magdalenian at La Vache is dated to just over 10,500 years BP.

Discovery and acceptance of Upper Palaeolithic cave art

The existence of cave art in the Upper Palaeolithic is now firmly established, and numerous caves and shelters are known in western Europe (see details below) which contain painted, engraved and sculpted representations from this period. The first discovery of cave paintings was nearly a century ago, but general acceptance of these paintings as genuinely Palaeolithic in date had to wait till the first decade of this century.

The first to suggest that the paintings on cave walls were of Palaeolithic date was a Spanish archaeologist, Don Marcelino de Sautuola. After his visit to the Paris exhibition of Palaeolithic bone and antler carvings in 1878, de Sautuola continued to search the

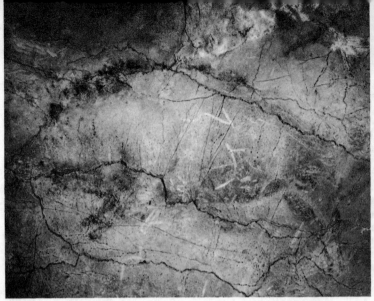

deposits of some of the caves on his estate in the Spanish province of Santander. One of these, the cavern of Altamira, yielded a rich deposit of middle Magdalenian tools and hearths with food debris of shells and animal bones at the entrance, but the cave became especially famous for the polychrome paintings of bison and other animals on the walls and roof inside the cave (figures 7 and 8). De Sautuola was struck by the similarity of style between his newly discovered parietal paintings and the animal carvings and engravings on bone from the French caves which had previously been recognised as Palaeolithic in date. In 1880 de Sautuola published his findings, with the suggestion that the paintings might be contemporaneous with the Palaeolithic deposits at the cave entrance. This suggestion was greeted with much scepticism.

In the following year, the French scholar Edouard Harlé visited Altamira to settle the argument about the antiquity of the paintings, and returned to France with sketches of the paintings and a firm conviction that they could not be of any great age. Harlé pointed out[23] the necessity for artifical light in the cave to carry out the paintings, and argued that with the torches or oil lamps or fat lamps used by prehistoric man a considerable amount of soot would have been formed, and that the roof and walls of the caves would have shown traces of darkening. Since the cavern walls were quite clear of soot, he considered that the paintings were carried out by means of modern (i.e. nineteenth century) lighting. Harlé further pointed out that certain signs at Altamira were painted on very

8 Painted and engraved
polychrome boar on the
ceiling at Altamira.

33

friable portions of the rock and that, had these been drawn in antiquity, they could not have survived practically intact. He also noted the freshness of some of the paintings, and the fact that some of the paintings covered stalagmite flow, whereas others were covered by thin layers of stalagmite and he argued, quite correctly, that a thin covering of stalagmite was not proof of great antiquity. Harlé's main reason, however, for denying the Palaeolithic age of the paintings was on artistic and stylistic grounds. He reasoned that the artists were evidently highly skilled, since animals such as deer were portrayed with great accuracy and artistic ability. The aurochs[24], however, he considered to be quite unlike true extinct aurochs, having strange humps on the back and neck and sometimes unrecognisable heads. They were drawn with clear sure lines and beautifully shaded in ochre and black. The inaccuracies were therefore not due to clumsiness and, had the artists been contemporaneous with the extinct aurochs (i.e. Palaeolithic hunters), they would surely have depicted them as accurately as the deer.

In the same year that de Sautuola discovered the paintings of Altamira, a French archaeologist, Chiron, was excavating stone age (Magdalenian) deposits in the cave shelter of Chabot. He uncovered a maze of scratched and engraved lines on the limestone rock just above the level of the Magdalenian floor. Chiron claimed that these were intentional engravings, though admittedly very crude, and represented either humans or birds. They were, in fact, later identified by Capitan[25] as mammoth. Similar claims were made by Dalaud for engravings in the cave of Pair non Pair in 1896.

The first paintings of Palaeolithic age in France were uncovered by Rivière in 1895 in the sealed cave of La Mouthe. Rivière's claim for a Palaeolithic date for these paintings was influenced by his opinion of the Altamira paintings which he had previously visited. All these claims were, however, received with little enthusiasm and Rivière was accused of being the dupe of forgeries. The main arguments against their Palaeolithic date were based on technological considerations: the absence of soot on the cave walls when the paintings, as at La Mouthe, were well beyond the reach of daylight; the necessity of having hardened steel tools to carve the limestone walls; etc.

So far the discoveries had been made by local archaeologists,

but Carthaillac, a famous archaeologist from Bordeaux, visited Dalaud's excavations at Pair non Pair and Rivière's excavations at La Mouthe where he himself uncovered part of a red ochre painting from beneath the Palaeolithic cave earth. The accusations against Rivière's discoveries at La Mouthe were then withdrawn. In 1901 Capitan and Breuil published the paintings and engravings of Les Combarelles and Font de Gaume and claimed a Palaeolithic date for them. Despite their fame, these publications of Capitan and Breuil did not go uncriticised. The following year (1902), however, Carthaillac publicly announced his acceptance of the Palaeolithic date of cave paintings and engravings in his famous 'Mea Culpa d'un Sceptique', and in the same year the members of the Congress of the 'Association Francaise pour l'avancement des Sciences' visited the caves. Following this, Harlé revisited the cave of Altamira and also accepted the paintings as genuinely Palaeolithic.

During the next two decades a deliberate search was made in France and Spain for Palaeolithic paintings, and important new discoveries came to light. In the Dordogne: Bernifal, Teyjat, La Calévie in 1903, La Grèze in 1904; in the Cantabrian mountains: El Castillo, La Peña de los Hornos, Covalanas and La Pasiega; in the Pyrenees: Gargas, Niaux, Le Portel, Le Tuc d'Audoubert and Les Trois Frères.

Already in 1904 Capitan had pointed out that Palaeolithic paintings would rarely be found unless they had been protected under deposits, or in sealed caves. Although new discoveries are indeed not common, they have continued, with such important recent additions as Lascaux in 1940, Cougnac in 1952 and Rouffignac in 1956. The most recent discoveries include those at Del Romito in Italy (1961) and Escoural in Portugal (1963) (figure 9). The total number of decorated Palaeolithic caves now known in Europe is more than one hundred.

9 *Left* Black painted horse with rounded belly from the recently discovered cave of Escoural in Portugal.
10 *Below* Low-relief sculpture of **a** a horse and **b** a boar-headed bison from Le Roc de Sers.

a

b

The suggestion that the engravings, sculptures and paintings might be Palaeolithic in date had first been proposed on the basis of similarities of execution between them and decorated objects of mobile art, which had been excavated together with the tools, hearths, and food debris of Upper Palaeolithic cultures. A second, and more conclusive, proof of the antiquity of these paintings and engravings was obtained from sites such as La Mouthe, Pair non Pair and others, where the wall art was actually covered by deposits of Palaeolithic age, and under which they had therefore been sealed since that period. In a few instances fragments of decorated limestone slabs fallen from the cave walls have been found in deposits of Palaeolithic age, for example the sculpted blocks of the frieze of Le Roc de Sers (figure 10), and their dates cannot be disputed. Sometimes as at Marsoulas the entrances of caves have been sealed by Palaeolithic deposits until opened in modern times, and the contents must, therefore, also be of Palaeolithic date. The representation of extinct animals such as mammoth, as well as animals no longer living in the Franco-Cantabrian region, such as reindeer and bison, can also be seen as proof of their Palaeolithic date.

Distribution of Upper Palaeolithic cave art

The search for parietal art spread outside France and Spain to other regions where caves and Palaeolithic cultures were known, but the distribution of Palaeolithic cave art has proved to be fairly restricted to western Europe.

The three main centres of Palaeolithic parietal art lie in the valleys of the Vézère and Dordogne in the region of Périgord, in the Pyrenees and in the Cantabrian mountains (see figure 5). Other groups have been found in the lower Rhone valley and smaller

11 Black painted signs, from La Pileta, showing Neolithic (?) superpositioning on Palaeolithic representations.

37

groups, or isolated occurrences, as far north as Arcy sur Cure, between Paris and Dijon, and as far south as Las Palomas, near Malaga.

Palaeolithic parietal art has also been reported, albeit very rarely, from countries other than France and Spain. In most cases these examples were not found in caves sealed since Palaeolithic times and were not covered with archaeological deposits. Differences in style between the Franco-Cantabrian works and the works claimed to be of Palaeolithic date in other countries can be viewed either as evidence of local stylistic diversity or as evidence against the ascription of a Palaeolithic date to the latter works. In several cases the original ascription of a Palaeolithic date has since been disclaimed; for example a row of red dots in the cave of Paviland on the Gower Coast of Wales[26], and an engraved deer in an Austrian cave.[27] Parietal paintings and engravings in Portugal, Turkey, Italy and Sicily may well be really Palaeolithic in date. A difficulty, in some of these caves, is to distinguish correctly Palaeolithic representations from later prehistoric representations on the same walls (e.g. figure 11, at La Pileta).

Recently[28] paintings of mammoths have been found in rock shelters in Southern Russia, for example at Kapova cave, and have been assigned a Palaeolithic date primarily because the mammoth has been extinct in this area since that period. The relationship between these southern Russian paintings and Franco-Cantabrian paintings remains unclear in view of the vast distances separating these two regions in which no Palaeolithic parietal art has been found, despite deliberate searching.

In central- and south-eastern Spain are distinctive paintings in rock shelters[29] which form a group of works that are artistically distinct from those of the Upper Palaeolithic both in style and content. Although at one time considered to be Palaeolithic in date[30] they are now generally[31] assigned to the Mesolithic or later Prehistoric periods.

Throughout most of the world (in Africa: Nubia, the Sahara, etc., in India, etc.) are parietal representations which have been claimed to be of Palaeolithic date. In almost no case is it possible to determine the exact date of the representations; in most cases where there is any evidence at all, the indications are that they are post-Palaeolithic (and in some cases, even modern) in date.

2 Palaeolithic parietal art

Characteristics

Palaeolithic cave art has been called an essentially 'animal art', and the vast majority of recognisable representations are indeed of various species of animals. Amongst the animals most commonly represented are the large mammals which lived in the late Pleistocene and whose remains have been found among the debris of Palaeolithic living sites. Amongst these some of the large herbivores are the most common: bison, wild ox, horse, ibex, deer, reindeer, the extinct giant deer and also the large pachyderms mammoth and woolly rhinoceros. There are also representations of carnivores such as cave lion and brown bear as well as occasional fish and very rarely birds. Human beings are also represented, less rarely than has sometimes been maintained. The majority of representations claimed as humans are crude and clumsy in comparison with many animal representations, but some are extremely fine. Palaeolithic parietal art also includes non-naturalistic representations which may be comprehensively grouped under the term 'signs' (and which include certain standardised variants called tectiforms, penniforms, etc.).

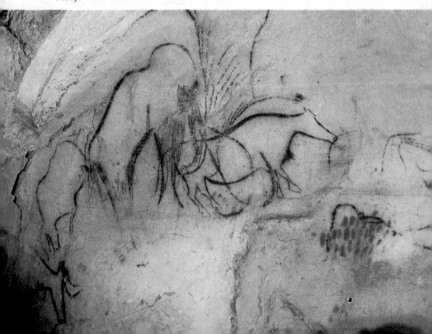

12 Black painted panel of animals at Pech-Merle,
including bison, mammoths, horses and wild oxen;
one ox is shown with head downwards and several animals
with lines from their mouths; some animals are
indicated by partial outlines only and one mammoth
is covered by red painted dots.

Animals, humans or signs are shown either in isolation or on panels which also contain several other animals (of the same or other species), humans or signs. These panels quite commonly contain combinations of animals which were not likely to have been found together in nature while they do not normally include combinations of animals of the same species and opposite sex.[1] Thus, bison and horse are commonly represented close together whereas, in nature, each lives entirely separate in pure herds; similarly, for example, mammoth, horse, oxen and bison on a panel at Pech-Merle (figure 12) and the bison, deer and wild boar on the ceiling of Altamira (figures 7 and 8). Although all caves contain a variety of animals, there are some in which one or a few species clearly predominate, such as mammoth in Rouffignac (figure 13), mammoth and bison in Font de Gaume and cow and horse in Lascaux (figure 14). In some caves greater emphasis is placed on different species in different sections of the cave – notably at Le Portel where one passage contains predominantly horses (figure 15) and another predominantly bison (figure 16).

Another characteristic of Palaeolithic panels with more than one representation on them is the frequent occurrence of superpositioning[2] (figure 17). It is not at all uncommon to find one animal or sign placed on top of another animal or sign either overlapping the previous representation in part only, or completely covering it. There exist numerous cases where the amount of superpositioning has been such that the immediate impression is of a mass of thousands of engraved or painted lines (figure 18).

As will be seen in subsequent chapters one of the most disputed questions concerning Palaeolithic parietal art has been whether or not Palaeolithic art is concerned with solitary representations or groups of associated representations. For a long time it was assumed that the existence of panels with more than one representation on them did not imply that the representations were intended to be associated. Those who favoured this view interpreted the common superpositions as evidence that the Palaeolithic artists were unconcerned about previous work and that each representation had a significance of its own[3], despite the fact that certain representations showed evidence of retouching (see chapter 3) (figure 21). It has been commonly stated that one of the distinctive characteristics of this art was that it was not concerned with scenes or groupings.[4] Nevertheless, in spite of this generally accepted view of the art, several exceptional scenes and compositions have always had to be allowed. Thus even in the early discoveries at Font de Gaume,

13 Engraved mammoth, from Rouffignac; the eye is shown by a natural flint nodule.

41

Breuil[5] recognised two reindeer (figures 19 and 20) as deliberately grouped together and at Lascaux most commentators have accepted as groups the 'frieze of galloping horses' (figure 14) and the 'swimming deer' (figure 22). Recently both superpositioning and close association have been interpreted as evidence of conscious association between two or more representations (see the following chapters for a discussion of the views of Laming and Leroi-Gourhan). Thus the fact that one representation is placed on top of another would be evidence not for lack of interest in previous work but for purposeful grouping of animals, humans and signs. In this view it would be a characteristic of Palaeolithic parietal art that it was concerned with scenes and associations.

One of the difficulties in assessing the likelihood of representations being associated or not arises from another characteristic of Palaeolithic parietal art: namely, the conspicuous absence of any attempts to indicate landscape or vegetation and virtually any attempt to show strict horizontal base lines. Although, in most cases, representations on walls are 'the right way up' this is by no means always the case. On the same panel animals, humans or signs may occasionally be shown variously orientated so that some are 'the right way up', some 'on a slope' and others 'upside down'. This characteristic does not make the interpretation of groupings any easier, and it is not justifiable to interpret the occasional upside-down animal amongst a group of other animals all the right way up (figure 12) as dead. The scale adopted for representations is not consistent within any one panel and large and small animals are shown close together irrespective of their correct proportions. On a panel at Pech-Merle (figure 12) one ox is represented in a vertical position with its head down, one mammoth is inclined upwards (virtually on its hind legs) whereas a horse, bison and several other mammoths are all approximately on the horizontal. Each animal on this panel is drawn with its own base line and not to scale. Compare, for instance, the relative sizes of the red dotted mammoth, an animal in reality around three to three and a half metres high, with one of the horses, in reality similar to a modern pony.

The difficulties involved in the interpretation can be summarised by looking at the attempts to make sense of a particular set of

14 *Top* Painted bichrome 'jumping' cow with small 'galloping' horses beneath, from Lascaux.
15 *Bottom* Small painted horse in red flatwash, from Le Portel.

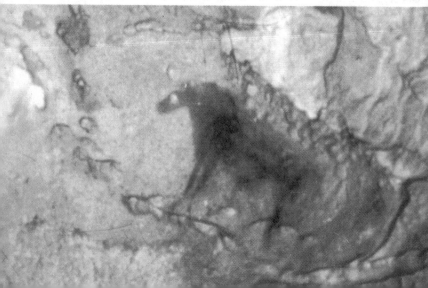

16 Three black painted bison, from Le Portel; one shows the combination of painting and engraving techniques.

43

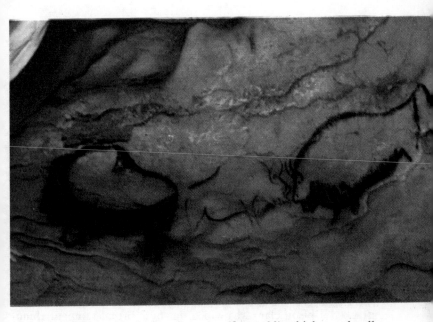

representations in the shaft at Lascaux (figure 23) which nearly all authors (even those who consider Palaeolithic parietal art to be in the main characterised by the absence of scenes) see as a pictorial composition. One of the main differences in the various attempts at understanding the meaning of this scene is the place assigned to the figure of the nearby rhinoceros. Breuil[6] saw it as a narrative hunting scene in which a dead man was shown lying between a rhinoceros which had killed him, and a wounded and furious bison. Nearby Breuil saw the representation of a throwing stick. According to this interpretation the rhinoceros had been victorious in killing the man who had previously wounded the bison. The bison, shown with a lance through him and his entrails hanging out from the wound, stands stationary with threatening head and lashing tail. On the basis of practices of modern tribes, Breuil interpreted the bird-headed stick as a funerary post. The dots below the tail of

17 Superimposed finger tracings on the
clay surface of the ceiling at
Pech-Merle; among the figures identified
from the maze of lines are several
human representations (female) and
mammoths (as shown in the detail below in brown).

the rhinoceros received no interpretation. Variations on this same interpretation stress that the man is shown falling backwards and that this man has a bird head 'precisely similar' to the bird on the stick.[7] The suggestion has been made that the rhinoceros was painted by a different hand from the other figures and may not be part of the scene at all[8] while another view is that the rhinoceros, an essential figure in the composition, is ready to charge having already trampled the man.[9] To Breuil the rhinoceros was in a tranquil mood, an interpretation with which Zeuner agreed, stressing that the rhinoceros was standing still and possibly defecating.[10] Various interpretations of the bird on the stick have been offered: as a hunting decoy,[11] as a dart-thrower[12] and as a totemic emblem. The man is often seen as wearing a bird mask. Not even the role of the bison has been agreed to, for it has been suggested that it is attacking the man who falls backwards away from it[13] despite Breuil's view that it cannot charge because it has already been disembowelled. One view is that the bison is caught in a trap and has turned its head away and therefore cannot even be considered a part of the same scene as the other representations, while others take the position of the bison's head as one threatening to the man. One interpretation of all Palaeolithic art as symbolic reads into this scene the message that an aggressive bird clan having attacked a bison clan, was wiped out by a brutal rampant rhinoceros, while another[14] (see subsequent chapters for explanation of the symbolic equivalences involved in this interpretation) takes the bird on the stick as equivalent to the human who is himself equivalent to the rhinoceros, all of which symbolise maleness and are in a meaningful relationship to the bison which is equivalent to femaleness.

In order to see that difficulties of interpretation are not found only when the representations are as numerous and complex as those in the Lascaux shaft it is only necessary to look at the row of 'swimming' deer (figure 22) at Lascaux. It is often assumed that only the tilted heads are shown because the rest of the bodies are submerged in the water of a stream but, as Graziosi has pointed out[15], there is at Lascaux another set of representations of painted and engraved ibexes (figure 25) and it is highly unlikely that these animals should be swimming. To Graziosi the representation of a

18 *Left* Maze of lightly engraved representations from the 'sanctuary' of Les Trois Frères which include the figure of a 'bison-man' supposedly playing a 'musical bow'.

19 *Top* Painted and engraved reindeer from Font de Gaume.
20 *Bottom* Abbé Breuil's drawing of the Font de Gaume reindeer.
21 *Right* Engraved lion on a stalagmite boss at Les Trois Frères, showing evidence of retouch in the pecking of the head and the various black painted and engraved attempts at showing the tail.

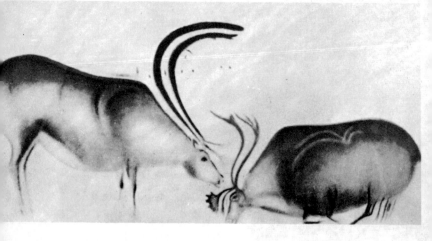

row of heads of deer and of ibex is a convention for showing herds (also a group composition) and does not imply that the bodies were immersed in water. The tilted heads and antlers of the deer can equally well be explained by a moving herd on land as in the water.

Animals are almost invariably shown in profile. There are a few exceptional representations such as the Levanzo deer (figure 24), the Lascaux-shaft bison (figure 23), the Trois Frères lions (figure 26) and the Trois Frères owls (figure 27) in which the head of the animal is turned more or less to face the front and is therefore shown in a three-quarter or front view. Although in many cases some of the extremities of the animal representations (hoofs and horns) can be seen as if they are not true profile views (see below), there is no doubt that the absence of animals facing towards or away from the observer is a striking feature of Palaeolithic art. The crude human representations are also almost all shown in profile but some of the more elaborate examples (those shown in low-relief) represent front and three-quarter views (e.g. frontispiece).

Despite the fact that the animals are represented from the sides only, the variety of stances to be found in this art are numerous. Some animals, such as the Portel (figure 16) and Niaux bison and Cougnac ibex (figure 28), appear stationary while others, such as the 'galloping' horses at Lascaux (figure 14) and the 'playful' ibex of Le Roc (figure 29) are full of movement and vitality. Both this vitality and the 'realism' of many of the representations have also been taken as characteristics of Palaeolithic parietal art. Just as it is an over-simplification to talk about this art as full of vitality because such a description ignores the conventional postures chosen by the Palaeolithic artists, so it is an over-simplification to categorise Palaeolithic art as 'naturalistic' or 'realistic'. All art is by definition 'stylised' and all statements about realism etc. must be couched within the context of stylisation. An enormous variety of styles and techniques (see below) were adopted by Palaeolithic artists to represent animals on cave walls. Generalisations about realism and vitality tend to gloss over these distinctions. Before it can be considered legitimate to deduce facts about Pleistocene fauna from Palaeolithic parietal representations these variations of style and technique must be explored. On the basis of these representations some authors[16] have suggested the existence of distinct breeds of horses, bovids, reindeer etc. in Palaeolithic times but to do so may be as mistaken as the suggestion that the models for these representations were dead[17], on the basis of the tip-toe position of several Palaeolithic representations, their raised tails, their tongues protruding from their mouths, the lack of weight in their legs, and the views of their bellies (see chapter 4 for assessment of this suggestion). One of the most striking single factors about Palaeolithic art is the variety: representations are sometimes finished; sometimes crude; sometimes detailed; sometimes simple; sometimes in isolation, sometimes superimposed; sometimes apparently concerned with movement, sometimes apparently static; sometimes painted, sometimes sculpted, and sometimes engraved.

Another characteristic of Palaeolithic parietal art commonly emphasised in the literature is the use made of natural rock shapes. These are said to have suggested the shape of an animal or part of an animal to the Palaeolithic artist. In support of this view some of the most commonly quoted examples are the Altamira bison, each painted on a natural projecting boss of the cave ceiling (figure 7); the bison on a stalagmite boss at El Castillo (figure 4) in which the line of the back, tail and hind leg and part of the belly coincide with the stalagmite shape; and the drip marks in the clay floor at Niaux (figure 32) which suggested the wounds of arrow-shaped projectiles on the body of the engraved bison. In the first two examples cited, the association between Palaeolithic painting and the natural rock formation cannot be disputed. In the third example such an association is less evident, for there are numerous other drip marks in the clay, some of which were left quite untouched by the artists and ignored although they are distributed both on the animal and near to the animal. A similar disregard of 'suggestive' rock features is found, for instance, at Rouffignac. In this cave one mammoth was 'drawn around' a projecting flint nodule in such a way that the nodule serves convincingly as the animal's eye (figure 13), and yet for another mammoth the eye has been carefully indicated by engraving while an equally 'suggestive' flint nodule has been ignored and left to protrude within the body of the animal (figure 30). In fact the majority of Palaeolithic representations are executed without any apparent regard to the natural shape of the rock surface. The natural rock walls have never been prepared by the Palaeolithic artists by planing or smoothing to provide a suitable working surface, and it is a real characteristic of the art that the artists chose to execute their works irrespective of the rock curvature, cracks and fissures, nodules, stalagmitic formations etc. In a few instances, as at Font de Gaume, a rock surface was covered in red ochre before painting, but such preparation was rare. The use of natural rock or cavern features was exceptional; when exploited it was done with great ingenuity as in the above examples as well as in figures such as a small red bison at Niaux and, if the identification is correct, the phallic man at Le Portel (figure 33). Examples such as the spotted horses of Pech-Merle (figure 31), in which the outline of the rock is said to have formed a first version of the horse's head, whereas the flatwash neck and tiny 'duck-bill' heads were a later addition, are less convincing. The identification of a feline head at Le Mas d'Azil within a natural rock form depends largely on the lighting employed, and the interpretation of paint on natural rounded stalactites at Le Combel as representing women's breasts is highly subjective.

Techniques. It is evident that some means of lighting was used in the caves in Palaeolithic times, and in some caves, for instance at La Mouthe and Lascaux, small stone lamps have been found. These consist of a roughly hollowed limestone slab in which oil or fat could be burned with a wick. Two lamps from La Mouthe are more carefully shaped, with a pear-shaped outline, and one of them is decorated with a delicate ibex engraving on the underside. Torches of resinous wood may well have been used, and the occasional traces of charcoal or small fires in decorated caves are likely to be the remains of sources of light.

Some of the representations are placed so high on the walls or cave roof, that they are well beyond reach of someone standing on floor level, and it is clear that to paint or engrave them Palaeolithic artists must either have clambered on the walls or, more probably in many cases, made use of some artificial aid. Leroi-Gourhan[18] mentions the probable use of a pole to paint one of the signs on the roof of Lascaux and quotes Glory as having found the remains of a very summary scaffolding in the same cave. Other representations, clay floor engravings, are situated in extreme corners of caves where the roof is only a few centimetres from the floor so that the artist must have crouched low on the ground.

The three basic techniques used in Palaeolithic parietal art are bas-relief sculpting, engraving and painting (e.g. figures 3, 13 and 14). These were used singly or combined; the combination of painting and fine shallow engraving was common (e.g. figure 16). It has been suggested that many of the sculptures may originally have been painted. Since these bas-relief sculptures are always situated in comparatively exposed areas within reach of external moisture, temperature and micro-organisms, paint if it had been applied would be unlikely to have survived until the present day. However the existence of paint on some sculptures (e.g. figure 60) which were protected from decay by cave deposits indicates that paint was sometimes applied to them. Sculpture in the round on a scale comparable to the bas-reliefs was very exceptional indeed. Although small modelled figurines are known in bone, ivory and

22 Black painted 'group' of swimming deer, from Lascaux, shown by tossing heads and antlers.

51

soft rock (mobile art), sculpture of this kind on a large scale is represented only by the fine limestone head of a musk-ox from Laugerie Haute (figure 35) which is about twenty-seven centimetres high. It is impossible to tell how far this apparent rarity is due to accident of archaeological investigation, to Palaeolithic inexperience in this technique, or to a genuine Palaeolithic lack of interest in this form of artistic expression.

Engravings and sculptures are all in limestone which, although they all consist largely of the same mineral, calcite, may vary considerably in their physical qualities such as purity, density, toughness and the degree of crystallinity. Many limestones in the Pyrenees are considerably harder to carve than the less compact, slightly sandy limestone of the Dordogne and it may be significant that bas reliefs and deep-outline engravings are much rarer in the former region (unless done on relatively soft stalagmites[19]). Limestone can be chiselled with tools of flint, and both flint picks (figure 2c) and chisel-like tools (burins) which could well have been artists' tools have been found in Palaeolithic dwelling sites. Some of the earliest engravings known are on the stone slabs from the Aurignacian levels at La Ferrassie. They are simple outlines of animals and 'vulvas', engraved in a single continuous deep and wide groove (figure 34). As in nearly all other Palaeolithic stone work the limestone is too corroded to be examined for actual traces of working technique (such as the cross-section of the groove, the

52

rounding of the ends of lines, etc.) and no detailed study of engraving or sculpting techniques in the Palaeolithic has yet been undertaken. Nevertheless it seems very likely that coarse and wide engraved lines were made by cutting with a stout flint tool in combination with some sort of punch, while shallow and fine engravings were made by pulling or pushing the chisel edge of a small burin along the rock surface. The early bas-relief sculptures such as the Laussel figures (figure 3 and frontispiece) are also outlined by a wide and deep groove. The relief modelling of the figures, though distinct and skilful, is shallow and body details such as breasts, leg division and stomach fold are often demarcated by grooving. For bas-reliefs it is known that stone picks (figure 2c) were used as well as stout burins for chiselling work for picks have been found beneath the sculpted frieze of Le Cap Blanc. On some representations, for example the 'lioness' at Les Trois Frères (figure 21), there is evidence for the use of pecking techniques. It has been said[20] that the final smoothing was accomplished with large-sized cores with bevelled ends. In some cases it is difficult to distinguish clearly between engraved figures and very shallow bas-reliefs; figures such as the Combarelles lion (figure 41) and Isturitz animals (figure 42) are intermediate in technique.

Some parietal engravings, like the middle and late Magdalenian engravings on objects of bone, ivory and antler, are made up of numerous sharp, often shallow, incisions placed either singly or in bands to mark the outline, and used also as cross-hatching to indicate modelling or details of fur and mane. Although, as is discussed below, the dating of parietal works of art to specific periods of the Palaeolithic is not yet securely established, it appears that this delicate engraving technique post-dates many of the deep engravings and may, perhaps, be more closely related to advanced painting techniques than to deep engraving-relief techniques.

The close connection between relief work and engravings is seen again in Palaeolithic clay works. Clay parietal works are very rare but some are known from floors and clay-covered walls of certain caves. The comparative scarcity of such work probably does not accurately reflect the Palaeolithic situation but is due to the easy disintegration of such material except under particularly favourable conditions. Breuil[21] considered finger tracings in clay of sinuous

lines and simple animal outlines, as at Gargas (figure 43), as the earliest artistic works in caves (see below). Finger tracings are produced simply by drawing with one or several fingers in the clay or soft rotten surfaces of some cave walls. An alternative technique, called 'cameo' by Graziosi[22] and others, was used in the cave of Les Trois Frères, where in parts of the cave the dark limestone is covered in a pale yellow clay. Between the fresh rock and its clay covering there is a thin whitish film of weathered rock. Thus by scraping with a hard and sharp tool either only the clay, or both the clay and weathering film, a three colour effect could be obtained, as for the two lion heads (figure 26) and the fine head of a bison in Les Trois Frères. The finger paintings of La Baume Latrone (figure 44), in which reddish clay has been used as a pigment and applied by the fingers have also commonly been called finger tracings. They differ from the previously mentioned finger tracings in that they are in effect a painting rather than an engraving technique. Since the fingers are used to apply the clay, the lines obtained are in broad parallel bands resembling the lines produced in true finger tracings in clay. It is the simple finger tracings which Breuil considered were replaced by parallel lines drawn with a comb and were the forerunners of engravings in stone such as those from La Ferrassie (figure 34). Although many of the clay engravings are simple finger traced outlines, some finely worked representations such as the fish and bison at Niaux (figures 32 and 45) are deeply engraved with a fine pointed tool in the clay. It is easy to envisage a technological development from clay engravings to shallow bas-relief work in clay, or even stone. In fact clay carving, although known from only very few sites, demonstrates this possible development. At Bédeilhac several small bison (figure 46) are carved and modelled in very low

26 *Left* Head of a lion in 'cameo' technique on disintegrated rock surface, from Les Trois Frères; the head faces the observer while the body is shown in silhouette.
27 *Right* Engraved owls, from Les Trois Frères, possibly two adults and a baby.

relief and only little removed from clay engravings. The magnificent carved and modelled clay bison of Le Tuc d'Audoubert (figures 36 and 37) could have developed from such beginnings.

These two animals at Le Tuc d'Audoubert, in unbaked clay, are placed leaning against a limestone block with small stones inserted behind them so that they are inclined at roughly forty-five degrees to the vertical and can be viewed from one side and also from the front, back and top. From the side the animals are skilfully modelled; the details of the head in particular are very fine, with the shape of the jaw, the nostrils, mouth and eyes all indicated in detail. Only one ear is modelled on each bison. On one bison the eye is indicated by a modelled projection, whereas on the other it is shown by a depression. The tail of one bison is broken off, but on the other it has been modelled deeply cut away from the body. The sexes of the animals are not indicated.[23] The heavy woolly fur of the neck and shoulders is accentuated by incision, but the feet are not shown. Seen from the top, the backs of the animals are also carefully smoothed and finished. However the far side, leaning against the limestone block, is untouched except for the addition of the second horn which is fully modelled and curves round so that it can be seen partially protruding beyond the level of the head. There was originally a third (figure 38), much smaller, clay bison with this group, but this had much deteriorated and was barely identifiable as a bison. A fourth, unfinished bison (figure 40) near the limestone slab confirms the link between the clay engravings and the clay models. This bison is no more than a roughly indicated outline in very deep incision on the clay floor, with the surrounding clay partially cut away. This shows that the bison were not modelled by

28 *Top* Red painted megaloceros (Giant Elk),
recognisable by its humped back and wide
palmated antlers, an ibex, another cervid
and an 'anthropomorph', from Cougnac.
29 *Bottom* Low-relief sculpture of two 'playful'
ibexes, from Roc de Sers.

building up and moulding the clay, but were cut out of a block of
clay and treated much as a very soft stone. The technique is that
of a stone carver and the plastic qualities of the clay were not
exploited, except perhaps for the addition of detail such as the final
shaping of the face and the addition of the horns. Not far from the
clay bison there are several hollows in the floor, where clay was
scooped out, and small shapeless mounds of clay. A group of small
clay 'sausages' (figure 39) in the nearby chamber could well be
prepared horns (or similar) for clay models of animals[24] (not unlike
the clay balls found at Montespan near clay models in that cave[25]).
The preservation of these clay bison may result partly from the fact
that the mass of the clay from which they were carved has not been
disturbed, as it would have been were they truly modelled, and
because the moisture content in the clay has not been altered
appreciably. Clay modelling normally requires wetter clay than that
out of which the bison were made. On drying again to the normal
moisture regime of the cave such a modelled figure would crack
appreciably more than is true of these bison. The cracks on these
figures result partly from stresses set up in the clay through leaning
against the limestone block and in one case, perhaps, from the
weakness resulting from an intentional incision.[26] During summer,
when the cave moisture decreases slightly these cracks widen and in
winter they nearly close up again. It is this nearly constant
atmosphere together with the difficulty of access which has ensured
the preservation of these bison. As soon as such clay models are
removed into different conditions of moisture and temperature they
are likely to disintegrate rapidly. If similar Palaeolithic clay sculptures had been placed in more exposed cave passages, where
draughts had caused greater variation in temperature and especially
moisture over the last 15,000 years or so, they are likely to have
disintegrated beyond recognition. The chances of survival for this
type of Palaeolithic art is therefore considerably less than for those
made of more durable rock or those which were painted.

The paints used by Palaeolithic man were all derived from
natural earth pigments. The colours used were various shades of
ochre which can vary from a clear red, through red browns, brown
and bistre, to a clear yellow. All shades of ochre were used in
various sites, but reds and browns are more common than yellow.

58

30 Engraved mammoth, from Rouffignac;
a natural flint nodule has been
ignored, cf. figure 13.

Red ochre occurs naturally, but could also have been obtained from pure yellow and brown varieties through burning. Black and a violet black were obtained from manganese oxides. Black pigments from charcoal or from the soot of fatty substances such as animal fat, bone etc., may have been used, but since they consist essentially of carbon they are under certain circumstances less likely to be well preserved than the manganese black. Blue and green are unknown in Palaeolithic art, although organic dyes may well have been used.

To execute the paintings, black, red and occasionally yellow pigment was used to draw a continuous outline in a more or less even line. The outline was sometimes sharp and well defined, but in some instances it was fuzzy round the edges and graded into broad bands of shading as in the small bison of Le Portel (figure 16). Outlines were occasionally indicated by a discontinuous line consisting of a row of dots merging into one another, particularly in some of the Cantabrian caves such as Covalanas (figure 47) where on the does and horse some of the dots merge into areas of shading. The bodies of animals were commonly left blank, but flat wash infilling in one colour was also used, as in the small red horse of Le Portel (figure 15). On the Lascaux and Font de Gaume paintings the outlines were filled in with carefully shaded tints using a combination of two colours on the same animal (figures 14 and 19) while on the Altamira paintings three colours were combined in one representation. Rarely, as on the Marsoulas bison (figure 48) the infilling consists of punctuated lines and on the Niaux and Le Portel animals detail and modelling are indicated by black lines and hatching (figures 16 and 49).

It is not always known whether the pigments were applied directly to the walls in the form of crayons (e.g. at Etcheberriko) or by rubbing on as powdered pigments or as a paste. The evidence suggests that there were several ways of preparing paints and different techniques were probably employed for sharp outlines, flat wash, etc. However, the slightly diffuse nature of some lines and the clear traces of running on paintings such as the black outline horse of Pech-Merle (figure 12) show that one form of paint was undoubtedly applied liquid and probably applied with a brush or tampon. Stencilling was also a technique known to Palaeolithic man as can be seen from the hands of Gargas (figure 50) and other

caves. How the stencil was achieved, whether by blowing powder paste or liquid, remains uncertain but it has been suggested that hollow tubes of long bone were used as blow pipes. In some instances, positive hand imprints were made, presumably by firmly applying the hand covered in paint against the wall.

Techniques and stylistic variation. Perhaps the most striking feature to emerge from a review of Upper Palaeolithic artistic techniques is the variety and adaptability of the means chosen. This variety of techniques resulted in many distinct ways of representing animals, and in varying degrees of detail indicated (from simple outlines to detailed engraving, modelling or shading). In many cases animals have been represented so ingeniously that their characteristic detail enables species to be identified. In certain cases which are drawn more simply, indicated by the outline only or merely partially sketched, characteristic features of the animal such as the hump-back and head of mammoth with its shaggy coat on the Pech-Merle panel (figure 12), or the elegantly curved horns of ibex at Lascaux (figure 25), and the massive forepart and humped shoulders of bison at Pech-Merle or El Castillo (figure 12 and 51), have been represented. Only a few animal representations are difficult or impossible to identify. Unfinished animals are in fact common in Palaeolithic art, and in many cases are not a result of partial destruction of the representation. Commonly the animal is

32 Engraving of a bison on the clay floor
of Niaux; several holes on and around it
are the result of water dripping from the ceiling
and 'arrow'-shaped signs have been
added to some of them.

31 Black painted dappled horses on a panel, from Pech-Merle; their hind quarters overlap and the dappling extends beyond the outlines of the horses; the panel also includes several black negative hand stencils and possibly a red 'fish' underneath the back of the right hand horse; the heads of the horses taper to a small 'duckbilled' shape.

indicated only by its head, or head and torso (e.g. figures 12 and 25), and at Bédeilhac there is a single leg of a horse engraved on the clay floor. Feet are quite commonly left unfinished but equally commonly are drawn with great accuracy (e.g. figures 49 and 54).

The stylistic conventions employed by the Palaeolithic artists to show details such as hoofs, horns and antlers, in particular, vary. Some are shown in silhouette outline as the Ebbou animals in which one front and back leg only is shown (and in the cows one horn only) (figure 53). In animals such as the Niaux bison and horses (figure 49) a full representation of the four legs and two horns are drawn in what approximates to true perspective with the farside legs and horns partially hidden by the body of the animal. In such cases the hoofs, if indicated, are generally also shown in true profile. An intermediate manner of showing all four feet and two horns or antlers is well illustrated by many of the Lascaux representations (figure 56), and has been called 'twisted perspective' by Breuil.[27] Although the animal is drawn in profile, both horns or antlers are shown as though from the front and not in perspective. The horns may be drawn symmetrically curved on the same side of the head, as at La Grèze (figure 54), or curved parallel, but still from the same side of the head as in many bovids at Lascaux (figure 14). Similar conventions are followed for the antlers. The ears may then be variously placed one between the antlers (or horns) and the second one behind the horns, half way down the neck, or simply omitted altogether (figure 22). Similar variations exist for showing the feet. In many instances the cloven hoofs of bovids and deer are shown face on, although the rest of the animal is in profile.

Other stylistic conventions used in Palaeolithic parietal art are less easily summarised. The disproportionately small heads of many representations is very characteristic of some Palaeolithic art (e.g. figures 31 and 52) but is not a feature of many finely engraved, outlined and modelled representations. The absence of small heads may well be associated with a more accurate use of perspective. The

33 Red painted outline of an anthropomorph, from Le Portel; a small stalagmite is generally interpreted to indicate his penis.

34 Engraved blocks, from La Ferrassie
showing signs usually interpreted
as sexual symbols and animals.
35 *Far right* Free standing sculpture of the
head of a musk-ox from Laugerie Haute.

latter has been referred to in the literature[28] as realistic or naturalistic. It is interesting to note, however, that this apparent 'realism' is often at the expense of 'movement' – so striking in representations such as the Lascaux frieze of horses (figures 14 and 52) – and 'power' – emphasised by the disproportionate rendering of the bison hump and head in the Pech-Merle outline drawings (figure 12).

In short, it can be said that Palaeolithic art is as much characterised by its diversity of stylistic conventions as by anything else. Although it is perhaps possible to talk about the 'overall unity'[29] of Palaeolithic art from the point of view of its content and the techniques involved in its execution, it is extremely difficult to isolate convincingly the stylistic conventions typical of all this art. In view of the length of time under consideration and the diverse origins of the Upper Palaeolithic cultures (see chapter 1) this is perhaps not surprising.

Chronology and styles. To date individual representations of Palaeolithic parietal art to the various cultural stages of the Upper Palaeolithic (see chapter 1) is often difficult or impossible, since they are not normally found in the same archaeological context as the tools by which these cultural stages are defined. Sometimes, however, parietal art is in association with other archaeological material as when, for example, carved limestone blocks have become embedded together with the flints, bone debris etc. in the deposits of the culture which produced them. When, rarely, such fragments of a decorated wall have fallen on to the cave floor and subsequently been buried under accumulating deposits this can give a minimum date for these works of art, for they cannot be later than the deposits in which they are found. Alternatively, the art on the walls of an inhabited cave may become buried by archaeological deposits. Such works must by definition be earlier than the deposits which cover them, and their minimum date is given by the highest archaeological deposits at their base. However it is important to realise that only a minimum date is given by such deposits for the works of art may well belong to earlier periods. In sealed caves, a minimum date is also given by the archaeological deposits which block the entrance.

A less direct way, and a less sure way, of dating Palaeolithic parietal art is by analogies with engravings found on pebbles, bone etc. stratified within archaeological deposits. Such dating must depend on comparisons of style and technique and must assume an equation between the artistic development of parietal art and mobile art. Looking, for instance, at the head of a parietal engraving of a deer at Altamira (figure 57a) and the heads of deer engraved on bone objects in the archaeological deposits of Altamira (figure 57b) and El Castillo, it is clear both that the subjects are identical and that the engraving techniques and styles adopted are so close that it is likely that in all three cases the artists belonged to the same cultural tradition. Unfortunately in this particular instance there is some doubt as to the exact date of the excavated examples, for at El Castillo the engraved bone was found in the early Magdalenian levels while at Altamira, Alcalde del Rio[30] found the engraved bone, below the early Magdalenian levels, in the late Solutrean level. To complicate matters still further, Breuil, on the evidence at El Castillo and the fact that at Altamira the Solutrean and early

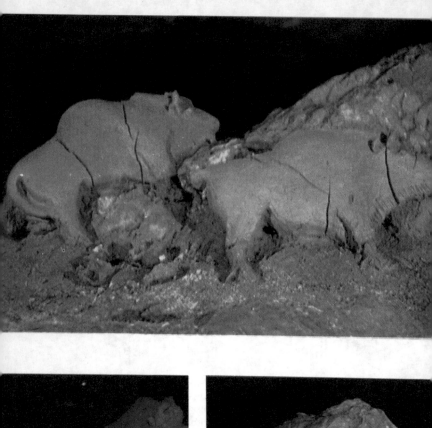

36 *Top left* Side views of two modelled clay bison leaning up against a limestone block in a chamber at Le Tuc d'Audoubert; the eye of one is shown by protusion and that of the other by depression.

37 *Below left* Front and back views of the two clay bison; both horns of each animal are fully modelled; traces of final smoothing by hand are visible on the backs and sides; they are separated from each other by nearly a metre.

38 *Right* Side view of a third small modelled clay bison, from Le Tuc d'Audoubert; originally close to the two larger animals it was removed to the museum of St Germain en Laye.

39 Modelled clay 'sausages' lying on the floor of a low chamber at Le Tuc d'Audoubert; these have been interpreted as representations of phalli.

40 Engraved rough-out on the clay floor at Le Tuc d'Audoubert for a fourth bison; this is situated close to the two remaining finished clay bison, figures 36 and 37.

Magdalenian levels follow each other without a clear break, suggested[31] that the engraved bone was intrusive, or mistakenly referred to the Solutrean levels. This example illustrates one of the difficulties of dating parietal art on the basis of similarities with mobile art for the cultural associations of the latter are often not as definite as could be hoped. It is always possible, after all, to argue that this or that particular piece was found out of its original context. In addition mobile art analogies to parietal art are, unfortunately, not very frequent, so that comparisons have had to be based on generalised stylistic similarities alone. It is obvious that it may not be possible to define broad stylistic similarities with sufficient clarity to characterise a particular culture, so that dating of parietal art on this basis must be much less secure than those based on parietal pieces which have become buried in an archaeological deposit.

Dated works of parietal art. There are no works of parietal art which can be securely dated to the first phases of the Perigordian i.e. the Chatelperronian.

Amongst the earliest securely dated Palaeolithic works of art are the engraved blocks from La Ferrassie (figure 34) which were found stratified in the Aurignacian II levels, and some blocks with traces of paint, engraved animals and symbols found stratified within the Aurignacian III and IV levels from the same site.[32] Similarly engraved blocks were found in the early Aurignacian levels at the Abri Cellier, at Arcy sur Cure and at Laussel. Some of the engravings on the wall at Pair non Pair were covered by Perigordian levels but not by the underlying Aurignacian levels, so that they must date also from the Aurignacian. Breuil[33] pointed out, however, that some of the engravings were so high on the wall that they could well date from the later Perigordian period. Since the entrance to this cave was sealed by a thin level of Solutrean material this gives a minimum date for the parietal art. At Le Poisson in Gorge d'Enfer, Peyrony[34] found some very fragmentary engravings on blocks which had fallen through intense frost fracturing from the roof, after the Aurignacian occupation of the site, but before the late Perigordian habitation. These blocks are too badly damaged to allow clear identification but it seems certain that some form of engraving or very shallow bas-relief, as well as ochre paintings, decorated the shelter before the Perigordian occupation. It seems that the Poisson blocks were executed in similar technique to Aurignacian engravings at La Ferrassie. However, neither the bas-relief of a fish (figure 55), nor the rings cut in the rock on the roof of this same shelter, can date from the same Aurignacian period. The later works were not destroyed by frost action and must, therefore, date to the Perigordian period for after the Perigordian period clay filled the entrance of the shelter and Perigordian bas-reliefs were well preserved.

The best known examples of Perigordian parietal art are the bas-relief figures from Laussel (figures 3, frontispiece, 58 and 60). These figures were executed on blocks of limestone in the habitation area at the foot of an overhanging cliff. The 'Venus' was carved on a large limestone block and the others are on smaller slabs of limestone. The base of the Venus block was found within the late Perigordian levels and Perigordian tools were found very close to the base of the figure. Not all the Laussel figures, however, are securely dated. One of the figures, the female with horn-shaped object in outstretched hand was secretly sold to a German collector by one of the workmen on the site, and the exact circumstances of its finding remain obscure. The double figure, which is said[35] to have come from the same Perigordian levels was first published by the excavator Lalanne[36] as Solutrean. There is, therefore, some doubt as to its exact context. At the time when the figure was discovered the flat retouch, which occurs on some late Perigordian tools (notably the Font Robert points) was believed to be a uniquely Solutrean characteristic, and Lalanne may well have mistaken a late Perigordian level (then known as upper Aurignacian) for an early Solutrean level. However, as a true early Solutrean level does exist at this site, a Solutrean date for the double figure from Laussel cannot be absolutely ruled out.

Perigordian parietal art is more securely dated in several rock shelters at Sergeac. Blocks fallen from the roof, with traces of engraved and painted animals on them, were found at the Abri Labatut between the Perigordian IV and V levels. The painted representations include an incomplete black outline deer painted with some indication of the detail of a hump and with large, elegantly curved antlers indicated with twisted perspective (figure 61). The engraved representation of a horse (figure 62) with the four legs shown is also securely dated to the Perigordian as is also a block which has been claimed[37] to have a hand representation on it. However the identification of this hand, the only dated example which could support Breuil's thesis of a very early date for hands (see below) is said[38] to be highly suspect. At La Grèze a bison (figure 54), engraved on the cave wall, with deep and clear outlines

41 Deeply engraved lion, from
Les Combarelles.
42 *Far right* Low-relief animals on a
stalagmite column, from Isturitz.

was found covered by a late Perigordian and Solutrean habitation
debris. The animal's horns are shown in twisted perspective and
only one front and one hind leg are represented.

Not many parietal works of art can be securely dated to the
Solutrean period. Mobile art is known from the late Solutrean only,
while there is no good evidence for any representational art in any
of the early Solutrean stages. The possibility of the engraved deer at
Altamira being Solutrean in date has already been discussed above.
The only painting which can be securely dated to the Solutrean are
the traces of black paint on a limestone block at Le Fourneau du
Diable.

At Le Roc de Sers a large frieze of animals (figures 10 and 29)
sculpted in relief on limestone blocks, was found lying in the middle
of a very rich late Solutrean level. The animals are carefully
sculpted and the rock around them has been cut away in deep and
wide grooves so that they stand out very clearly. Similarly sculpted
blocks were found in the late Solutrean levels at Le Fourneau du
Diable (Bourdeilles) (figure 63). The low relief frieze of La Chaire à
Calvin (Mouthiers) (figure 64) may also date from this period.
However, the account of its discovery is not entirely unambiguous,
for it was found within Magdalenian deposits with only traces of
Solutrean industry. The low relief animals (figure 42) carved on a
wide column of soft stalagmite at Isturitz have been ascribed to the

Solutrean levels of that site. The carvings were covered by all but the first ten centimetres of the middle Magdalenian levels. Therefore they belong either to the very beginning of the Magdalenian occupation of this cave, or to the earlier rich Aurignacian and Perigordian deposits. The latter are separated from the Magdalenian levels by a thick layer of water-deposited clay in which there is a thin and rather poor layer of Solutrean tools. However, since the Solutrean occupation of the cave was short-lived, during a temporary drying up of the site, it seems possible that the engravings should in fact be ascribed to the considerably more important underlying Aurignacian and Perigordian deposits or more likely to the rich middle Magdalenian levels which included low relief mobile art.

Surprisingly little is known about art in the Lower Magdalenian period, for no parietal example is known and most Magdalenian mobile art belongs to the later phases, particularly IV and V.

The sculpted frieze of animals and female figures (figure 65) at Angles sur l'Anglin were partially buried by deposits of late Magdalenian, and has therefore been dated[39] to the underlying middle Magdalenian (Magdalenian III) which does not cover it. At Abri Reverdit and Le Cap Blanc Magdalenian levels were excavated belonging to a middle Magdalenian (probably Magdalenian III). In the latter case[40] the association between low relief sculpture (figure 66) and archaeological deposits is less direct, for the deposits did not cover the frieze. However, since there is no evidence that the shelter was inhabited at any other time, the likelihood is that the frieze does indeed date from the middle Magdalenian. A somewhat similar situation is found at Les Combarelles, but here the association is still less direct. The middle-late Magdalenian habitation of this cave is restricted to the smaller of two branches of the cave which diverge at the cliff face. The engravings (e.g. figure 41) are all in the second, deeper and narrower part of the cave. On stylistic grounds and the study of superpositioning (see below) Breuil[41] dated these engravings to a period only slightly later than the Cap Blanc bas-relief frieze, and thus concluded that the habitations and engravings could not belong to the same culture. This is a tenuous conclusion for the fact is that the Combarelles evidence suggests a Middle-Late Magdalenian date for the engravings in the same way as the Cap Blanc evidence suggests an early Middle Magdalenian date for the sculpted horses there. At Marsoulas, again, Breuil has departed from consistent deduction. In this cave the main deposits at the entrance contain Magdalenian III and IV levels with a poor Perigordian level below the Magdalenian and 'traces of a later Magdalenian and Azilian'[42] above the main levels. These final deposits sealed the entrance to the cave. On stylistic grounds Breuil dated most of the paintings and many engravings to the later Magdalenian periods, whereas he tentatively assigned only a few black-line drawings and several of the engraved horses to an earlier Magdalenian.

The engravings on stalagmite at Teyjat (figure 67) are securely dated to the late Magdalenian. They were executed partly on a wall of stalagmite flow and partly on broken blocks of stalagmite which were placed on the ground against the walls of the shelter. The bases only of the blocks and the engravings were found covered by Magdalenian v levels, while many of the blocks were covered by the succeeding Magdalenian VI level.[43] One engraved deer at Teyjat still retains traces of paint.

Breuil's stylistic and chronological evolutionary scheme. The number of sites where parietal art can be directly dated to various archaeological stages is very small. In many cases only indirect associations

43 Finger tracing of a bison on the clay surface of the wall at Gargas.

between habitation debris at, or near, the cave entrance and the paintings and engravings inside the caves can be established. At a very early stage of his study of cave art, Breuil interpreted the superpositioning of different representations as evidence of a basis for a floating chronology which he hoped to anchor to the known archaeological chronology by comparison with the instances where direct dating was possible.

Breuil worked on the reasonable assumption that when one painting or engraving covered another it had been executed at a later time than the original. However, the time gap between the execution of two superimposed representations need not be great; in fact, it need be no more than the moment between the completion of the one and the beginning of the other. It is implicit in some of Breuil's work that the time gap could be very short for, when two superimposed works of art appeared to him to have been executed in the same technique and style, he did not use the fact of their superpositions to assign them to different archaeological periods. Thus Breuil's floating chronology depended to a large extent on the definition of different styles and techniques and on the assumption that only one style and technique of painting or of engraving was in use at any one time. In his early work on the caves of Cantabria, Breuil[44] evolved a four-stage evolution of Palaeolithic art which started with the simple 'primitive' representations and ended with the more detailed and complex representations which made use of 'correct' perspective. At a later date[45] Breuil, on the basis of much further work, modified his original scheme and suggested a more complex two-cycle evolution of parietal art. He considered these two cycles to have developed independently from each other, each beginning with simple representations and evolving to more accurate and complex works. The first cycle is the Aurignacian-Perigordian cycle and the second the Solutreo-Magdalenian cycle

44 *Top* Red clay finger paintings of mammoth, 'snake' and other animals, from La Baume Latrone.
45 *Middle* Engraved fish on clay floor at Niaux; usually identified as a salmon.
46 *Bottom* Low-relief sculptures in clay of bison, from Bédeilhac; they form part of a larger composition including signs and are situated on the floor of a small chamber at the end of a very low and narrow passage.

each of which includes painting, engraving and sculpture. It can be summarised as follows:

Aurignacian-Perigordian cycle: This cycle, as well as the earliest art, starts with stencils of hands and rows of dots followed by simple finger drawings in clay of meandering lines. With these lines are found simple traced outlines of animals, 'intensely natural',[46] with the legs either omitted or very stiff and the horns shown full face in twisted perspective. The earliest paintings are partly contemporaneous with these early tracings and develop from them: large red signs such as claviforms and red and yellow meanders; and red 'barbarously'[47] painted animals in broad red bands and flatwash. The clay finger tracings further evolve to simple, first shallow, then deep-cut rock engravings such as those from La Ferrassie, and finally culminate in the low relief sculpture such as those of Laussel. Painting evolves to animal outlines in blotted or dotted lines; to the use of flatwash in red, black or sepia; and culminates in bichromes in which the twisted perspective of earlier works is much attenuated. These are followed by 'good' black outline and brown animals such as those from Sergeac.

Solutreo-Magdalenian cycle: This cycle starts in the Magdalenian with simple black outline animals, followed by animals with wide blotted outlines and black flatwash. Subsequently modelling is shown with areas hatched in black filled in with either red or black dots and leads to fully polychrome figures which are first partly outlined, and later fully outlined, in black. Sculpture of this cycle begins with the magnificent reliefs of the Solutrean and early Magdalenian periods which are later replaced by very delicate engravings with details finely hatched in.

Critique of stylistic and chronological evolutionary schemes. Laming[48] stressed the remarkable degree of parallelism in the development of painting in Breuil's two cycles. She also pointed out the embarrassment to this two-cycle theory, of Solutrean sculptures such as Le Roc de Sers which, in technique and style, can be considered as intermediate between the Perigordian sculptures (such as Laussel and Le Poisson) and the early Magdalenian sculptures (such as Le Cap Blanc and Angles sur l'Anglin). As will be seen in chapter 3, Laming considered superpositioning to be the

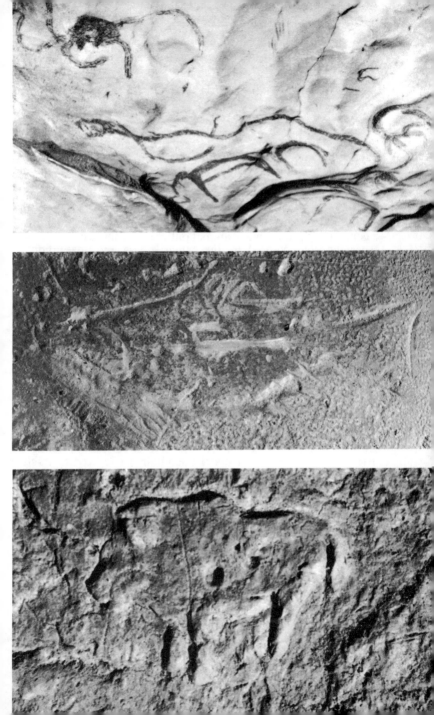

usual Palaeolithic means of representing a group or scene and, with this very different approach, suggested a single line evolution for Palaeolithic art, broadly classifiable into three stages: 1 an archaic stage which comprises Breuil's earliest groups as well as simple tentative animal outlines and dates entirely to the Aurignacian-Perigordian period; 2 a middle stage in which are included Breuil's later phases of the Aurignacian-Perigordian cycle as well as the earlier phases of his Solutreo-Magdalenian cycle (including all bas-relief sculptures, black animal outlines and the use of flatwash; especially characterised by the extensive use and adaptation of twisted perspective); 3 a final stage which culminates in the Magdalenian polychromes and the black painted and engraved animals shown in true perspective.

Laming's scheme resolves the problem of the apparent separation of the Perigordian bas-reliefs from the Solutrean and Magdalenian ones. But, like Breuil's, it is based on the fundamental assumption that an artistic tradition will show a single and unified development over a period of many thousands of years which proceeds from the simple and primitive to the elaborate, complex and detailed.

Leroi-Gourhan[49] has also formulated a single-line evolution of Palaeolithic art styles. This was based primarily on the dated examples of parietal art and on stylistic comparisons with mobile art for he, like Laming, considered superpositioning to be conscious association (see chapter 3). Like Breuil and Laming he arrived at the conclusion that Palaeolithic art represents a single artistic tradition. Like the others he saw Palaeolithic representational art as having progressed from simple beginnings to a climax of accuracy and detail, although he admits that not all apparently 'primitive' representations need necessarily be the most ancient. However, for non-representational 'signs' he allowed a very different development, from the simple but 'naturalistic' to the abstract and 'stylised'.

In each of these developmental schemes it is the uniformity of Palaeolithic art which is being assumed. One of the striking characteristics of Palaeolithic art is, however, its heterogeneity. As has already been stressed, this makes good sense when the heterogeneity of the archaeological cultures of the Upper Palaeolithic (see chapter 1) is remembered. The stylistic and chronological evolutionary schemes reviewed above have all tended to minimise the diversity of the artistic conventions and techniques which exist in Palaeolithic parietal art; in talking about a single, or even two-fold, artistic tradition they are bound to gloss over the variations of the Palaeolithic art and to stress its uniformity. The archaeological record reveals the Upper Palaeolithic period as a complex interplay of varying traditions, with some apparently sharp cultural breaks between them. That it is possible by 'content' and 'technique' to 'recognise' an individual representation as Palaeolithic does not conflict with such an archaeological record.

When traditions of Upper Palaeolithic flint working are examined they reveal the sort of picture that could be expected from the general archaeological picture of the Upper Palaeolithic and not one of progressive evolutionary improvement over thousands of years. For a clearly defined culture such as the Solutrean its distinctive flint technique can be traced for about four to five thousand years; for the Magdalenian about five to six thousand years; and for the Aurignacian no more than eight thousand years. A more pertinent example is the development of the Magdalenian mobile art for this may well be thought to have changed more rapidly than the functional stone tools. In most general terms Magdalenian mobile art can be seen to have had a slow beginning during the early Magdalenian and to have attained a peak of artistic and technical excellence during the middle Magdalenian. The late Magdalenian, however, is characterised by stylistic and technical standardisation together with a simplification of certain forms and an increased use of geometric decorative design.

There are four fallacious assumptions at the basis of evolutionary schemes of development of Palaeolithic parietal art. First, it is obvious that artistic expression when it starts for the first time will be more simple in technical competence than artistic expression with a long history of trial and error behind it. As has been seen in chapter 1, Palaeolithic art appears in the archaeological record suddenly together with the Upper Palaeolithic. Because of this it has been assumed that it is legitimate to take the most simple examples of this Palaeolithic art as the oldest examples, from which more complex examples were derived. However it is not at all certain that the beginnings of Palaeolithic art are represented in the parietal and mobile art known to the modern world. Experiments in artistic expression may well have started on organic materials, long since perished. It is not at all unreasonable to imagine many thousands of years of art-work on skins, bark-cloth, wood, etc. behind the first Palaeolithic parietal art in caves. That the Perigordian period includes such complex works as the Laussel Venus and male figure (figure 60 and frontispiece) shows conclusively how far removed from the first attempts at artistic expression, Perigordian man at least, was. There are remarkably few later Solutrean or Magdalenian works which can rival these in technical or conceptual achievement. In any case it is perfectly reasonable to imagine that the first attempts at portrayal were more detailed than later ones, for only with experience behind them could the spectators be expected to comprehend the meaning of a representation.

The second fallacious assumption follows straight on from the first. The Palaeolithic period represents human activity over something like twenty thousand years. During this time literally thousands of influences can be assumed to have affected cultural activity; results of experimentation, results from accidental discoveries, diffusion from outside sources, etc. It is ludicrous to expect to find 'simple' artistic expression throughout this period simply because the archaeologist has been unable to differentiate the sources and cultural affiliations of the sub-periods. Even if it be true that change and innovation was much slower in Palaeolithic times than in later periods,[50] it is clearly pointless to search for clear-cut improvement in artistic aptitude and expression over many thousands of years, except in the most general terms.

The third fallacious assumption is closely linked to the first two. Not only can it be correctly assumed that many influences will have affected Aurignacian artists (let alone Magdalenian, Solutrean and Perigordian artists) but it must also be recognised how unlikely it is, on the basis of many typological studies from all over the world, that any development will be one of continuous steady improvement from the 'simple' to the 'complex'. As is well known from many fields of study development is often interrupted by 'stagnant' periods, by 'standardization', and even by regression. It is absurd to assume that this did not happen with Palaeolithic art; in fact there is evidence for the same process in the Magdalenian mobile art (see above). Thus, it is clear, that not only can one expect a variety of different influences on artistic expression, some of which may well have been self-contradictory, over a period of many thousands of years but one can also expect to find many 'beginnings' and many 'climaxes' of artistic expression at different points during these thousands of years.

The fourth assumption so commonly found in evolutionary and chronological schemes of development is a more complex one. If, for the sake of argument, it would be granted that the three assumptions mentioned above were indeed justified it would remain to construct a valid scale of artistic achievement. Consideration of the schemes of Breuil and others shows that the height of artistic achievement by Palaeolithic artists is assumed to be the polychrome paintings and the fine delicate engravings, while the 'simplest' works are those with painted outlines only and with deep engraved outlines. Again this may well be a fallacious assumption, based on the visual impressions of people living in the nineteenth and twentieth centuries. When considering the achievements of Palaeolithic artists it is more realistic to evaluate the technical and conceptual difficulties of the work of art than its visual impact on the modern connoisseur.

A ranking of the Palaeolithic techniques used in parietal art (see above) must recognise that the one which requires the least effort and the least technical skill is clay finger-tracing. The next easiest technique is painting for, whether the pigment was used as crayons, paste or liquid paint, considerably less effort and technical ingenuity is required to apply paint than to cut rock. Bas-relief sculpture, on the other hand, requires considerable effort and also considerable skill. The higher the relief and the more clearly the forms are undercut, the greater the effort and skill required. Thus it follows that sculptures such as the friezes of Le Cap Blanc (figure 66), in which the animals are deeply cut out, are amongst the greatest technical achievements of Palaeolithic artists. Deeply cut out engravings, though requiring considerably less effort than true bas-reliefs, must be ranked as more difficult than the fine, lightly engraved, figures, which were executed by light scratching of the rock with a sharp tool. Of course, to draw up such a scheme of technical difficulty in any detail, it would be necessary to consider the hardness of the rocks on which engravings were made (see the geographical distribution of bas-reliefs, above).

The situation is, in fact, considerably more complex for evaluations of 'difficulty' must be based not only on physical effort and technical skill but also on stylistic complexity and sophistication of concept. By the time the variables are all listed together (hardness of material; technique employed; daylight or darkness; number of legs/horns/antlers represented; twisted or 'true' perspective; front or three-quarter view; detail and accuracy of features represented; etc.) it becomes quite clear that any scheme which assumes the steady progression over thousands of years from a simple outline engraving or painting to a polychrome painting or detailed engraving must be a gross oversimplification of what is likely to have been the true state of affairs.

No attempt is made here to suggest how Palaeolithic parietal art may be evolved; there is absolutely no point in trying to deduce a straight evolutionary line when the time span under consideration represents thousands of years and the available evidence suggests that during this time many different cultural influences and movements were at work.

Before moving on to the content of Palaeolithic parietal art, however, it may be profitable to summarise what is definitely known about the various styles and techniques used by the artists of the archaeologically defined cultures.

Some of the earliest known art forms are deeply engraved simple animal outlines and symbols on limestone of early and middle Aurignacian date. Both technically and chronologically these are followed by similar, but more detailed, engravings and also by bas-relief sculptures of the late Perigordian. In the Perigordian bison engraving of La Grèze the animal is shown in simple outline, but the horns are in twisted perspective, whereas the bas-relief humans are modelled in detail in front or three-quarter views. The bas-relief technique is found again in the late Solutrean and middle Magdalenian, when it was used for long friezes of animals and humans, carved either directly out of the living rock, or on blocks placed side by side.

Painting was practised throughout the Upper Palaeolithic, but the Aurignacian paintings of La Ferrassie are too worn to determine details of style. In the Perigordian a black outline painting with twisted perspective is firmly dated from Labatut, and paint was used on the bas-reliefs at all periods. The comparatively more rapid decay of paint in exposed zones has meant that far fewer Palaeolithic paintings than engravings have been preserved in datable contexts, and the many painting styles cannot be dated on stratigraphic evidence. Combination of fine engraving and painting is found in the late Magdalenian site of Teyjat and may date back to the middle Magdalenian, as at Angles sur l'Anglin where the sculpted and engraved frieze also has traces of paint.

There is no sure stratigraphic evidence to support Breuil's theory that the simple Aurignacian engravings developed from clay finger tracings, nor that hand impressions are amongst the earliest artistic manifestations.

Content

Animals: The apparent accuracy of representation and frequent indication of characteristic detail, has led several people[51] to try to identify the animals more closely; to identify not only species but also subspecies. Specific identifications of animals such as elephants or rhinoceros have been used in attempts to date the paintings either to fully glacial or to interstadial periods, and finer differentiation into subspecies have been attempted particularly for horses, oxen and reindeer. Before considering in individual detail each group of animals represented, one general characteristic of Palaeolithic representations of animals deserves especial mention. Very few cases are known where sure identification of baby animals can be made (possible examples are ibex, owl and rhinoceros – figures 68, 27 and 69) and no definite case of animal copulation is known. Unless the primary sexual organs of the animals are shown it is difficult to distinguish between the male and the female of most species. Since the scale adopted for showing animals varies from one representation to another, even within a single panel, size dimorphism between the sexes cannot be taken as a criterion for identifying male and female animals. Only in a few species are secondary sexual differences sufficiently distinctive to be easily recognised from Palaeolithic representations, and these will be discussed under the relevant sections.

Elephants. The majority of elephants represented are quite characteristic of the mammoth (*Mammuthus primigenius*). This elephant was especially adapted to life in cold climatic environments. Apart from its distinctive coat of long shaggy hair, it also had a thick woolly coat and a considerable layer of subcutaneous fat (and other physiological adaptations to cold conditions). In profile its fat hump on the shoulders and the steeply sloping back are characteristic, as is also its strongly rounded head. The mammoth was smaller than earlier elephants, standing approximately three and a half metres at the shoulder, but it had massive tusks, elegantly curved outwards and slightly up at the tip. Mammoths first appear at the beginning of the last glaciation and persist until the end of this glaciation, gradually becoming more restricted to north-east Europe as the glaciers retreated. They finally became extinct in Siberia around 10,000 BC. During the last glaciation they spread throughout Europe, replacing the straight-tusked elephant of the temperate zones. The mammoths roamed in large herds on the open steppes and tundra of east and central Europe where they were hunted, and reached south of the Alps into Italy. They were also common in the sparsely wooded regions of western Europe, but probably did not penetrate south of the Pyrenees. In Spain the earlier type of elephant, the straight-tusked elephant (*Palaeoloxodon antiquus*) survived at least for part of the last glaciation. This elephant was adapted to living in temperate forested country, as much of Spain would have been during the glaciations of Europe. The straight-tusked elephant was rather larger than the mammoth, without the fat hump, and with a slightly less steeply sloping back. Nothing is known of its coat, but there is no reason to suppose that it differed considerably from the nearly hairless condition of modern elephants. One of its most obvious differences from the mammoth lies in the shape of its tusks which are nearly straight, with only a very slight curvature, first outwards and then inwards.

Among Palaeolithic representations of elephants, a few have been identified as belonging to the straight-tusked elephant, and not the mammoth. Two Spanish elephants, at El Pindal and at El

Castillo (figure 70), both in the Cantabrian mountains, have been identified as the straight-tusked elephant on the basis of the absence of a hairy coat and the shape of the back. In neither case are the tusks indicated. In this region, the existence of *Palaeoloxodon antiquus* during the Upper Palaeolithic does not raise any serious problems of ecology or chronology. The elephant of Cougnac (figure 71) in France, however, is also shown hairless, but here the shape of the back and the curvature of the tusks are consistent with those of mammoth. It is more likely that the hair was omitted than that the Cougnac elephant represented *Palaeoloxodon antiquus*.

Rhinoceros. The woolly rhinoceros (*Coelodonta antiquitatis*), like the mammoth, was particularly well adapted for life in arctic conditions. Its coat of wool, long shaggy hair on a thick skin and insulating layer of subcutaneous fat are its most obvious adaptations to cold climatic conditions. These are accompanied by other physiological adaptations to cold. The woolly rhinoceros spread across Europe from Asia at the beginning of the last glaciation, and replaced the temperate woodland form of rhinoceros, Merck's rhinoceros (*Dicerorhinus kirchbergensis*). Apart from its insulating coat there are two more characteristics which serve to distinguish woolly rhinoceros from Merck's rhinoceros. The nose horn of the woolly rhinoceros is set far forward and is comparatively long and slender, ending in a point while a second, shorter and stouter, nose

49 Black painted horse
from the 'Salon Noir' at
Niaux; details such as
beard, hoofs and body
hair are indicated in
great detail.

horn is set a short distance behind this. In Merck's rhinoceros
the nose horns are shorter and stouter than those of the woolly
rhinoceros and not set as far forward on the nose. A second major
difference between the two forms is the angle at which they hold
their head at rest. The woolly rhinoceros, which is adapted to
feeding on open steppe vegetation of low lying plants, has the head
swung low (like the present-day African white rhinoceros which
also feeds on low lying plants), making a wide angle with the line of
the back and so accentuating the humped shoulders. Merck's rhinoceros, which is adapted to woodland vegetation, held its head more
or less in a straight continuation of the line of the back (as in the
present-day black African rhinoceros).

The majority of representations of rhinoceros are undoubtedly of
the woolly rhinoceros as typified by Rouffignac rhinos (e.g. figure
69). The rhinoceros of Lascaux (figure 23), however, has been
interpreted by Zeuner[52] as Merck's rhinoceros. Zeuner considered
the entire cave fauna of Lascaux as that of a woodland environment, and hence the identification of the rhinoceros as a woolly
rhinoceros would be inconsistent with the rest of the fauna represented. Zeuner used the faunal representations to date the Lascaux
paintings to the very beginning of the Aurignacian, when isolated
specimens of Merck's rhinoceros still probably survived in western
Europe. On purely morphological grounds, however, there is no
reason to suppose that the rhinoceros at Lascaux is of a different
species from all the others known in Palaeolithic art. The angle of
the head and the humped shoulders, though not as strongly accentuated as in some Rouffignac examples are not inconsistent with a
woolly rhinoceros identification, and this is further indicated by the
rather slender and long nose horn. Although the forelegs and belly
of the animal are not clearly indicated, faint vertical lines under the
neck and belly could well be taken to represent the shaggy coat of
the woolly rhinoceros.

Horses. Horses are among the most commonly represented animals
in Palaeolithic parietal art. The European wild horse of the late Pleistocene is *Equus caballus*, from which all modern horses derive. Until
the middle of the last century one wild form of *Equus caballus* (*Equus
gmelini*) still lived in Europe. It is difficult, on palaeontological

evidence, to distinguish this wild horse from the Przewalski horse which still survives in Mongolia, and therefore to determine to which the Pleistocene wild horses of Europe belonged. The identification of several subspecies of horse in Palaeolithic paintings has been claimed from time to time, including the Przewalski horse, the recently extinct tarpan and various hypothetical forms from which some of the modern breeds are believed to be derived.

Since the Przewalski horse is the best known wild horse, it has generally been taken as the living representative of the Pleistocene horse. Like all wild horses it is smaller than most modern breeds, with a massively built body and neck, round belly, short slender legs ending in heavy hoofs and an upright mane. The tarpan horse differs from the Przewalski in its slightly smaller size, its more slender form of the neck and head and in its colouring which is mouse-grey. Both have a paler belly and dark legs. The tarpan's tail was more fully haired and its mane less upright than that of the Przewalski horse. Both have a dark mane which continues as a dark stripe along the back to the tail. Both forms of wild horse had thicker coats than most modern breeds and grew a distinctly thicker, slightly woolly, coat in winter. The Przewalski horse lives in arid steppe country and can withstand severe winter temperatures. The tarpan is known to have existed in the forests of Poland, but appears to have been particularly prominent in the less arid grassland plains of the Ukraine.

Zeuner[53] has suggested that some, at least, of the horses represented in Palaeolithic art are more like the tarpan than the Przewalski horse. He refers particularly to the frieze of small bichrome horses of Lascaux (figures 14 and 52). In this identification he is, however, again strongly influenced by his interpretation of the entire faunal assemblage of Lascaux as belonging to a forested environment. Bourdelle[54] found that he could recognise three horse subtypes in Palaeolithic art; one of which corresponds quite closely to the Przewalski, one of which resembles the present-day 'nordic' horses which are larger and, especially, longer in the back than the Przewalski horse, and a third type which he compared with the present-day 'celtic' horse. However, as Windels[55] has shown, for the Lascaux horses the characteristics of the different forms isolated by Bourdelle and others are by no means exclusive, for features

50 *Top left* Red and black negative hand stencils, from Gargas; some have shortened fingers and/or thumb.
51 *Top right* Black painted bison, from El Castillo.
52 *Bottom* Painted bichrome horse with rounded belly and short legs, from Lascaux, with arrow-shaped or barbed signs nearby.

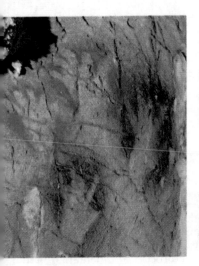

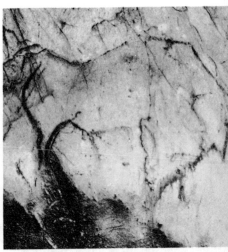

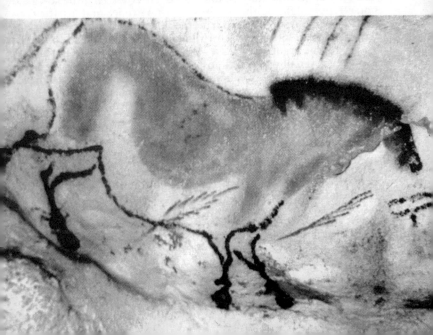

86

53 Engraved ibex, from Ebbou.
54 *Far right* Engraved bison,
from La Grèze; the horns are
shown in 'twisted perspective';
only one front and one hind leg
are indicated.

such as the position of the head, the position of the mane and the position of the tail overlap considerably. Windels suggests that this overlapping of characteristics could be explained if different subspecies of horse had been in the process of differentiation and had not yet become fully characterised. Alternatively, the so-called horse types might be the result of artistic licence and artistic conventions. One has only to look at the different stylistic conventions employed in different caves for showing the horse's head to see the weight of this argument (figure 72). Thus, in Pech-Merle the head is shown as a small narrow almost shapeless projection on the neck, the 'duck-bill' head of Laming;[56] at Lascaux the horses' heads are generally disproportionately small and narrow, but with the nostrils, and sometimes the eye shown; in contrast the horse's head from Niaux, for example, is carefully outlined and shaded, with detail of nostril, mouth, eye and chin hairs shown with little or no distortion.

The only other known equid to have existed in late Pleistocene Europe was the wild ass, *Equus hydruntinus*. Wild asses were particularly common in Italy and the Mediterranean region where they are found among the food debris of Palaeolithic habitations. They also penetrated into the less extreme cold regions of France, but asses are essentially animals of temperate climate and cannot withstand the very cold conditions of the tundra. There have been

occasional reports in the literature of the hemione (a half ass, *E. hemionus*) in European Palaeolithic sites, but Stehlin and Graziosi[57] consider that many of these are in fact true asses or true horses. A few equid representations on cave walls have been identified as asses on account of their slender build, particularly the slender neck and head and long pointed ears as shown in the examples from Lascaux (figure 73), a doubtful one from Montespan and a few others. Wild asses appear to have been rare in France and Spain, and they are amongst the more rarely represented animals.

Bison.[58] Bison are almost as common as horses in parietal art. They are clearly distinguishable from other animals by their massive neck and shoulders, and comparatively slender hindquarters. The European bison of the Upper Palaeolithic period is *Bison uriformis* (Hilzheimer) which differs from the earlier *Bison priscus* primarily in the curvature and size of its horns.[59] It is from the size and shape of their horns that Zeuner identified the Lascaux bison as the early form *B. priscus*.[60] He considered this to be evidence for an early date of the Lascaux paintings, and to support his identification of the rhinoceros. Laming, however, ascribes the large horns of the Lascaux bison as due to 'lack of skill on the part of the artist'.[61]

B. uriformis differed in appearance from the modern American bison in two respects. Its horns were somewhat larger, and they

55 *Top* Low-relief sculpture of a fish,
from Gorge d'Enfer.
56 *Bottom* Large, black painted bull,
from Lascaux; its horns and hoofs
are shown in 'twisted perspective'.

89

curved outwards and upwards in a light S-curve, projecting out of
the thick fur of the animal's head, whereas in the American bison
the horns are curved close to the head. A more striking difference is
in the shape of the head and neck. The American bison has a short
rounded head and a massive fat hump on the shoulders which gives
it a double-humped profile. In *B. uriformis*, as in the modern
European bison, *B. bonasus*, the fat hump was continuous over the
neck and shoulders. The horns of *B. bonasus* are, however, smaller
and differently curved from those of the fossil European form.

Bison live on open steppe and in lightly forested regions, and
although they are not adapted to arctic conditions, they were
common throughout the Upper Palaeolithic and were extensively
hunted. It is often difficult to distinguish bison from aurochs
remains, so that in many cases one can only tell that large bovids
were hunted, and the relative importance of these two animals in
Palaeolithic times is difficult to ascertain.

Wild Oxen. Wild oxen are frequently represented in Palaeolithic
art. The late Pleistocene wild ox is the aurochs, *Bos primigenius*,
which became extinct in Europe during the seventeenth century. Its
appearance is therefore known from descriptions of that period,
and also from experiments at the Munich and Berlin zoos where
animals with the characteristics of aurochs have been bred back
from certain breeds of domestic cattle. The aurochs were considerably larger than modern cattle, the bulls reaching as much as two
metres at the shoulders. The bulls were massively built with long
curved horns, generally pointing upwards and forwards, but some
depressed horn forms are also known from the fossil record. The
horns were pale with black tips and light curly hair between them.
The bulls were very dark in colour, brown or nearly black whereas
the cows were smaller and considerably more slender in build than
the bulls and had slightly shorter horns. They were often paler in
colour, with a dark head and had a pale stripe along the back (e.g.
figure 74). Wild cattle lived in open woodland or parkland but not
on arid steppes. Although they did grow a woolly winter coat they
could not survive the extreme cold of tundra winters.

Although the oxen in the cave paintings have generally been
assumed to represent the aurochs, it has been said[62] that at Lascaux

57a Head of an engraved deer, from Altamira, closely similar to a mobile engraving, figure 57b.

two distinct species of Bos were represented: the aurochs and a smaller species of Bos, which is only known from post-glacial sites in Europe. This short-horned cattle, *Bos longifrons* (= *Bos brachyceros*) differs from the aurochs primarily in its more graceful build with slender head, shorter horns, and a bony ridge between the horns. Its wild ancestry is not certainly known, but it seems to have been derived from the aurochs through domestication. In the absence of any fossil evidence for the existence of *Bos longifrons* in Europe during the Pleistocene[63] it cannot be assumed that the Lascaux cattle represent this short-horned species. The differences between the massive Lascaux oxen (figure 56) and more slender forms (figures 14 and 74) is better explained as the representation of sexual dimorphism of the aurochs. In fact, in some of the representations the detail of colouring and even the pale stripe along the back and curvature of the horns agree very well with what is known of the appearance of aurochs bulls and cows.

Deer. The most commonly represented deer of the late Pleistocene is the red deer, *Cervus elaphus*, which typically lives in forests but also thrives in the more open regions north of the forest zones, as in present-day Scotland. During the coldest periods of the Upper Palaeolithic red deer were rare and were largely replaced by reindeer (*Rangifer tarandus*). During the interstadials and at the end of the Pleistocene, red deer again became more common (e.g. at the end of the Magdalenian and during the Azilian), and reindeer became rarer and finally became restricted to more northerly regions. There are two distinct ecotypes of reindeer which have somewhat different habitats. Both the tundra and the forest reindeer probably existed in Pleistocene France but never spread south of the Pyrenees.

Male red deer have branching antlers which are shed annually in the autumn and grow larger, more elaborate, forms each year as the animals grow older. The females have no antlers. These deer are frequently represented in many caves, particularly in the Cantabrian ones; an artistic distribution which coincides well with their actual distribution. At Lascaux it is generally the males which are shown, with a fine display of antlers (figure 22), but representations

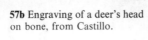

57b Engraving of a deer's head
on bone, from Castillo.

of does are also known, again particularly in Spanish caves (figure 47). In many representations (e.g. figure 75) the male antler spread is shown in fine detail; in fact the detail is exaggerated and must, in many cases, be accepted as artistic licence, not realism.

Both the male and the female reindeer have antlers, which are shed annually in autumn by the males and in spring by the females and immature males. The female antlers are somewhat smaller than those of the full-grown male, but the differences are too slight to be used for assessing secondary sexual characteristics without careful measurements. The tundra reindeer, which now lives in the open tundra of northern Europe and Asia, can be distinguished from the forest reindeer by the shape of its antlers. The tundra reindeer has slender rounded antlers which are lightly palmated, whereas the forest reindeer has shorter flatter antlers which are clearly palmated. Despite their actual distribution in France, reindeer are not commonly represented in parietal art, except at Le Gabillou (figure 76), although they are better known from mobile art.

Palaeolithic art also includes representations of an extinct form of deer, *Megaloceros hibernicus* (e.g. figure 28) (also known as Irish elk or giant deer) which was about the size of a horse, with a humped back and a magnificent spread of palmated antlers. This deer lived in open steppes north of the forest zones. Artisitic representations are rare.

The elk, which also lives in northern forests, is known to have lived in Europe during the Upper Palaeolithic. There are, however, no Palaeolithic parietal paintings, engravings or sculptures which can certainly be identified as representing the elk.

Ibex and Chamois. Ibex (*Capra ibex*) are now restricted to mountainous country but during the Upper Palaeolithic they occurred abundantly throughout south-west France and Spain, and were hunted by Palaeolithic man. The chamois (*Rupicapra rupicapra*) which, like the ibex, is now also restricted to mountainous country is much less frequently represented and is not known from parietal art. This animal has two short upward-pointing horns and a steep and concave head profile, whereas the ibex can invariably be recognised by its gracefully curving horns (e.g. figure 25) which are shorter in the female than in the male.

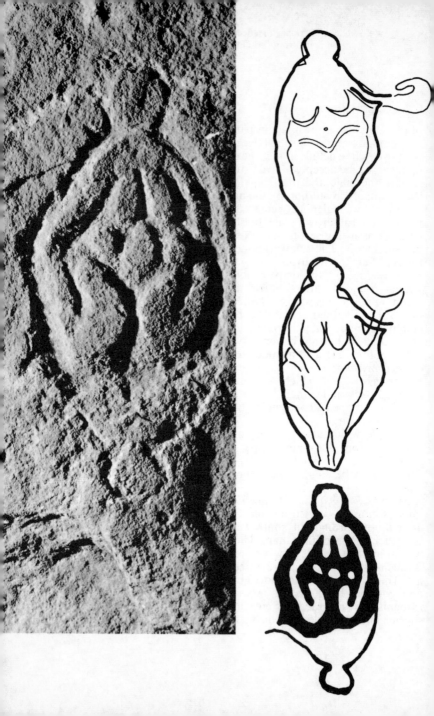

58 *Far left* Deeply engraved figure usually interpreted as a coitus or parturition scene, from Laussel.
59 *Left* Comparison by Leroi-Gourhan of the 'coitus' figure from Laussel with two finished figures from Laussel.
60 *Below* Low-relief sculpture of a female figure with traces of red paint, from Laussel. (Ht. 43 cm).

Musk-ox. During the Pleistocene musk-ox (*Ovibos moschatus*), which is exclusively a tundra animal, was much rarer in France than in central Europe and it features only rarely in Palaeolithic art (figure 35).

Carnivores. Representations of carnivores are rarer in Palaeolithic art than are those of herbivores. Many of them are of the cave lion (*Panthera* (*Leo*) *spelaea*) (e.g. figure 41) which can be identified by a rather squarish muzzle, round ears and large canines (as in the Labastide head of a lion with open mouth). It is not known whether the male cave lion had a mane like the present-day African lion (*Panthera* (*Leo*) *leo*), and it is therefore unjustifiable to identify all the maneless representations as females. No Palaeolithic lion representations have a mane indicated, with the possible exception of the cameo lion of Les Trois Frères (figure 26), where several faint lines around one side of the head might, perhaps, indicate a mane. Other carnivores include a few representations of wolf (*Canis lupus*) (figure 78) (e.g. at Les Combarelles), a glutton (*Gulo gulo*) (figure 77) (at Los Casares) and several representations of bear (figure 79) (e.g. at Les Combarelles). The bear shown in Palaeolithic art is presumably the brown bear (*Ursus arctos*) and not the large cave bear (*Ursus spelaeus*) which had become extinct by then. Brown bear, like the cave bear, used caves in which to hibernate and to give birth to its young. Remains of bears are not infrequent in caves, and their claw marks on the rock walls are found occasionally interspersed or overlapping with cave art, thus showing they were more or less contemporary with the artists.

Boar. Wild boar (*Sus scrofa*) is a forest animal and cannot survive in open regions. They were consequently not very common in Upper Palaeolithic France, except during the milder interstadials. In Spain, boar was hunted throughout the Upper Palaeolithic and representations of wild boar are known from Spanish caves, for instance at Altamira (figure 8), and also from French caves, such as Niaux.

Other Animals. Palaeolithic representations of fish are known for instance from the sculpture of Gorge d'Enfer (figure 55) and the clay engraving of Niaux (figure 45), and have been identified as salmon and trout respectively. The many sinuous lines (e.g. figure 44) which have been called snakes by some[64] have been seen as eels by others.[65] Breuil[66] cautiously refers to them as 'snake-like lines', or 'macaroni' when they are interlaced. Two rather round-bodied marine animals with pointed snouts from the south Spanish cave of Nerja (figure 80) are probably dolphins.

There are occasional representations of birds but it is often difficult to identify the species accurately. Snow owls have been identified at Les Trois Frères (figure 27) and Le Portel and a more doubtful interpretation is that of the bustard at Le Roc de Sers (figure 82) and goose at Labastide (figure 81). The sharp-beaked bird on the ceiling reported from Rouffignac turned out to be a rhinoceros viewed upside-down (figure 84).

Among other rarely represented animals is a delightfully engraved hare at Le Gabillou (figure 83).

Imaginary creatures. In the literature there are many references to 'fantastic' creatures. In many cases these are due to the misreading of superimposed lines; photographs in Breuil's *Four Hundred Centuries of Cave Art*,[67] for example, show a strange backward-looking horse from Pair non Pair which was called 'Agnus Dei' by its discoverer. In different lighting[68] it becomes clear that this representation is in fact made up of two different animals: an ibex whose head is invisible in Breuil's photograph, and the back of a horse which faces in the opposite direction.

A few Palaeolithic representations of 'animals' are quite unlike any known animal, and must have been intended as imaginary compound beings, mythical animals or monsters, for in many cases they are carefully engraved or painted, and the lack of resemblance to known animals cannot be attributed to artistic ineptitude or misinterpretation. The best known of these imaginary beings is the spotted representation at Lascaux (figure 85). Its saggy, tail-less body, humped shoulders and long neck ending in a square head are quite unlike any animal known, living or extinct. It has been called a unicorn, although there are clearly two parallel 'horns' rising straight forward and upward from its forehead. Leroi-Gourhan[69] has suggested that its horns are not part of the mythical being, but this seems improbable since the lines clearly start from the animal's head and are not joined to the ox. Another imaginary creature is engraved in a narrow passage at Le Tuc d'Audoubert (figure 86). It has a strongly rounded back and the body is entirely covered in finely engraved hatching. The head has a thick drooping muzzle, not unlike an exaggerated elk muzzle, or the thickened nose of the saiga antelope, but instead of antlers or antelope horns it has short curved horns, and a large ear. A drawing by Breuil[70] of an 'animal' at La Pileta shows that a similar head profile is combined with the body of a bovid with sagging stomach.

In the Combel extension of Pech-Merle is a unique painted composition of a row of compound animals (figure 88). Their most striking features are large ballooning bodies on slender legs. The three foremost animals have slender, disproportionately small, heads resembling those of antelopes. The body of the foremost animal has been omitted and it only consists of the head and neck and is joined on to the next animal by an arc of dots. The fourth and last animal is indicated only by the hindquarters, belly and one foreleg and it appears to 'share' the back, neck and head with the third animal.

As a final example of an imaginary creature it is interesting to note the sculpted bison with boar's head from Le Roc de Sers (figure 10). Breuil[71] considered the head to be a later alteration, for he found all except one of the bison of Le Roc de Sers unfinished or 'altered in shape'.

There are also part animal, part human, figures which are more logically included here under the heading 'imaginary creatures' than under the heading 'human representations' (below). The figures of Los Casares in Spain which Breuil[72] described as part human and part frog-like may also be classed among compound or mythical beings. Although it is difficult to follow Breuil's description, the rounded heads with open, blunt beak-like mouths and a large eye (figure 87) are clearly not representations of any real animal.

The compound creature from Les Trois Frères (figure 89), called a sorcerer by Breuil and many others (see chapter 3), is equally unlike any known creature, and embodies features from a large number of animals. The tail and curvature of the back could belong to a horse, the legs and feet are human but the forelegs and palmated hands are closer to a bear's paw than to any other animal and the penis and testicles are wrongly positioned for any animal or human. The head is not easy to identify. On Breuil's drawing (figure 89) the head is shown bearded with round owl-like eyes, tufted ears and stag's antlers.

Human representations. Human representations, although in no way a conspicuous part of Palaeolithic parietal art, are very varied. The most detailed and accurate of the human representations are some of the bas-relief figures at Laussel and the two reclining figures at La Magdelaine. The bas-relief technique used for these human figures is no different from that used for animal figures but in some the artistic sophistication is greater. The La Magdelaine figures (figure 90) are shown in reclining posture with the head supported on one arm, one leg extended and the other bent at the knee (recently a somewhat similar engraving has been published from Le Gabillou[72]). At Laussel the figures are standing (figures 3, frontispiece, 58 and 60): one female figure has one hand on the abdomen and the other raised, holding an object resembling a horn; her legs appear to be shown in profile view, facing each other. A second figure also holds an object in outstretched hand, while a third has the arm bent at the elbow and raised, but is too damaged to tell whether she also held a horn-shaped object; the male figure from Laussel (frontispiece), unlike the female figures, is shown in three-quarter profile view, except that the torso is twisted face-on to show the shoulder and part of the outstretched arms. None of the intact bas-relief figures have any facial features indicated. One further figure from Laussel (figures 58 and 59) is unique in that it represents a double figure, one of which, at least, has breasts. This relief has been interpreted[74] either as a copulation or a parturition scene, but since the rock is very worn the details of this figure are difficult to make out.

In several instances, low relief or deeply incised representations of humans are reduced to part of the body alone. At Angles sur l'Anglin three female torsos, from the waist down to the ankles, are modelled in bas-relief with the navel, sexual triangle and vulva indicated by incision (figure 65). On blocks at La Ferrassie, the female form is even further reduced to a more or less triangular or oval form with short vertical slit (figure 34) generally interpreted[75] as the female sexual triangle and vulva, and similar representations are very occasionally found engraved on cave walls.

Another manner of representing the human figure is shown both by the engravings on limestone blocks at La Roche (figure 92a) and Les Combarelles (figure 92b) and the painted figures of Pech-Merle (figure 92c). The recognition of these as anthropomorphic representations rests on their resemblance to the profiles of small pendants from Petersfels (figure 92d) which themselves are not easy to interpret. It has been suggested[76] that all these schematic figures were evolved from drawings such as the clay tracings on the ceiling of Pech-Merle (figure 17) where female figures are supposedly shown in profile with bodies bent slightly forward, broad buttocks, pendulous breasts and arms and legs barely indicated. On one of the ceiling drawings the head is said to be shown in outline, but two others are said to be headless.

At Lascaux a male figure is drawn very stiffly, unlike the animals (figure 23). In one instance at Le Portel a roughly human outline enclosing a stalagmite protrusion (figure 33) has been interpreted as a phallic representation. In the majority of so-called human representations, however, no clear sexual characteristics are indicated.

The 'human' representations are very varied in execution and the manner, however sketchy, adopted for showing the human anatomy; it is difficult to isolate any common denominator beyond the extremely crude and sketchy execution of many of them. On the most elaborate examples details of hair styles may be indicated (buns (?) on representations from Laussel (figure 60) and Pech-Merle (figure 17), for example) while others have no hair shown at all. On the most elaborate, postures and limbs are clearly shown while on others no identifiable posture can be made out and limbs are not differentiated. Until recently all of the so-called human representations were supposedly nude, except for those said to be wearing masks (figure 94, and see chapter 3), but at Le Gabillou there is an engraving of a human wearing an 'anorak'[77]; examples of mobile art (figurines and engravings) are shown' with possible examples of anklets, bracelets and other ornamentation.

The crude nature of so many 'anthropomorphs' may, in part, be due to the misinterpretation of superimposed lines by many archaeologists; there has been a tendency over the past one hundred years for any obscure painted or engraved line to be taken as evidence of one more Palaeolithic representation of a human.[78]

Hands. Palaeolithic parietal art includes representations of hands (and perhaps feet) which were painted on the rock walls, and are quite distinct from the footprints and occasional hand impressions on the clay floors of caves. The hand representations are not frequent but are very characteristic of certain caves; they occur in more than twenty caves in France, Spain and Italy. Hands are often shown as negative prints – that is, the hand shape itself is left clear of paint while the surrounding rock is coloured, probably by stencilling (e.g. figure 50); less commonly as positive prints – the hand shape itself is coloured, and exceptionally with only the tips of the fingers represented – as at Cougnac. It has been claimed for a few of these representations[79] that fingers have been retouched after their initial painting. Painted hands are most commonly red or black/brown/violet but are also known in yellow and white.

The most striking caves with hand representations are Gargas and El Castillo where hands are shown in isolation on the walls, in niches, or occasionally superimposed in large panels containing numerous hand stencils (e.g. figure 50). In other caves such as Les Trois Frères and Pech-Merle, for example, hands are much less common and are often shown close to representations such as dots, animals, etc.

It has been claimed for Gargas that left hands are found on the left-hand walls of the cave (as one enters the cave) and right hands on the right walls of the cave.[80] On the basis of representations at Gargas and El Castillo it was noticed that left hands were much more frequent than right hands (about 159 as against about 23) and in the former that the hands are small.

On some of the hand stencils, one or several of the fingers are considerably shorter than normal. Some authors[81] have interpreted this shortening as indicative of actual hand mutilation, others[82] as evidence of disease (e.g. Raynaud's), and others[83] as evidence of the artists having, for some unknown reason, held the back or the palm of their hands against the cave walls with one or several of the fingers bent forwards away from or towards the cave wall.

Some painted representations at a few caves such as Santian have been interpreted as feet and hands with forearms, but their forms are not at all clear.

Signs. The many characteristic non-representational signs in Palaeolithic art are engraved or painted but never shown in bas-relief. They are found either with animal representations, singly, or in groups of signs apart from the animals. Unlike the other Palaeolithic representations, signs are not frequently super-imposed on other signs (except at La Pileta where they are probably of post-Palaeolithic date (figure 11)) or on animals. One exception to this generalisation are the signs shaped like feathers which are found engraved or painted on the bodies of some of the animals (figure 93l). These particular signs have often been considered to represent arrows (see chapter 3) but real Palaeolithic bone projectile points were either not barbed or were mounted to produce only a single barb, and fully biserial barbed harpoons only appeared in the final Magdalenian. These feather-shaped signs as well as many others such as dots and ovals, which have frequently been given a representational interpretation (see chapter 3) are here all classed as non-representational.

Parietal signs vary greatly in shape and complexity (figures 93a–l); they appear to be both more numerous and more complex the farther south they are found,[84] especially in Spain.

Various names have been used to refer to different signs: tecti-forms, claviforms, scutiforms, penniforms, aviforms, etc. These terms are derived from a representational identification of items such as huts, clubs, shields, feathered objects, birds, etc. Since their original application, however, they have been commonly used as names simply to refer to various sign-shapes, without prejudice to their significance or identification.

Many of these forms will be referred to in more detail in later chapters. They vary from the simplest painted single or grouped dots or lines (figure 93a) to more complex square or rectangular shapes, often divided into sections by parallel vertical divisions (figures 93a, h and i). One complex form consists of a bar with a rounded protrusion on one side, about half way along (figure 93g).

Another complex sign is oval and boat-shaped, commonly with a central protrusion and divided by hatchings and strokes into geometric designs (figure 93k).

Context

Palaeolithic parietal art gives an impression of variety not only by its content, styles and techniques but also by its contexts. At first sight the various contexts seem to have little in common; the newcomer to Palaeolithic art may be surprised to find that having seen the sculptures of Le Cap Blanc, for example, situated on the walls of an open-air shelter, his next visit to the parietal art of Marsoulas, for instance, will necessitate examination of the walls of a tunnel-like cave extending beyond the reach of daylight. His third visit may well take him to the cave of Rouffignac, where he is saved several kilometres of walking in the dark till he reaches the first parietal art, by a train service. Once arrived at the Palaeolithic representations he can easily walk upright in galleries devoid of stalagmites and stalactites so that he will again be surprised that, at a cave such as Le Portel, he is forced to scramble and slide around numerous boulders to see the wall engravings and paintings.

In the literature this variety of parietal contexts has been largely ignored in interpretative essays (see chapter 3) for, in most cases, all Palaeolithic parietal art has been considered to have the same meaning. One aspect of this variety has been considered by many authors; thus Breuil[85] noted the association of bas-relief sculpture with daylight shelters and stressed the difference between representations in daylight and in dark caves. In fact bas-relief sculptures are nearly always found in daylight contexts (but see figure 95) and never deep down inside caves.[86] Recently Laming[87] has, on the basis of contexts, distinguished two traditions of Palaeolithic parietal art, and she divides all the art into 1 open air shelters, associated with habitation debris, and 2 deep down in caves, not associated with any habitation. It is not clear how she would classify caves in which decoration starts with habitation debris at, or near, the entrance but where only the decoration continues far down inside the cave. Leroi-Gourhan[88] has attempted to include such 'intermediate' contexts by postulating a chronological

61 *Above* Black painted deer, from Labatut.
62 *Left* Engraved horse, from Labatut.
63 *Below* Low-relief sculptures of oxen, from Le Fourneau du Diable.

significance to the depth penetration of caves. He considered that the earliest art is found at the cave entrance or in open shelters and that, subsequently, people penetrated progressively farther into the depth of caverns until the middle Magdalenian. In the late Magdalenian, according to Leroi-Gourhan, there was a return to the decoration of shallow caves and shelters. This scheme is based on dates obtained by stylistic comparisons and ignores the association, or non-association, of works of art with human occupation debris.

Before any real attempt to assess the variety of contexts of Palaeolithic parietal art can be undertaken two important points must be considered: whether the present-day entrance to a cave was also the Palaeolithic entrance to it, and whether the apparent distribution of the art within the shelter or cave is the same as in Palaeolithic times or has changed through the effects of weathering and differential preservation.

Any valid discussion about the context of Palaeolithic parietal art must not only be based on knowledge of the route which Palaeolithic man used to carry out his artistic works but also on the sort of activity which was carried out in the decorated regions of the caves. Knowledge about entrances to caves depends almost entirely on the extent to which the caves have been fully explored. Although it can be assumed in the majority of cases that any cave passages and tunnels which existed in Palaeolithic times will also exist today and that no new passages will have formed since Palaeolithic times, it is a frequent occurrence that passages become filled with debris and that entrances become blocked with rubble from falls. Unfortunately competent spelaeological exploration of caves with Palaeolithic parietal art are all too frequently missing. In many cases a chance visit to a cave has revealed the existence of a second or third possible entrance and in many cases the apparent existence of only one entrance to a cave may be explained by the lack of comprehensive exploration. In many caves the full extent of passages and corridors is not yet known, for they are frequently blocked by rubble which would have to be removed at great cost and effort before their extremities could be explored. In several cases the passages between a cave entrance and decorated region are obstructed in this way (e.g. at Pech-Merle and Cougnac).

When Palaeolithic habitation debris is found at the entrance it may be presumed that the particular entrance to the cave was the one used by Palaeolithic man. In several cases such debris had to be excavated before anyone in the nineteenth or twentieth century was able to penetrate into the caves. However, even in such cases it is not certain that only one entrance was used in the past. The greatest difficulty, however, is found with caves where no Palaeolithic habitation has been found at any of the known entrances. In such cases it is not yet known whether other entrances with habitation debris existed but have since become blocked, or which, if several possible entrances are known, was the entrance used by Palaeolithic man. The cave of Villars is interesting in this respect, for although its original entrance has probably not been found there is one narrow, and rather difficult, passage marked with occasional red dots which leads to the decorated chambers with hearths and a scatter of flints. Because of these ochre dots, Leroi-Gourhan[89] suggests that this was presumably part of the original path of access.

Rock-shelter sites by definition contain habitation debris and only sometimes parietal art as well. As has been mentioned, cave entrances have also frequently been inhabited. It is a general rule, however, that habitation does not normally extend far down inside caves. This statement does, quite clearly, need further elaboration for some signs of Palaeolithic activity (apart from the parietal art) do exist inside caves. Normal Palaeolithic habitation debris, be it in open air sites or in cave entrances, includes animal bones (from food), hearths (from cooking), ochre (for colour etc.) and flint fragments and tools (from knapping and use). In many caves with parietal art the entrance was used as a habitation site. In a few cases habitation is found quite far inside the caves, for example Gargas and Isturitz, but still just in reach of daylight or not far beyond it; the Palaeolithic entrances of these caves were far larger than those of today which have been artificially walled in. Evidence of Palaeolithic activity deeper inside caves is usually confined to parietal art, the rare flint tool, the rare piece of ochre, the occasional lamp, the rare footprint and sometimes traces of fire. Although very few decorated caves have been adequately explored or excavated it does seem certain that their dark interiors were not normally inhabited in the same way as rock-shelter sites or cave entrances. In general it is clear that Palaeolithic man did not cook, or work tools, in these dark places but either confined his activities to those which left virtually no traces or did not visit them after having decorated their walls. Although untrustworthy, the rarity of Palaeolithic footprints in the clay of cave floors seems to support the view that Palaeolithic man was not in the habit of making frequent visits to these places, although Vallois[90] reported that in a lateral gallery at Montespan 'one had the impression that there had previously been considerable stamping of the ground there' and at Aldène a long passage, apparently far from any parietal art, was covered with Palaeolithic (?) footprints.

A typical example where habitation is found in a cave entrance is Altamira. Here Palaeolithic habitation debris occupied the cavern entrance as well as the first part of the painted gallery, whereas the only signs of habitation farther down the cave were fragments of bones, shells and tools. A much less typical situation is found at Le Tuc d'Audoubert, for example, where despite the lack of excavation in the dark galleries it seems on the surface that Palaeolithic remains in these galleries are confined to parietal artistic works, the occasional footprints, the occasional imprint of a hand which has clutched at the ground to stop the Palaeolithic man from slipping on the wet clay, the very occasional flint tool, and several bears' skulls from which Palaeolithic man had removed the canines (there were no postcranial bones). At Lascaux, excavations have revealed a slightly different picture again. It must be remembered, however, that even the partial excavations which have been carried out at Lascaux are more than has been attempted at many other caves with parietal art; the apparently exceptional nature of Lascaux, therefore, may be more apparent than real – only more scientific excavations in such caves will tell. From inside the cave of Lascaux come numerous lamps, atypical but not infrequent blade tools, some bones of animals, a piece of rope, antler spears and frequent evidence of hearths from which radiocarbon dates of 17,000 and 15,500 BC have been obtained. A further feature of interest about this evidence from Lascaux was the concentration of lamps, flint tools, spears and much charcoal found in excavations in the 'shaft of the Dead Man'. Even more exceptional is the evidence from Labastide. Here excavations (largely unpublished) apparently revealed evidence of numerous hearths, bones, flint blades and numerous engraved plaquettes, all deep inside the cave (close to parietal representations) far from daylight. Whatever the activities by Palaeolithic man which could explain many of these remains it is clear that they do not correspond to those which produced the normal Palaeolithic habitation debris.

Only a few more features of Palaeolithic man's activities in the caves can reveal evidence about the sort of person who went into these deep galleries.[91] It has been claimed on the basis of the size of painted hand impressions that the artists concerned were women or children. Even were it true that the majority of representations of hands were very small the overlap between the dimensions of male and female hands is so great that sexing on this basis is bound to be dangerous.

Footprints, also, have been studied with a view to determining which sections of the Palaeolithic population penetrated the caves. In a study which assumes that the maximum length of a Palaeolithic foot was roughly equal to 15 per cent of stature, Vallois[92] deduces from footprints at Cabrerets, Montespan and Le Tuc d'Audoubert that many of the visitors to the deep galleries were children (between 1m 24 and 1m 61 tall) of between ten and thirteen years of age. Also at Le Tuc d'Audoubert Vallois deduced that five or six children had intentionally walked in files across a small chamber using their heels only and with toes in the air (the significance of these findings for the interpretation of the function of the art is considered in chapter 4). It must be recognised that until the range of stature of Palaeolithic man is more fully known some doubt must remain about the ratio of foot length to total body height. Furthermore sizes of male and female feet, as with the sizes of hands, overlap considerably. Despite the dangers in Vallois' approach it does seem as if, not only at Le Tuc d'Audoubert and Cabrerets but also at Aldène, both adults and children penetrated the dark passages of the caves.

No less important than the knowledge of cave entrances and activities in caves to the assessment of contexts of Palaeolithic art is the accurate knowledge of the positions of parietal representations. Even when such detail is known, it is clear that conditions of preservation of Palaeolithic parietal art must be understood before any apparent relationship between cavern features, habitations and the occurrence of cave art can be fully accepted. Absence of art in a particular part of a cave may not, in some situations, be the result of Palaeolithic man's inactivity.

Corrosion is most rapid on rock faces exposed to changes in atmospheric conditions and to the action of micro-organisms, algae and plants. A greater proportion of parietal art at cave entrances than further inside caves is likely, therefore, to have been destroyed by natural agencies. But the problems concerned with preservation are considerably more complex than this.

At a cave entrance changes in temperature, moisture, etc. cause rock to break up and corrode, thus resulting in slow filling of cave entrances with rock debris, clay residue of limestone solution and soil from cliff sides and habitation debris. When a decorated rock wall is exposed to such factors it flakes off or becomes corroded beyond recognition. However when a cave fills up comparatively rapidly a decorated wall is buried under a layer of soil and is partly protected by it from extremes of temperature changes, vegetation and other destructive forces. A certain amount of corrosion, due to ground water, the penetration of plant roots, etc., does still take place and engravings or bas-reliefs lose their original sharpness of outline and smoothness of surface; painted works will, in any such condition, be the first to suffer.

The extent to which destruction of cave walls will proceed inside a cave depends very largely on the local conditions of shape and size of the cave entrance, and especially on the absence or presence of subsidiary entrances to the cave through which a draught is caused. In some circumstances, depending on the amount and acidity of percolating moisture, the concentration of carbon dioxide in the air and the presence of micro-organisms, corrosive conditions which cause rock to disintegrate will occur well beyond the 'entrance regions' of a cave. In such conditions corrosion of limestone results in the solution of lime which is washed out and either a clay residue is left as a coat on a cave wall, or clay accumulates as a deposit on the cave floor. Alternatively, ground water may be overcharged with lime which is then either deposited from water flowing over the rock surface which it covers, or is deposited from water oozing out of rock pores usually as a white powdery precipitate; in either event parietal art may be partly, or even entirely, obliterated.

With these considerations in mind analysis of the contexts of Palaeolithic parietal art can be attempted. The first recognisable category consists of parietal art which is in association with habitation debris in rock shelters and the entrances of caves (open-air sites cannot, by definition, have parietal art associated with them for they are really in the open and the walls of the dwellings, which might have had parietal art on them, no longer exist). Most of the works in this category are in direct daylight, however weak (for example at Isturitz), and it is in this category that bas-relief sculptures mainly occur. The other frequent form of parietal art in this category, at rock shelters and cave entrances such as Isturitz, Chabot, Ouillins, Le Figuier, Teyjat, La Grèze, Murat and Sergeac, is engraving. The apparent scarcity of painting in this category is undoubtedly due to conditions of corrosion (see above), for traces of ochre on bas-reliefs, engravings and painted blocks buried in deposits show that painting had been practised in

rock shelters and cave entrances.

Details of the associations between the parietal art and the habitation debris of works in this first category vary considerably, and in several cases corrosion has resulted in the Palaeolithic association being disturbed. Frequently engravings and bas-reliefs were placed on walls around or above the actual habitation debris; on the roof directly above habitation at Le Poisson, on the wall against which occupation deposits accumulated at Le Cap Blanc, Angles sur l'Anglin, La Grèze, La Magdelaine, and many others. At Isturitz decoration was placed on a stalagmite column in the middle of the inhabited chamber. In many rock shelters works of art were also executed on blocks of limestone or stalagmite which do not form part of the solid rock walls. In such cases the blocks were often found lying face downwards, or haphazardly, in the deposits suggesting that they had fallen from their original positions. Some, however, were found standing upright, propped up against the rock wall or standing supported by small stones in such

65 Low-relief and engraved
frieze of women and bison, from
Angles sur l'Anglin; the women are
shown from the waist downwards only.

a way that it was clear that they were still in their original positions. At Laussel the sculpted blocks were roughly placed in a semicircle; one block had been carved on both sides, and several blocks still had traces of red ochre on them. At Roc de Sers the decorated blocks had fallen from their original positions but many of them were found on a nearly horizontal platform under the overhanging cliff while others were found a short way down a nearby slope. The excavator, H. Martin,[93] considered that their original positions could be safely determined as having been propped up against the wall of the shelter, forming a roughly ellipsoidal frieze which surrounded the habitation area. Similarly, at Le Fourneau du Diable, Peyrony[94] found sculpted blocks, as well as a painted block, arranged as part of a series around the edge of the habitation area. At Teyjat some of the engravings were made directly on the stalagmite flow around the habitation zone while others were engraved on the naturally fractured blocks from the same stalagmite and were placed up against the shelter wall.

It is clear that the first category of parietal art, bas-reliefs, engravings and paintings in rock shelters and cave entrances were carefully placed to be in full view of the habitation area where all normal day-to-day activities, such as cooking, eating, flint knapping, etc. took place.

The second category of Palaeolithic parietal contexts includes all the art which starts around, or very near, habitation but which also penetrates farther into the cave, into an area where hearths and kitchen debris are not normally found. Many caves with parietal art clearly belong to this second category. Apart from Altamira, which has been described above, other caves which have the same distribution of parietal art include La Peña de los Hornos, El Castillo, Gargas, Bédheillac (one gallery at least), Marsoulas, Mas d'Azil, La Mouthe, Pair non Pair, Salitré, and El Pendo. It is, of course, essential for the correct recognition and definition of this second category that the cave entrances used by Palaeolithic man be known and, in all the above cases, the entrances were filled with Palaeolithic habitation debris. In many other cases the position is not at all clear for in some the Palaeolithic entrances are not definitely known, and in others the parietal works do not nowadays start near the habitations but may well have done so in Palaeolithic

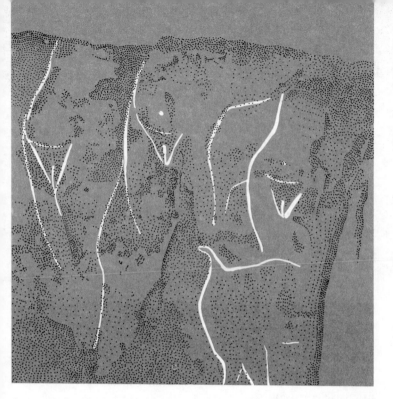

times. At Le Portel, for example (a cave which, in the literature, is usually classed as one in which the parietal art is situated deep down inside the cave and far from habitation), the original Palaeolithic entrance was very probably nearer to the beginning of the paintings than is the present entrance. A Magdalenian IV occupation level has been found in this possible entrance region (and an even earlier possible entrance was blocked by deposits containing Mousterian tools). It seems likely that Le Portel should be classed within this second category of Palaeolithic parietal contexts. As has been mentioned, a complicated situation exists with those caves where parietal art does not appear to start until some way away from the areas which were actually inhabited. Such a case is Font de Gaume, the present entrance of which is known to be the same as that used by Palaeolithic man. Here Breuil[95] has convincingly explained the absence of any trace of art for about sixty-five metres from the entrance by the effects of corrosion and weathering for in this cave a small passage joins the main passage and leads to

66 Low-relief sculpture of horses, from Le Cap Blanc.

the cliff face a short distance from the main entrance. Since the two entrances are differently orientated and are at slightly different altitudes, there is a temperature difference between the two; although this is very slight it is sufficient to cause a continual draught of air and to create conditions most likely to favour extensive corrosion.

The third category of parietal contexts is the one most usually referred to in the literature, where parietal decoration is far down in the darkness of a cave and in no way associated with habitation. As has already been seen the cave of Le Portel is much more likely to belong to the second category than to this third one. The same is true of quite a number of other caves; it is a fact that close study of the possible entrances used by Palaeolithic man and conditions of corrosion move many caves from the third category, as assumed by most authors, to the second category. In the largest number of instances, unfortunately, the true situation does remain obscure. In caves such as Les Combarelles, Le Gabillou, El Buxu, Los Casares and perhaps El Pindal it is likely that, as at Font de Gaume, parietal art which was situated near the cave entrances has been destroyed by natural agencies. In many of these caves excavations have shown that the cave entrances had been inhabited. In caves such as La Pasiega, where several entrances are known to exist it is likely that the entrance used by Palaeolithic man was much closer

to the regions in which parietal art begins than are the present
entrances, so that they too may belong to the second category and
not the third. At Niaux (a cave usually classed within the third
category) the present entrance is known not to be the original one
and, even as late as Neolithic times, several other entrances still
gave access to the cave.[96] It is extremely difficult, however, without
scientific exploration and excavation to tell which of the potential
passages, now blocked through roof falls etc., leads to the original
Palaeolithic entrance. The Trois Frères-Tuc d'Audoubert cave
system is a very large and complex one, and the late Magdalenian
cave-entrance site of Enlène undoubtedly belonged to it. The present-day entrances are almost certainly not the ones used in
Palaeolithic times to reach all the decorated galleries, for other
entrances, now blocked, are known to exist and to lead into these
galleries.[97] As no accurate surveys are published it is impossible to
determinte with any certainty whether the cave should be assigned
to the second or the third category.

Caves such as Montespan, Rouffignac, Pech-Merle, Ebbou, La
Baume Latrone and many others, appear to contain parietal art
which is far removed from entrances and habitations. In almost
every case, however, these caves have not been sufficiently well
documented or explored for it to be possible to say where the
original entrances were situated. In caves such as Santian, La

Clotilde, Covalanas, Etcheberriko and others the present entrance seems to have been the one used by Palaeolithic man but it is difficult to tell whether the absence of art close to the entrances was always so or is the result of natural destruction.

In caves of categories two and three the parietal paintings and engravings are found in an enormous variety of positions. Relatively few are known from the floors of caverns but this may be due to their having disintegrated, for the ones known are frequently in sheltered positions near to the rock wall. At Niaux several engravings (figures 32 and 45) were found under the shelter of an overhanging wall, while at Bédeilhac bas-reliefs (figure 46) have survived in a tiny chamber, difficult of access. It is a striking feature of the contexts of Palaeolithic parietal art that the walls and roof of caves are not uniformly decorated. Often representations are executed on natural panels, where the rock is both fairly even and more or less vertical, as in the large panel with black outline animals at Pech-Merle (figure 12), the panel with dappled horses (figure 31) in the same cave and the Salon Noir panels at Niaux (figure 49). Equally frequently, however, engravings and paintings were executed on uneven surfaces with apparent total disregard for natural protrusions or recesses, veins or cracks (e.g. figure 30) (but see above for the occasional use of natural rock features in Palaeolithic parietal art). Many natural rock panels and large stretches of apparently suitable rock surfaces were left plain whereas, elsewhere, representations are so closely crowded that they overlap into a virtually indecipherable maze of lines (e.g. figure 18) sometimes only a few centimetres away from blank spaces. As has already been noted, such extensive superpositioning is a particular feature of parietal art of the second and third categories.

Another variable feature of Palaeolithic parietal art inside caves is its visibility (and see chapters 3 and 4 for the importance of this feature for any interpretation of the function of the art). In many cases paintings and engravings on natural rock walls in caves as Pech-Merle, Niaux and Gargas, friezes on walls and ceilings in caves as Lascaux and Castillo, and paintings and engravings on natural cave roofs in caves as Altamira and Pech-Merle, are clearly visible to anyone standing in the appropriate areas of the cave. At

Cougnac, where the cave is particularly rich in stalagmitic and stalactitic formations, many of these concretions were broken in antiquity. It has been claimed[98] that these breakages were made to enable the painted panels to be easily viewed before they were actually reached, for they are more extensive than was necessary for the actual painting activities. In other instances, on the contrary, representations are 'hidden' away. Thus, in many cases in the Trois Frères 'sanctuary' engravings are situated in a narrow twisting tunnel which can only be entered when one is lying, and in which the engravings can only be seen when the visitor presses his back right up against the engravings behind him; even the Trois Frères sorcerer (figure 89) is partly obliterated from view by a tongue of rock which projects into the small 'sanctuary' chamber. Caves cannot be classed according to the way in which parietal representations are arranged. The same cave often includes examples which are easily visible on 'panels' and examples which are 'hidden away'.

3 Historical review of interpretations

In chapter 1 the discovery of Palaeolithic cave art was described. In this chapter the most important attempts at interpreting the meaning of this parietal art are reviewed. From time to time in this review the connection between the discovery of a new decorated cave and a new interpretative hypothesis will be obvious.

The earliest discoveries (c.1840) of Palaeolithic art were not of parietal works but of mobile pieces (e.g. figure 2g). These small pieces (at that time ascribed to the work of the Celts) were later often found in clear-cut contexts where an association with other Palaeolithic material could not be doubted. Thus, once the Palaeolithic period was accepted and its great antiquity acknowledged, no one could seriously doubt that the art was of the same age. But this knowledge created its own theoretical implications, which have concerned archaeologists right up to the present day.

It was in the nineteenth century that the Palaeolithic period was first recognised by archaeologists and the recognition of Palaeolithic art was not long delayed (see chapter 1). The acceptance of the antiquity of the Palaeolithic is usually attributed to the work of Boucher de Perthes (1788–1868) although his first major documentation of Palaeolithic man in 1846 had been foreshadowed by several earlier workers.[1] At this time archaeologists had a theoretical framework into which they could fit the concept of the Palaeolithic for already during the sixteenth to eighteenth centuries it had been believed that historic civilisations had been preceded by uncivilised or barbarous periods. The Palaeolithic period could, therefore, be seen as one of the representatives of these barbaric periods. It was not very long after the work of Boucher de Perthes that archaeologists first developed the more elaborate sequence of human cultures which is still the basis of modern archaeological thought.

Already by 1836 Danish archaeologists divided archaeological material into those made of stone, those made of bronze and those made of iron. With Boucher de Perthes' work it became necessary to attribute the stone material to two periods, and in 1863[2] Sir John Lubbock named them the Palaeolithic (Old Stone Age) and the Neolithic (New Stone Age). Subsequently archaeologists have inserted a Mesolithic period (Middle Stone Age) between these two and this sequence, followed by the Metal Ages, is still the framework of human cultural development accepted by archaeologists.

It is not surprising that the assumption in the nineteenth century was that Palaeolithic men were still at a very primitive cultural level; as could, after all, be clearly seen from the fact that they had not yet been able to invent metal tools. What could be more primitive than the fact that they relied entirely upon hunting for their food, and had not yet hit upon the ideas of agriculture and stock breeding (characteristic features of the Neolithic)? Added proof of Palaeolithic barbarism, if any were needed, was provided by the ethnographers,[3] travellers and missionaries of the nineteenth century who recounted frightening tales of the primitiveness of many tribes still living in remote corners of the world. There resulted a tacit equation in the minds of both archaeologists and ethnographers between the primitiveness of hunters and gatherers living in the remote times of the Palaeolithic and the primitiveness of hunters and gatherers still living in the remote corners of their own world (see chapter 4 for further discussion of this equation).

Art for Art's Sake

With the knowledge that Palaeolithic man was responsible for works of art, it became essential to explain, somehow, how such an apparently 'advanced' activity could possibly have existed among such obviously 'primitive' people. Already in 1864, on the basis of mobile art only, Lartet and Christy made the first attempt at explaining this apparent theoretical contradiction. In a study in which they accepted as proven that Palaeolithic man had lived contemporaneously with several extinct animals, had known only the use of stone-tools and had relied entirely upon hunting, Lartet and Christy[4] attempted to explain the phenomenon of Palaeolithic art in terms of exceptionally rich environmental conditions. Thus they maintained that although it was evident that culturally Palaeolithic men could hardly have been more primitive, it was clear that abundance of wild game could have made economic activities so easy that they had plenty of leisure and that leisure was the nourisher of the arts. As their hunting activities did not take all their time they could well afford not only to decorate their weapons but also the luxury of wearing ornaments.

Although this explanation of Palaeolithic art preceded the recognition of Palaeolithic parietal representations and was only accepted for a short time its indirect influence has been considerable (see below). Twenty years after Lartet's and Christy's original thesis, discussion of Palaeolithic art was still sometimes couched in terms of the impossibility of religion in the Palaeolithic period (because, for instance, Palaeolithic man did not even manage to represent a cross – the simplest of symbols) so that Palaeolithic 'art' was purely a matter of ornamentation.[5]

Towards the end of the nineteenth century ethnographic reports from Australia made it clear to the world that people lived there in a cultural condition very similar to Palaeolithic men and produced a remarkable number of complex paintings, some of which were on rock shelters (e.g. figure 96). These reports proved of the utmost significance for the study of Palaeolithic art (see below) and they showed conclusively that Lartet's and Christy's assumption that artistic activity by hunters and gatherers required exceptional environmental conditions was ill-founded. Already in 1889[6] Cartailhac pointed out that although the agricultural Polynesians might be said to have a relatively easy life, the same could not be said about either the Bushmen or the Australian hunters and gatherers. Nevertheless the approach propounded by Lartet and Christy lives on in numerous works dealing with Palaeolithic parietal art which maintain that the glorious representations of animals and the occasional human being to be seen in caves of France and Spain are essentially aesthetic. Some have maintained that human beings have an inherent wish to express themselves artistically; others have interpreted Palaeolithic parietal art as the wish for decoration and joyous surroundings. All such interpretations are known colloquially (and rather inaccurately from the art historian's point of view) as 'Art for Art's Sake'.

One of the few people to accept this interpretation in more or less the same terms as stated by Lartet and Christy was the great French prehistorian Piette who had been one of the first influential archaeologists to accept de Sautuola's dating of the parietal art to the Palaeolithic (see chapter 1). In his magnificent documentation of mobile art Piette[7] described Palaeolithic art, at various places in his book, as 'exclusively artistic' and Palaeolithic artists as 'seeking perfection in art' and 'eternally concerned with the cult of beauty'. General uncritical acceptance of this interpretation is found in various works of Boule,[8] whereas Graziosi[9] appears to restrict such an interpretation to only some representations when 'the Palaeolithic artist sought to fulfil an instinctive desire for pure artistic creation, apart from all material consideration', and likewise Breuil[10] for certain specific representations such as the Magdelaine Venuses (figures 90 and 91) which would give pleasure to Palaeolithic man during his meals.

Art for Art's Sake was still the basis for further elaboration in the works of Luquet[11] who accepted Magdalenian art as a functional activity for the same reasons as outlined by Breuil and others, see below, but insisted that Aurignacian art was 'exclusively a figured art dictated by the pleasure that the artist took in creating images of actual beings, the idea of which occupied his mind'. Another variation can be found in the work of Riddell[12] who maintained that only in the winter could Palaeolithic man find the leisure to be artistic while relying on the hoards of food preserved by the ice.

The Art for Art's Sake interpretation still finds echoes in specialised discussion on various aspects of Palaeolithic art (e.g. Van Gennep[13] who maintained that Palaeolithic artists were in no way different from modern artists and had nothing to do with any kind of magical rituals) and in the generalised writing of some present-day authors (e.g. Giedion[14] who wrote 'there is no difference whether the basic impulse [of the urge for artistic expression] rises from a cosmic anguish, the urge to play, art for art's sake or . . . the desire to express in signs and symbols the realm of the unconscious').

As has been mentioned above, the early and middle nineteenth century still relied mainly on travellers and missionaries for its understanding of modern non-literate tribes. Towards the end of the century, however, a great change took place and the first analytical reviews of modern primitive life appeared, coinciding with the first reliable studies and reports on the every-day life of tribes which could still be studied by ethnographers. By 1880 the French already felt the impact of Sir Edward B. Tylor's *Primitive Culture*[15] and in 1890 Frazer produced the first volumes of his *Golden Bough*[16] which, for the first time, provided a synthesis of the

67 Engraving of wild oxen and horse, from Teyjat.

complexity of modern primitive peoples' thoughts and actions and grouped together the cultural activities of men both in antiquity and in the present. Both these works were destined to have the profoundest influence on all works on human societies from that time till the present day. Frazer's work had been preceded only a few years before by the first detailed and reliable work on the Australian aborigines[17] which gave to the world its first warning against simple generalisations about modern primitives. In all three of these works considerable attention is paid to totemism. Totemism as a social phenomenon among American Indians had already been reported in the eighteenth century (the word totem is an American Indian term) but it was the much later nineteenth century ethnographic reports from Australia which really forced ethnographers to devote their attention to this system of beliefs and practices. The essential criterion of this phenomenon was supposed to be a special relationship between man and natural species such as plant or animal.

The first of these authors, Tylor, published a revolutionary classification of primitive culture in the latter years of the nineteenth century in which he formulated his definition of religion as a belief in spiritual beings, deriving from the primitives' experiences and memory of dreams; for dreams, according to Tylor, proved to the primitive that the spirit was able to leave the body at will and

journey around by itself. On the basis of this formulation Tylor took a belief in ancestor cults as the most basic of religious beliefs and totemism was to him simply an extension and particular form of ancestor cult. According to Tylor primitives made little distinction between man and animal, rather wondering at the human characteristics (albeit the more base ones) which could be observed in certain animals,[18] so that it was easy to explain totemism in terms of some kind of sharing of spirits between man and animals. Likewise the worship of animals by some people could be understood as the reincarnation of dead humans in animal form.

That totemism was in fact a more complex social phenomenon than was suggested by Tylor was made clear by the first of the classic ethnographic reports by Spencer and Gillen on the Australian Aborigines.[19] Although this work gave detailed information of the variation in totemic practices among different tribes, only certain of these practices were picked up by the ethnographers interested in classification and evolution and even fewer by the archaeologists interested in the interpretation of Palaeolithic art. As will be seen in the following chapter, one of the most difficult problems in understanding anthropological writings on totemism is the problem of finding a common denominator of all the social phenomena which have been grouped together under this name: totemism. The glossing-over of variations in totemic practices began already in the very early years of the twentieth century.

In 1887[20] Frazer published the first of his general works on totemism giving all available evidence for totemic beliefs from all over the world, for by now it was the beliefs which were the main concern of the anthropologist. Considerable time and space were devoted by Frazer both in this early work and in subsequent writings to explanation and description of the precise nature of the relationship between a human and his totem which was the criterion by which totemism was recognised. This totemic relationship, and also the way in which Frazer summarised its content, became fundamental to many of the totemic interpretations – and criticisms (see chapter 4) – of Palaeolithic art. He wrote of 'the relationship of an individual to the clan totem . . . [that] he will not kill it, he speaks of it as his brother, and he calls himself by its name'.

It is necessary to follow one more step in the historical development of anthropological work on totemism for the work of Durkheim is contemporary with the work of the archaeologists and their first essays in the interpretation of Palaeolithic art which were not based on the theory of Art for Art's Sake. Durkheim was the first to have a decisive influence on anthropologists moving their interests away from the study of totemism as a self-contained system of beliefs to a consideration of it in relation to social behaviour. Nevertheless, despite his change of emphasis, Durkheim did still consider both the theological and the sociological aspects of totemism. Concerned almost entirely with Australian totemism, Durkheim rejected the explanatory and classificatory works of Tylor and Frazer and saw totemism as the most fundamental of human religious expressions, from which all other religions such as 'animism' and 'naturism' had evolved, and as explicitly associated with clan identification and clan exogamy (marrying outside the clan). In his view[21] the Australian aboriginal 'civilisation [is] most rudimentary . . . [and] also their organisation is the most primitive and simple which is actually known'. They possessed the 'most primitive and simple religion which it is possible to discover'. Their totemic beliefs could therefore be assumed to represent the prototype of all religion, and what could be said of totemism could be applied to the understanding of religion in general. Durkheim concluded that as many totems were in themselves insignificant objects (and in many cases the reverence of Australians was not directed to the totemic animals at all but only to the totemic symbols), therefore the ritual sacredness involved in totemism had to come from some other source. This was 'Society' itself and this explained the connection with the other feature of totemism already noted, namely clan exogamy and clan identification. 'Social organisation on a clan basis is the simplest which we know' so that the symbolic power of Australian totemism and religious beliefs must be the expression of the clan and, in Durkheim's analysis, 'totemism and the clan naturally imply each other'. (For more recent work on totemism and its relevance to interpreting Palaeolithic art, see chapter 4 below.)

Sympathetic magic and totemism

Early ethnographic works were used as reference books by both archaeologists and ethnographers and used as the justification for wide generalisations about primitive cultures. Under the influence of the new ethnographic knowledge Reinach, who had previously[22] regarded Palaeolithic mobile art as a luxury activity devoid of symbolic meaning, put forward for the first time in 1903[23] detailed reasons for the interpretation of Palaeolithic art as evidence of beliefs in the efficacy of magic. In the context of Palaeolithic sympathetic magic Reinach had, earlier, also been the first to make allusion to totemic beliefs. Of all interpretations of Palaeolithic parietal art Reinach's views are those that have been most widely accepted and quoted.

Reinach's views on 'sympathetic magic' are of the utmost importance for they already incorporated the two major aspects of sympathetic magic developed in more detail by later writers: that of hunting magic, and that of fertility magic. Later theories which account for Palaeolithic art in terms of sympathetic magic do, in some details, make closer use of various features actually represented by Palaeolithic man, but all the essentials of the later theories are to be found in this first of the sympathetic magic theories. One more notable feature of Reinach's interpretation is that it was based primarily on parietal art with the assumption that mobile art might have had the same functions.

The following points about Palaeolithic art were basic in Reinach's thesis (see also chapter 4 below, for critique of these views): 1 that most of the Palaeolithic representations were of animals; 2 that only animals which were potential food were ever represented; 3 that the Palaeolithic representations were placed in contexts which were difficult of access.

To Reinach, and most subsequent authorities, the third point was enough to demolish once and for all any interpretations of these works of art as acts of luxurious enjoyment, for their positions deep down in caves showed that a deep and powerful intention must have driven the artists concerned. The fact that only food animals were represented suggested the same conclusion, for the absence of dangerous predatory animals and birds from the Palaeolithic artists' repertory could not be reconciled with an interpretation of the art as purely decoration.

Basing his further interpretation of these facts on the ethnographic information available at his time Reinach drew attention to the widespread belief among living primitive peoples in sympathetic magic by which the human could gain control over, or at least exercise a fundamental influence on, whatever subject was represented. For early ethnographers, no less than these early archaeologists, the subject of magical beliefs was of paramount interest, and led to Frazer's[24] classic division of all magic into two 'principles of thought' – 1 'that like produces like, or that an effect resembles its cause' and 2 'that things which have once been in contact with each other continue to act on each other at a distance after the physical contact has been severed'. As one of numerous examples of 1, Frazer mentioned the North American Indians who 'believe that by drawing . . . in sand, ashes or clay . . . and then pricking it [the representation] with a sharp stick or doing it any other injury, they inflict a corresponding injury on the [subject] represented'. For Reinach it was the first of these principles of sympathetic magic, 'homoeopathic' magic, which underlay the phenomenon of Palaeolithic art.

Further support for the magical interpretation of parietal art came from specific parallels, with Australian aboriginal practices, for not only did the Australians also paint but their reasons for doing so were supposedly known: as acts of sympathetic magic. Furthermore the Australian paintings were situated in places where the uninitiated, women and children were not allowed to venture; another possible parallel with the contexts to Palaeolithic parietal art, as Reinach pointed out.

The first two points of Reinach's observations on the content of Palaeolithic art revealed to him the ultimate aim of Palaeolithic sympathetic magic. Food animals only were represented so that the artists must have wished one of two things: either to increase the number of food animals available to them, or to gain control and facilitate capture of the already available food animals. Reinach was prepared to see both aims as the basis for the art and stressed that sympathetic magic paintings were used by living Australian aborigines for both these very same reasons.

As will be seen later several of the arguments put forward by Reinach cannot be accepted both on theoretical grounds and because subsequent discoveries of parietal art have shown that his initial premises were not entirely accurate. Nevertheless, the influence of Reinach's interpretation of Palaeolithic art as a practice associated with sympathetic magic has been profound – those who have visited any of the Palaeolithic decorated caves in the company of a voluble guide will recognise the source of much which they heard! – and most of the subsequent interpretations in terms of magical acts have done little more than elaborate the fundamental arguments of Reinach.

Before considering some of these later elaborations a few further points of Reinach's approach to the interpretation of Ice Age art should be noted for they will be seen later to recur in very different approaches. Reinach started from facts to be inferred from the contents of parietal art, as far as they were known at the time, and proceeded from there on the basis of ethnographic parallels (similar activities and beliefs among modern peoples living similar lives to those of Palaeolithic man). In this context he made much use of Australian Aboriginal beliefs and practices and recognised the connection between many of the sympathetic magic practices (which he found so illuminating for his own work on Palaeolithic art) and the Australian beliefs in totemism. Despite this Reinach refused[25] to assume lightly that Australian-type totemism was a

Palaeolithic belief accounting for Palaeolithic art. The impression that one gains from reading this phase of his work is that he was primarily impressed by the Australian aboriginal beliefs in sympathetic magic, which formed the basis of his interpretation of Palaeolithic art, and only secondarily in totemic beliefs, which he suggested might possibly have existed in some form in Palaeolithic times. It is surprising that this tentative statement regarding Australian totemism (and especially another slightly less cautious remark by Reinach published elsewhere[26]) had also a profound effect on later workers.

As has been shown above, the ethnographic works which had the greatest influence on early interpretations of Palaeolithic art not only provided information about the range of 'primitive' peoples' ways of life, but also all included discussion or reports about totemism. It is important to realise when considering such early interpretations that in the early part of the twentieth century the concepts of magic and totemism were not divorced. To Reinach and to several other later workers they were complementary beliefs and not distinct analytical alternatives. For this reason it was possible for Reinach and others to favour a sympathetic magical interpretation of Palaeolithic art and yet at the same time to include totemism as a possibility (indeed this distinction was explicitly made in a revealing article by Capitan[27] who pointed out that the only thing certain about Palaeolithic art was its magical basis and that any further elaboration of interpretation on the basis of analogies with Australian practices might be true but remained entirely hypothetical). For the same reason it is misguided to discuss a totemic interpretation separately from a sympathetic magical interpretation as is commonly done by several modern authors.[28] Those who have adopted the latter course have found that they have had to discuss the separate aspects of the same author's work in different contexts and have thus tended to overstress particular isolated features at the expense of the cohesion of the early hypotheses.

A further peculiar feature resulting from this dual nature of the early magical interpretations is that few facts have been adduced by the early workers to support an explicitly totemic interpretation of Palaeolithic art. In fact, insofar as Reinach (and a few others) supported a totemic interpretation at all, he did so for the very same reasons as have been reviewed above in support of a magical interpretation. As Laming has pointed out[29] more attention has been devoted to criticising totemic interpretations (see chapter 4 below) than to advocating them in any detail. This in itself has led to a strange situation whereby Reinach himself has been accredited not only as the originator of the sympathetic magic interpretation but equally so with the totemic interpretation. It is even possible to find authors referring to Reinach's exposition of his magical interpretation for the original documentation of the totemic interpretation.[30] It can well be claimed that Reinach was the first to suggest the magical interpretation but his support of a totemic explanation has to be seen in historical perspective and the fact that his allusions[31] to totemism were almost asides has to be recognised.

Insofar as he thought of the Palaeolithic art as based on sympathetic magic Reinach was quite ready to envisage both the increase and the hunting magic within the context of totemic ceremonies, all the more so as his ethnographic parallels were based on the practices of Australian aborigines who themselves were totemic. Furthermore, as did also his contemporary Durkheim (although for different reasons[32]), Reinach accepted totemism as a cultural feature which was derived and evolved from a more fundamental and universal taboo against killing one's fellow, so that in his view totemism in one form or another could be found in many, otherwise very dissimilar, human societies. Almost all the features stressed by the early ethnographers' writing on totemism, such as the role of humans as the agents of multiplication of totemic species and the role of the totem animal as protector and guide to humans of the same totem, feature predominantly in Reinach's twelve-rule codification of totemism.[33]

Thus acceptance of totemism as a fundamental form of religious expression, recognition of the vital role of sympathetic magic within the context of totemic ceremonies and the knowledge that Australian aborigines painted complex scenes in the course of totemic rituals are the factors which, as has been seen above, influenced a few authors to make allusion to totemism in the course of their expositions of magical interpretations (Reinach himself, Capitan and Breuil[34] and Hamy[35]).

68 Low-relief sculpture of a young ibex, from Angles sur l'Anglin.

One further general point should be noted about Reinach's views and that is the cautious note, all too often absent in later interpretations, by which he admitted the possibility that individual pieces of art (inept or incomplete work) might well have been the works of novices and never used in ritual. One of the few early workers on the interpretation of Palaeolithic art to follow up this general point was Capitan.[36] In an admirable theoretical statement he said that many different, and complex ideas may have lain behind the fact that Palaeolithic man painted. He went even further in pointing out that similar results may well evolve from very different intentions, and in deploring any assumption that one single theory could suffice to explain Palaeolithic art, just because 'art' was interpreted as one single given fact.

It would not be profitable to present all the views of the many people who have accepted sympathetic magic as the *raison d'être* of Palaeolithic parietal art for they are almost all derivative, adding little of interest to the views of the few major workers on Palaeolithic archaeology.

Without doubt the man who has had most direct influence on all aspects of the study of Palaeolithic art is Abbé Breuil. Starting in

1901 Abbé Henri Breuil began to publish the results of his study and copying of Palaeolithic art. With his death in 1961 the world lost the man who alone was responsible for more documentation of Palaeolithic art than all other workers put together. As the whole world recognised the pre-eminence of this figure it is not strange to find that Breuil's views on the significance of the art became the most widely accepted of all interpretations and his influence is seen not only in almost all general books where sympathetic magic is unquestionably accepted as the basis of the representations, but also in works scattered in learned journals.

It is perhaps more surprising that Breuil's views of the significance of parietal art were neither particularly original, well thought out, nor concerned with specific, as opposed to generalised, comment. In a sense Breuil was more important a figure for the documentation and dating of Palaeolithic art (see chapters 1 and 2) than for its interpretation. Yet, because of his exalted standing, even his smallest contributions to the interpretative puzzle had the most long lived and widely felt influence. It is significant that as his long career proceeded Breuil appeared to become less and less interested in the question of the significance of the art and more and more in the evolution of the various Palaeolithic art styles.

From the very beginning Breuil was convinced that the explanations of Lartet and Christy were too simple to explain the complexities of Palaeolithic art. Like Reinach, he considered the context of Palaeolithic parietal art, often placed in inaccessible corners and corridors, as the most revealing feature. Again like Reinach, Breuil relied on ethnographic parallels to reveal the real meaning of the Ice Age art and at an early stage in his career accepted the significance of Palaeolithic art as possibly being religious, 'fetishistic' or totemic.[37] In his last great general work, Breuil wrote[38] 'when we visit a painted cave, we enter a sanctuary, where, for thousands of years, sacred ceremonies have taken place, directed no doubt by the great initiates of the time, and introducing the novices called to receive in their turn the necessary fundamental instruction for the conduct of their lives'.

By the time of Breuil's last works knowledge of Palaeolithic parietal art was much richer than at the time of Reinach. Since Reinach, therefore, various features revealed by the art itself had to be incorporated into the sympathetic magic interpretation. Thus Breuil added to Reinach's thesis of increase ceremonies and hunting magic of food animals the idea that the sympathetic magical rites were also directed to the destruction of beasts of prey, for several such (e.g. figures 26 and 41) had since been recognised in paintings and engravings. In a work with Capitan and Peyrony[39], Breuil pointed out that any interpretation of Palaeolithic art must take account of the existence of representations of carnivores and stressed that the existence of such representations in no way conflicted with a totemic interpretation for there are not only 'people who seek possession of an image of their quarry to ensure success in the hunt but also those who, on the contrary, expect to gain the qualities of a predator through its image, and in this way be endowed with its skill in catching game'. For some considerable time, too, it had become known that not all Palaeolithic parietal art was situated deep down in caves beyond the confines of habitation but that some was also found in shelters open to the air and in living sites (e.g. figure 66). Breuil himself had been responsible in 1904 for the documentation[40] of one such rock shelter, La Grèze, when he drew attention to the parallel with living primitives who also painted rock shelters, but only much later (see page 119) did he offer a particular interpretation of these open-air examples of parietal art; he included them within the general magical interpretation of all Palaeolithic art.

At the time of Reinach's interpretation certain signs, described as sexual symbols (figure 34) had not been discovered. These 'sexual symbols' led Breuil, and many others who supported the sympathetic magic interpretations to include in their schemes the Palaeolithic intention magically to increase not only the number of animals (already stated by Reinach) but also the number of human beings. On the other hand, some representations of humans were seen as masked or half human and half animal and were variously interpreted as officiating priests or sorcerers, spirits, or disguised hunters (see below).

Specific representations were, throughout the twentieth century, taken as special evidence in favour of the sympathetic magic interpretation. Not all these originated with Breuil but all can be found faithfully repeated and accepted in Breuil's last general work.

Male animals were seen to follow closely behind female animals while certain representations (e.g. horses at Escoural and Lascaux) were interpreted as pregnant (figures 9 and 52) and, to those in favour of magical intentions, both these features were clearly evidence of increase ceremonies and reproductive rites.[41]

The discovery of the cave of Montespan in 1923 became one of the strengths of the sympathetic magic interpretations. Not only to Breuil did this seem one of the discoveries to clinch his arguments but also Count Bégouen, perhaps the most convinced supporter of this interpretation, considered it worthwhile to devote a new article in 1929[42] to press home the way in which these recent discoveries ousted any interpretations based on aesthetic considerations alone and confirmed, once and for all, a magical basis for the art. In the cave at Montespan several clay horses and a 'lion'[43] had been found riddled with holes, as well as a crude model of a small headless bear with smooth body and an actual young bear's skull lying between its feet (figure 97). The holes were clear proof of stabbing by spears or javelins; the smooth body evidence of a model covered with an actual animal skin; and the whole group clear documentation of destructive magic.

Breuil fully supported the interpretation of 'feather'-like signs (figure 93l) on some engravings and paintings as the representations of arrows or other weapons while others, such as Count Bégouen, interpreted painted marks on animals as wounds and lines from the mouths or nostrils of animals (figures 12 and 77) as blood. Pointing to ethnographic parallels, once again, and especially to an early report by Frobenius concerning the Pygmies, all these features were taken as evidence supporting the interpretation of hunting magic. It must, however, be recognised that some authors have gone considerably further than Breuil in their hunting magic interpretations. Thus the animals on the ceiling of Altamira (figures 7 and 8) were seen by Breuil[44] as 'sometimes simply standing resting, sometimes lying down or stretching, sometimes strolling lazily, sometimes galloping' whereas Graziosi[45] interpreted the crouching bison on the ceiling as dying with buckling legs (presumably killed in the hunt).

Perhaps the most individual of Breuil's interpretations concerned the numerous parietal 'signs' which he called tectiforms. In 1910

Capitan, Breuil and Peyrony devoted one whole chapter in their book on Font de Gaume to various geometric signs which had no immediate recognisable human or animal features. Thus had started the labyrinth-like enquiry into the meaning of these signs which continues till this day and which exemplifies best of all the various approaches which have been brought to bear on the possible significance of Palaeolithic parietal art. Already in 1897[46] Rivière interpreted one such geometric sign (e.g. figure 93f) as the three-quarter view representation of a dwelling and this was to be the interpretation finally favoured by Breuil himself, although he added a personal twist to this interpretation. The discussion of tectiforms in 1910 made it evident that many different types and varieties of geometric signs exist in Palaeolithic paintings and engraving (figure 93). In nearly all cases it was possible to find ethnographic parallels for these signs from somewhere in the world and in all cases these signs could be related to the various primitve houses and shelters employed by living primitive tribes. In the 1910 discussion,[47] Capitan, Breuil and Peyrony could write 'all the world was agreed, our tectiform signs did represent primitive huts'. Thus, again, ethnography seemed to give the clue to the meaning of these signs. But from an early date other ethnographic parallels seemed to offer a very different interpretation of the tectiforms, as traps. This second interpretation was favoured by many supporters of sympathetic magic for the clear support it gave to their ideas on hunting magic, but this proved one of the few points of disagreement between Breuil and other supporters of this interpretation. Two distinct approaches arose amongst those who interpreted tectiforms as traps: those who saw the traps, and also the arrows as destined to secure the animals which were the livelihood of Palaeolithic man, and those who considered the traps to be used against evil spirits. At one time Breuil thought that this second interpretation might be valid but finally came out in favour of the tectiforms as the residences of ancestral spirits. He rejected the interpretation of tectiforms as traps for any kind of animals because the animals and tectiforms supposedly associated were in fact frequently superimposed and therefore, according to Breuil, of different dates, and because the tectiforms were frequently placed alone in various parts of the caves well away from animal representations.

Within the general category of tectiforms certain distinctly shaped signs have, at various times, been given specific names and individual meanings. Thus, for example, some have seen certain tectiforms as pallisades; Breuil himself interpreted[48] certain isolated panels of tectiforms in the cave of Niaux (figure 98) as topographical sign-posts for 'brave explorers of the Reindeer Age to find their way'; Count Bégouen interpreted red and black dots painted in lines or in circles (e.g. figure 93g) within the context of sympathetic magic as the representation of projectile stones. Probably the most far-fetched of all attempts at giving a sympathetic magic interpretation to tectiforms was the suggestion for two particular groups of tectiforms by Astre[49] (and see chapter 4 below) that the red dots in lines and circles represented heaps of 'apples, cherries, raspberries and strawberries' to aid collection of these fruits and increase their numbers; 'worm-shaped' signs as edible roots; barbed and pointed signs as harpoons; 'hut'-shaped tectiforms as fish or animal traps made of vegetable matter; scutiforms as shields; and pediforms as maceheads.

This survey of the general lines of Breuil's interpretative work has shown that, basing himself on the significance of ethnographic parallels, he differed only in subsidiary details from the sympathetic magic interpretations of many other authors. Yet his treatment of tectiforms illustrates the slight individual twist that he gave to this interpretation for, to Breuil, the painted caves were religious sanctuaries and, in his later works especially, it is a sense of the religious which pervades the implicit assumptions of his suggestions. As has been seen Breuil had already introduced the concept of ancestor spirits into the interpretation of Palaeolithic parietal art, albeit in a generalised way, and this tendency for interconnecting religious expression and sympathetic magic is further reflected in his interpretation[50] of the 'sorcerer' of the cave of Les Trois Frères (figure 89), considered by most authors to be no different from other rare representations of magicians, as a 'God', 'Sorcerer' or 'Spirit controlling the multiplication of game and hunting expeditions'.

In most ways Count Bégouen's approach was the same as Breuil's, except for the interpretation of the significance of tectiforms, but he attempted more detailed explanations of various

69 Black painted rhinoceros, from Rouffignac; one possibly a baby.

features of the cave representations. Thus he stressed the significance of Palaeolithic man having added representations of darts to natural drip marks on the flanks of clay engraved animals (figure 32) as support for the hunting magic or destructive magic interpretation.

His views on the magical intent of parietal art led Bégouen to a very individual interpretation of engravings on the wall of the Montespan cave. In one of the dry galleries of this cave are engravings of horses and many coarse holes and vertical lines. Bégouen interpreted the holes as stones thrown to drive the horses towards, or into, the vertical strokes, which he took to be the representation of a stockade. He concluded: 'It would appear to be a regular hunting scene, all the more remarkable because up to the present we do not know of any other picture in prehistoric art showing a definite grouping of animals'.[51]

Despite his belief that all Palaeolithic art was magical in intent Bégouen, as did also Breuil, allowed that Palaeolithic men must have been true artists and had, quite obviously, enjoyed their work and had aimed at the most perfect results possible (a view not all that far removed from the supporters of the Art for Art's Sake interpretation). In this context we can understand Bégouen's statement that the better the resemblance, the better the magical efficacy. Nevertheless Bégouen realised as well as anyone else that many examples of parietal art were not as finely finished as others, and even that some representations lacked certain details such as head, limbs, or facial features (e.g. figure 12). Having observed that for all hunting people it was sufficient to see footprints to identify a particular animal, Bégouen proceeded to develop his explanation of the missing details on many representations; namely that omissions were intentional. Thus, the absence of eyes or ears on a representation was to make the animal deficient in its normal activities, the absence of head was to make the animal weak, and so on. Bégouen was therefore led into the position whereby he maintained that there were three ways of representing an animal for the purposes of sympathetic magic: 1 as accurately as possible; 2 as schematically as possible; 3 with various details deliberately omitted.

It is strange to find how few explanations of Palaeolithic

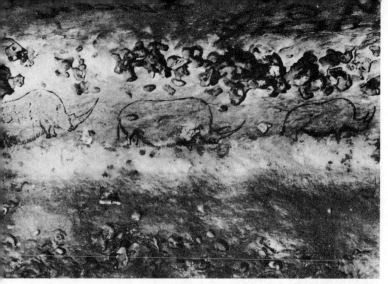

sympathetic magic consider the question of how the rites might have been carried out. Incidental and purely hypothetical statements do exist scattered in the literature. Thus, Astre[52] inferred from the similarity in style of all Palaeolithic art that painting and engraving must have been a specialist activity of the sorcerers, passing from father to son, and aimed at 'attracting the admiration of their special clients'.

The most important author to deal with this problem in any explicit way was again Count Bégouen. On the basis of certain of the parietal representations, and accepting the ethnographic parallels and the assumptions connected with the hidden contexts of many such representations, Bégouen formulated an explicit hypothesis as to how the magical rites of Palaeolithic man might have been carried out. He noted that certain paintings and engravings had been altered at various times; in the case of the 'lioness' of Les Trois Frères (figure 21) both the head and the tail had apparently been shown in various different ways. He postulated, therefore, that Palaeolithic magical rites consisted of either making new images for each purpose or adapting anew images made on previous occasions. From this position the important contention developed that it was the act of painting or engraving itself which had been the essential act of the sympathetic rites. Thus, as had already been noted by Breuil and others, the 'hidden meaning'[53] of sympathetic magic could account well for the superpositions so noticeable in Palaeolithic art (see chapter 2); for 'artistic' effect on the viewer was not the concern of Palaeolithic 'artists'. How important this interpretation of the significance of superpositioning was to become, will be seen below.

Anthropomorphic representations featured in some way or another in most of the interpretations of the significance of Palaeolithic art. Reinach interpreted their significance on the basis of Australian aboriginal fertility representations while Breuil and others saw them, and especially the Trois Frères figure, as sorcerers, magicians or spirits. Interpretation of the function of representations of anthropomorphs must form one of the most important starting points for any interpretation of what actually happened during a sympathetic magic rite, for the human is clearly the originator of the rite in the first place.

All the reviews of human representations in Palaeolithic parietal art were forced from the beginning to recognise the fact that animal and human representations were of very different character (but see chapter 2 for the different treatment of humans in engravings, paintings and bas-reliefs). This difference was based on three factors: 1 the rarity of human representations, 2 their schematic nature and 3 their 'masked' features. In the context of the magical rites the last two features became both the main basis for interpretation and the main point of disagreement.

Already by 1908 the identification of features shown on representations of 'anthropomorphs' (see chapter 2) had divided authors into two schools; a division which has lasted throughout the works of the classical interpreters. Some maintained that the humans were masked (e.g. figure 94) and/or clothed in animal skins while others have preferred to see the same works as evidence of ineptitude, of caricature, or of a primitive mentality unable to distinguish clearly between man and animal. The views of the second school have little relevance in the discussion of magical rites. One of the main supporters of this view, Luquet, saw[54] the gestures and the 'animal'-like heads simply as the result of the artistic evolution of Palaeolithic art which, he thought, had started from animal representations and only later arrived at human representations. This evolution, according to Luquet, explains not only the occurrence of ineptly drawn human heads on anthropomorphic figures but also the curious, forward-bent, stances of these figures (figures 89 and 92), still connected to the four-legged stance of animals.

The supporters of the first school, however, have rejected any evolutionary view and placed the anthropomorphic representations in positions of importance in their magical interpretations. Some, like Breuil, who accept that they may be masked and are covered with animal skins have interpreted them as officiating sorcerers, as mythical beings who had to be propitiated, or even as the representation of spirits. Others who also accept the mask and skins interpret them as representations of hunters in disguise approaching their quarries. For both interpretations much attention has been focused on ethnographic parallels.

Count Bégouen interpreted the large Trois Frères human (figure 89) as the arch-sorcerer of magical rites and offered various other more specific interpretations for other anthropomorphs. On one occasion[55] he saw them as representations of the artists themselves while on another[56] he reasoned that they represented the sorcerer as people had seen him in the course of a ritual dance. Bégouen rejected the arguments of followers of the second school by pointing to the elaborate and finely finished representations of some Palaeolithic humans (e.g. the Trois Frères 'sorcerer' (figure 89). He therefore argued that, when he wanted to, Palaeolithic man was fully capable of a high standard of human representation. The large number of instances when this was not so (e.g. figure 92) showed only that he had not wanted to. In such cases it was impossible to explain 'animal'-like faces by stylistic ineptitude; the figures were intended to be shown masked. It was equally impossible to ascribe their horizontal or stooping postures to stylistic evolution from animal representations; the figures were intended to be shown dancing, with arms outstretched, and the dance must have been an essential element of sympathetic magic rites (and see chapter 4 for the evidence for ritual dancing in Le Tuc d'Audoubert).

Fertility magic

The views of Reinach, Breuil and Bégouen encompass the basis of the sympathetic magic interpretation. Various additional interpretative details are scattered through the writings of a vast number of authors who have accepted this basic interpretation. Many authors who have accepted the views of the classic authorities on Palaeolithic art have elaborated the suggestions of an interest in fertility magic for humans as well as animals out of all proportion to its original formulation. Initially referring to the rare representations of female figures and the symbols interpreted as sexual organs, those who support this sexual theory have dragged into its scope all the female human figurines of Palaeolithic (and even later) date (sometimes as Mother Goddesses[57]) and have given a sexual interpretation to a vast number of indeterminate amorphous signs on cave walls, to a number of animal representations which might conceivably represent an association of male and female animal (e.g. figures 36 and 67), to many animal representations with slightly swollen bellies (figure 9), and to the unknown subconscious drives of Palaeolithic man. The idea of animal fertility in Palaeolithic art is already present in Breuil's description[58] of the nature of the two clay bison in Le Tuc d'Audoubert (figures 36 and 37) 'destined to obtain multiplication of the species' (thus ignoring the significance of a third smaller bison nearby). This sexual imagery developed into descriptions[59] of these bison as a 'male and female following each other; the male is in the act of rearing up on the other's hindquarters' and[60] 'a male bison and female bison, whose nervous widespread nostrils may indicate her excitement just before the moment of mounting' (thus ignoring even the presence of the third bison) (figure 38). For these later authors obsessed by the interpretation of sexual magic, the Palaeolithic world was often dominated by the worship of a Mother Goddess to which all Palaeolithic art could ultimately be related.

Recent work

Certain consistent interpretative and methodological assumptions can be isolated from the 'classic' works reviewed above. Almost all of them have stressed certain generalities of Palaeolithic parietal art (e.g. the predominance of animals over humans; the division of animals into potential food and dangerous species) and at the same time made much use of certain individual representations (e.g. the Trois Frères sorcerer (figure 89); the Montespan horses and bear (figures 97 and 101)). From these starting points they have proceeded to examine (and in many cases to search for) practices of

modern primitives to form the basis of possible explanations of
Palaeolithic art. Of course, within this general scheme specific
authors have stressed different features of the art and have made
different allowance for Palaeolithic variation (compare the cautious
note of some of Reinach's and Capitan's statements with the
generalisations of Breuil and Giedion) but the same methodological approach underlies all their works. In recent years a new
approach to the interpretation of Palaeolithic art has arisen which
explicitly rejects almost all these working hypotheses of the 'classic'
authorities.

Laming and Leroi-Gourhan refuse to accept the use of ethnographic parallels (and see chapter 4 for a full discussion of the
use of ethnographic parallels), insisting that all interpretations must
in the first instance be based exclusively on the evidence of the
Palaeolithic art itself. Nor are they content with the way in which
previous workers have set about their generalised assessments of
the content of Palaeolithic art.

Rejecting these two 'classic' approaches, Laming and Leroi-
Gourhan have departed from previous practice and undertaken
their work on Palaeolithic parietal art by detailed recording and

compilation of the facts of the art itself. Leroi-Gourhan is responsible for the first systematic analysis of the distribution of animal species in the caves. Both insist that interpretation can only be based on the results of such scientific analysis. They both maintain that only categories and consistencies revealed by accurate records of associations of animals in as many caves as possible can be taken as reliable clues to the meaning of the art while the 'classical' assumptions about the nature of Palaeolithic art and the 'classical' use made of one or two specific representations only can be nothing but misleading. On the basis of this approach ethnographic parallels are simply irrelevant to the interpretation of Palaeolithic art. [61]

The recent analyses of the facts of the art itself have revealed certain features which greatly affect the validity of the 'classic' interpretations (see chapter 4) and have stressed many features of Palaeolithic art which themselves demand interpretation but which were not specifically considered by the classical authors; for example the many differences between bas-reliefs and paintings/engravings (see chapter 2). [62]

Like many of his predecessors, Leroi-Gourhan bases his interpretation primarily on parietal art for this art alone gives definite contextual evidence whereas mobile art was, presumably, carried about for all sorts of different reasons. Taking only the parietal art Leroi-Gourhan has drawn up a detailed inventory of subjects to be seen in many caves (over sixty-five) and his analysis is based on these facts as well as the contexts of each subject noted.

His analysis has two starting points which come together finally in his overall view of the meaning of parietal representations; the first is the frequency and spatial distribution of animals in caves, the second the analysis of the signs in Palaeolithic art. Leroi-Gourhan notes that well over half of the animals shown are horse and bison. These, he concludes, must represent two coupled or juxtaposed themes, 'A' and 'B' respectively, whereas other animals must have played subsidiary roles.

For the analysis of the distribution of the animals he divided up the caves into seven different regions which are frequently determined by natural topographical features such as sharp bends, constrictions, chambers, etc.: 1 the first point where representations begin; 2 passages and shafts which connect up the large galleries; 3

points at the beginning of fissures, diverticules and alcoves; 4 the furthest region which is decorated; 5 the central part of decorated walls in large galleries; 6 marginal zones around the central part; and 7 points inside fissures, diverticules and alcoves. From the distribution of animals in these seven regions he finds that all the animals represented can be divided into the two groups A and B which correspond to the horse and bison groups and which are consistently used in particular regions of the caves. From this Leroi-Gourhan concludes that caves must have been systematically organised sanctuaries.

Group B animals (which are bison, aurochs and women) are found in the central panels (5 above). In most cases group B is represented by one animal, aurochs or bison, and only rarely by both although in a bison cave aurochs may play a subsidiary role, and vice versa. With one exception group A animals are found in all the other areas (1–4 and 6–7 above) only. The one exception is the horse which is also very commonly found in area 5 together with 'B' animals, thus forming the basic theme of 'man-woman and (or) horse-bison'.[63]

This fundamental differentiation of group A and B representations is not always easy to make out for animals of either group are frequently shown in twos: 'one sees that it is couples of couples which are represented; male and female bison opposed to mares and stallions'.[64] The whole theme is made much more difficult by the presence in some scenes of a third (or even fourth or fifth) animal belonging to group A which Leroi-Gourhan himself admits may sometimes dominate, numerically, the whole scene.[65]

On the basis of this dichotomy of parietal representations and the fact that in some places the central 'B' animals' place is taken by the representation of a woman, Leroi-Gourhan sees the whole theme of Palaeolithic 'naturalistic' representations as the 'juxtaposition', 'opposition', 'coupling' or 'association'[66] not of two groups of animals *per se* but of the female and male principle, B group animals representing the female and A group male. It is at this point that the first part of Leroi-Gourhan's analysis joins up with the second part, the analysis of 'signs'.

On the basis of a detailed inventory of the 'non-naturalistic' signs, tectiforms, etc., of Palaeolithic parietal art Leroi-Gourhan has constructed an evolutionary series which he thinks divides up the signs into two groups which show a clear derivation either from the whole female figure and the female sexual organs, or from the male sexual organs.[67] Once again Leroi-Gourhan sees the two groups of signs as opposed, coupled or juxtaposed; those of 'a' (lines, dots, etc.) representing the male, and those of 'b' (ovals, triangles, etc.) representing the female.

As with group B representations 'b' signs are predominantly found in central panels whereas 'a' signs are predominantly peripheral. Leroi-Gourhan[68] sees the relationship between male 'a' signs and female 'b' signs as the same as that between horse and bison. Similarly, signs are frequently coupled; group 'b' signs 'accompanied by "a" signs which complete it'.[69] The place of an animal representation is often taken by an equivalent sign, while the place of a sign is sometimes taken by an equivalent male or female human representation.

Leroi-Gourhan admits that 'the relationship between the group a-b and the group A-B is difficult to define clearly'.[70] The juxtaposition and coupling of the male and female principles is symbolically expressed not only by group A and B animals but also with group 'a' and 'b' signs, as well as by one group A or B representation with a sign of group 'a' or 'b'.

Leroi-Gourhan's thesis is clearly far removed from all previous interpretations in which the virtual absence of any scenes was considered a significant feature of Palaeolithic art. Both Leroi-Gourhan and Laming, on the contrary, consider that although 'narrative' scenes are uncommon, or even absent, all panels with more than one single representation should be viewed as meaningful scenes (see below). Whereas earlier authors took frequent superpositions to mean that the final appearance of the panel was not important and that the actual act of depicting each individual animal had an essential magical purpose, Leroi-Gourhan and Laming both consider that superpositioning on a panel was used as a means of showing the association between figures, thus forming a composite picture. According to these authors, except in cases where they were short of suitable rock walls, the Palaeolithic artists were careful to avoid destroying earlier works with more recent paintings and engravings.

From his analysis of the distribution of animals and signs within caves, Leroi-Gourhan concludes that the caves were decorated according to a systematic plan and he has reconstructed the elements of the 'ideal' composition in the 'organised world' of Palaeolithic man[71]: 'a group of large herbivores of two species, one of which is nearly always a horse. One of the two species is numerically predominant. This central composition is flanked by complementary animals, most frequently deer and ibex. Juxtaposed with these are the usually abstract representations of man and woman or of the male and female principles'[72], the whole being a true 'metaphysical system'[73], a mythology based both on the opposition as well as the complementary nature of the two sexes:—

Gone are the wounded animals so important to previous interpretations, for wounds are group b signs (female), frequently associated with male signs. Gone are the frightening impersonal caves where magical rites took place, for male signs are frequently placed in particular natural cavern features and the cave itself is therefore female. Gone are the animals which can be classed as edible or dangerous, for the animals themselves are sexual symbols. Gone are the traps for animals or spirits, the houses, weapons or projectiles, for tectiforms etc. are also themselves sexual symbols. Instead Leroi-Gourhan has introduced the idea that Palaeolithic parietal art expresses, in abstract form, a whole complex system of fecundity. 'In the last analysis (which is still provisional) we may conclude that Palaeolithic people represented in the caves the two great categories of living beings, their corresponding male and female symbols, and the symbols of death which feeds the hunter. In the central zones the system was expressed by the aggregate of male symbols around the female principal figures, while in the other parts of the sanctuary the male representations were exclusive, apparently complementary to the cavern herself.'[74] Palaeolithic 'representations are concerned with an extremely rich and complex system, much richer and much more complex than anyone had previously suspected'.[75]

The main emphasis of the work of Laming is on the definition and recognition of two groups of parietal art.[76] In one group she places the paintings, engravings and bas-reliefs which are within reach of daylight and in the other the engravings and paintings deep down in caves (but see chapter 2 for criticism of this grouping). Laming is mainly concerned with the interpretation of the significance of the first group. By definition, therefore, the argument of the 'classical' authorities that the hidden contexts presuppose a religious, sacred or magical meaning does not apply. Although she recognises this in theory, Laming proceeds to stress the different artistic traditions between the bas-reliefs (e.g. Laussel (figures 3, 58 and 60)) and the paintings/engravings and stresses that the open-air representations form a relatively homogeneous group. The fact that these bas-reliefs are situated in, or near, habitation sites cannot, according to Laming, distinguish between a sacred or profane function. It is therefore to the content of these representations that she next turns.

The representations open to daylight differ, in the analyses of Laming, from the deep-situated paintings and engravings by the absence of 'feather'-like signs and tectiforms. They frequently feature horse and bison (figures 10 and 66) but not dangerous animals such as rhinoceros, mammoth or feline. In addition there are more humans represented than in deep caves and they differ in character from the painted and engraved humans and are also larger. Furthermore there are many sexual symbols on bas-reliefs and the humans represented are predominantly women.

Laming recognises four major themes of content for the open-air sites: bison and boar; horse, reindeer and bear; so-called 'masked' humans and animal; woman and bison or horse. Unfortunately at this point, instead of continuing with the analysis of this group of Palaeolithic parietal art, Laming continues her work by offering comments about subterranean Palaeolithic art leaving the reader with the thought that daylight parietal art suggests 'calm, peace, harmony. It seems that if there were ceremonies carried out around these extraordinary bas-reliefs, they were perhaps concerned with love and life. No terror, no violence, no weapons, no wounded animals, but rather an extraordinary grouping of animals and humans sculpted in daylight, on the sides of cliffs, perhaps the most ancient evidence of man's efforts to understand the meaning of life, in order to recreate what seems to them a real image of it'[77](!).

In her less detailed analysis of Palaeolithic parietal engravings and paintings which are situated deep down in caves, out of reach of daylight, Laming also challenges the basic assumption of 'classic' views that superpositions are 1 evidence of relative dating, and 2 evidence that 'artistic' effect was not important to Palaeolithic man. She drew attention to the fact that cave walls, and blocks of rocks, frequently have blank spaces on them but that, nevertheless, Palaeolithic man chose to represent a new subject on top of a previous representation and ignored the blank areas. Furthermore she noted that it could be shown that various animals had been consciously superimposed (e.g. two bison at Lascaux, figure 100), for it could not be due to chance that their tails and back legs formed a balanced composition. On close analysis Laming also noted that various animals were frequently associated with each other, and that such associations could be found repeated not only in different places within the same cave but also in different caves. Thus she also favoured the revolutionary view that Palaeolithic art was concerned with scenes reflecting an overall unity of composition, an interpretation previously admitted only for certain rare groups of representations (e.g. the deer and horses at Lascaux, figures 14 and 22) and favoured by Count Bégouen for only one large hunting scene at Montespan (see above). Rejecting the view that superpositions were always evidence of the magical nature inherent in the actual act of painting she concluded that 'the Palaeolithics composed groups of animals and that in places where one had supposed juxtaposition or superposition, one must deduce composition'.[78]

Referring to the significance of Palaeolithic art Laming inferred from the themes on bas-reliefs that the 'woman, universal principle of fertility, occupied the central place' and that the 'male principle was represented by the bison' while the horse in such scenes might correspond to 'a female principle'.[79] This female personification was, to Laming, 'conceived, perhaps, not only as the source of life, but also as the link binding humans to animals and nature'.[80] For subterranean parietal art, she sees a different emphasis. Here the main themes are concerned with the complex relationships between different animals and with the insignificant role of the human (a view based on the accepted 'classical' view of the difference in treatment between small schematic anthropomorph and large naturalistic animal) who in a few cases takes his place in the animal world as a man-bison or man-cervid.

Despite the revolutionary nature of many of these suggestions Laming did in fact accept several of the conclusions and deductions made by the classical authorities. One such (and for others see the critical review of chapter 4) was the basic unity of style and content which runs through all Palaeolithic art, whatever its context (see chapter 2, Critique of stylistic and chronological evolutionary schemes). To Laming, therefore, the same cultural traditions are responsible for both the open-air and the subterranean Palaeolithic parietal art, each containing evidence of similar fundamental themes of associated representations: bison and horse; bovid and horse; etc. It is in a way ironical, therefore, that despite her theoretical recognition that the contexts of open-air parietal art suggest as much a profane as a magical/religious intent, she concludes her most detailed work with the statement that these themes 'might be mythical representations of, for example, the origin and history of some human group and its relations with animal species; they might be the concrete expression of a very ancient metaphysical system and the explanation of a universal system where each species, animal or man, has his own place and where the sexual division is primordial; they might be religious depicting supernatural beings. They might be all these at one and the same time, mythical, metaphysical and religious'.[81]

Of one thing she is certain and that is that, just as Breuil and others were sure that Lartet's and Christy's views were simplistic, the classic views of Palaeolithic art being founded on magic could not accurately reflect the complexity of the Palaeolithic mythical world which already then was rich in its own traditions and which was the basis of Palaeolithic parietal art.

Thus, both Leroi-Gourhan and Laming are convinced that Palaeolithic art is the result of a very complex system of beliefs and practices.[82] Both reject the use of ethnographic parallels as an aid to the interpretation of Palaeolithic art and both base their arguments and analyses on the contexts and contents of the art itself. Despite these similarities it must be admitted that their conclusions, on a superficial level anyway (see chapter 4 for a more detailed consideration of their respective interpretations), appear to be contradictory. As has been seen Laming equated the female

71 Red painted mammoth and two 'anthropomorphs', one red and one black, often said to be pierced by lances, from Cougnac.

principle with the horse and the male principle with the bison while Leroi-Gourhan, on the other hand, is inclined to see the reverse, with the horse as the male principle and the bison as the female principle. Writing about Laming's findings, he says[83] that the important feature of Palaeolithic parietal art is the one recognised by both Laming and himself, namely that the bison and the horse are the most important 'coupled' subjects of the art which represent opposed or juxtaposed conceptual elements of Palaeolithic thought. Leroi-Gourhan himself supports the identification of the female with the bison and the male with the horse but does not appear to rule out altogether the possibility that Laming's preference for the opposite identification might be correct.

The clue to this strange situation where two 'rebel' workers appear to arrive at the opposite conclusions can probably be found in the fact that they have concentrated their researches in slightly different fields. As has been seen Laming's important contribution lies really in her analysis of the art of the open-air sites, whereas Leroi-Gourhan's analyses are concentrated on the paintings and engravings of animals and 'tectiform' signs deep down inside caves. Of the two, it is the work of Leroi-Gourhan on parietal paintings of animals and signs which is the more detailed and better documented.

Hands

Before moving to a critique of all the intepretations reviewed, this chapter ends with a short resumé of the interpretations offered at different times for one specific Palaeolithic representation: the hand; for this gives ample evidence of the changes in emphasis which have taken place together with the specific interpretation favoured.

The vast literature on the subject of hands (figure 50, see chapter 2) has been equally divided into those dealing with their date and the way in which the representations were executed, and those seeking to interpret their meaning. Of the latter discussions many have been concerned with establishing whether or not they represented mutilated hands, whether the 'artists' responsible had been right or left handed, and whether they were the hands of men, women, or children (see chapter 2).

One interpretation of these hands, ignoring the analyses of many who have maintained that the hands belonged to women and children only, states that they were simply painted for enjoyment and aesthetic appeal (Art for Art's Sake) while another has taken several of these hands as accidental markings which had occurred while work went on on another representation[84], ignoring the panels devoted to hands alone at caves such as Gargas.

Authors who have accepted the hands as mutilated have carried out exhaustive research into modern primitive ways in order to find parallels for this practice. They have found mutilation of the hands among North American Indians, amongst the Bushmen, and elsewhere (Ethnographic Parallels). Basing his interpretation on his analysis of the practices among such primitive tribes, Giedion wrote[85] that 'the cloud of mutilated hands at Gargas stands there like a tragic chorus eternally crying out for help and mercy'.

Perhaps the most usually accepted interpretation of such Palaeolithic hands sees the clue to their meaning in the relationship of the hands to animal representations. Ignoring the isolated examples at caves such as Gargas the hands are taken as evoking the 'magical hold of hunters over symbolised prey'.[86] Others have been less explicit referring simply to such hands as 'no doubt magical in origin'[87] and others still have taken them either as giving power 'to take possession of the prey'[88] or as power to increase the number of animals (Sympathetic Magic).

It has been suggested[89] that the representation of hands was evidence of man's prayer to link himself with the Mother Goddess (Fertility Magic).

Leroi-Gourhan has accepted[90] that hands were those of women and his analysis has shown that they are almost always accompanied by such 'male' signs as points and short strokes and are found in central panels when the signs considered by him to symbolise the female are absent. Ignoring both ethnographic parallels for the painting or mutilation of hands, as well as the fact that it is hands which are represented at all, Leroi-Gourhan deduces that they belong to group B (or b?) representations and symbolise the female (Recent work).

4 Critical analysis
of interpretations

The previous chapter has shown how different authors have stressed different aspects of Palaeolithic art in their search for an understanding of its significance.

Content and locality (context)

The insistence by recent workers that any worthwhile interpretation must be based on two features of the art: its content and context, is clearly very important. Although Leroi-Gourhan and Laming both present this approach as something new, many of the supporters of the sympathetic magic interpretation (Reinach, Bégouen and Breuil, for example) already attempted to do just this. They took what they thought were the most important features of the content of Palaeolithic art (the animals, the arrows, etc.) and, stressing the locality of the art (deep down in caves far from habitation) inferred a secret magical function.

What is needed, therefore, is not so much a new approach as a systematic appraisal of the content and context of the art. It is no longer sufficient to consider any one or two representations from a particular cave to support an interpretation. What is important is accurate recording and detailed description of the positions and characteristics of every representation in as many caves as possible. Only then can one be reasonably sure that one is dealing with a true picture of what the Palaeolithic artists were about. The recording of cave representations by Leroi-Gourhan and rock-shelter representations by Laming has done a great deal to remedy the lack of accurate documentation.

Ethnographic parallels[1]

But this must not be the end of the process; content and context may or may not suffice to give a correct interpretation. It is here that the 'recent' approaches break down, for at this point Leroi-Gourhan and Laming do not admit the use of ethnographic parallels as aids to interpretation. However, something must be substituted for ethnographic parallels; and the substitution of a postulated metaphysical system of male and female symbolism, both rooted in a certain school of analytical thought, is not satisfactory.

The effects of this substitution will be considered in detail later. It suffices here to point out the essential differences between the 'ethnographic' and the 'recent' approach.

The aim in considering the practices of living 'primitive' (or 'non-literate') peoples should be, primarily, to avoid predetermining the type of explanation that one can offer for the interpretation of archaeological material by basing it exclusively on experience derived from one's own cultural heritage. In other words, reference to the practices connected with Australian aboriginal paintings, for example, should prevent one from offering an interpretation exclusively based on the reasons behind contemporary painting. This is not to suggest that a worker such as Leroi-Gourhan is interpreting Palaeolithic art on the basis of his own culture's artistic activities. What he is doing, however, is not so far removed. He (like many others before him) assumes that one can tell what was of interest to Palaeolithic men (e.g. hunting, gathering, fertility, etc.) and the interpretations of the juxtaposition and coupling of male and female symbols are greatly influenced by this view. So, instead of offering an interpretation drawn directly from their own culture's preoccupations, Leroi-Gourhan and Laming offer one based on their assessment of the preoccupations of Palaeolithic cultures.

The difficulties inherent in such an approach are many. For many centuries it has been popular in Europe to assume that from the knowledge of a people's economic activity it is possible to deduce something also about that people's attitudes to life, artistic achievements, marriage practices, etc. (see chapter 3 for some of the assumptions concerned). This view has, however, been shown by much modern anthropological analysis to be simplistic and highly misleading. An examination of living hunters and gatherers shows the range of activities and interests which may form part of a culture with a 'Palaeolithic' economy. On the level of material equipment there could be nothing more divergent than the simplicity and standardisation of Australian aboriginal stone celts, rough shelters, etc. and the elaboration and ingenuity of Eskimo ivory harpoons, knives, snow igloos, etc. On the artistic side, the Australians are among the very exceptional hunters and gatherers of today who still paint rocks. In terms of religious and metaphysical thought the Australian aboriginal system (see chapter 3 and below) is one of the most complex known among any people (including pastoralists and agriculturalists) living today, while other hunters and foragers have little religious elaboration and none of the complexity of kinship organisation which accompanies Australian totemism. To know that a people live by hunting and gathering does not, therefore, enable one to generalise about many other features of their culture.

Since the Palaeolithic 'cultures' which are the subject of this book started about 30,000 years ago (see chapter 1) any assumption that people living in the nineteenth or twentieth centuries AD can know *a priori* about the Palaeolithic 'ethos' must be ill-founded. Thus, interpretation of the meaning of Palaeolithic art must, as is stressed by the modern French workers, rely to a great extent on the facts revealed by the art itself. However, problems arise when it comes to interpreting these 'facts'. And the problems become extremely difficult when it is assumed, for instance, that the art is concerned with symbols and not with naturalistic representations (for example, the equivalence of bison with woman or man, and not just a bison).

Although the generalised attack by Laming and Leroi-Gourhan on the profitable use of ethnographic parallels to arrive at the meaning of Palaeolithic art must be rejected, there is, nevertheless a very real objection to the use of ethnographic parallels made by most of the twentieth century workers on Palaeolithic art. There are two fundamental points: whether all ethnographic parallels are of the same value, and whether ethnographic comparison is in itself any more illuminating than any other.

It may well be true that many of the specific ethnographic parallels adduced by followers of the classic sympathetic magic and totemic interpretations were ill chosen. Thus there can be no justification at all for the type of suggestion which led Breuil[2] to infer some meaningful connection between the (very questionable) ' "rain-making rites", reflecting a fundamental anxiety ... all through Africa' and the human representations in Spain (figure 87) which are akin to 'something resembling Bactracians or Fish'. The facile suggestion that a mass of finely engraved lines coming from an apex, at Lascaux, should be compared to the figure of a New Guinea costumed sorcerer[3] helps one to understand the origin of generalised attacks on the value of ethnographic parallels.

Very similar artistic outputs from two different cultures do not imply identical significances and causes. Comparisons can only suggest the variety of possible factors which may lie behind a certain representation. This is the essential point to be borne in mind when making use of ethnographic parallels. First, it is necessary to remember that one draws upon ethnographic parallels simply to avoid over-emphasis of one's own experience based on one's own cultural conventions. Second, that ethnographic parallels cannot produce simple answers but can only be used to demonstrate the range of possible factors underlying human activities.

With this in mind it is possible to make two generalisations. Useful ethnographic parallels may be based on two sorts of similarities: 1 the generalised, non-specific, activity of two cultures (e.g. that two cultures have at different times and in different places painted representations of hands, or that two cultures have been interested in painting at all), and 2 the specific results of certain activites in two different cultures (e.g. that culture X in their paintings often associated two species of animals in certain hidden recesses of caves, and that culture Y did likewise). There is a positive value to both these kinds of ethnographic parallel.

As has already been said, Leroi-Gourhan and Laming may well be right in that the generalised twentieth century use of ethnographic parallels may have been badly conceived and executed. Indeed the documentation of Palaeolithic art by these two workers has, for the first time, made it possible to search for more detailed and specific ethnographic parallels. It is all the more wrong, therefore, to react, as Laming and Leroi-Gourhan have done, to the increased knowledge of the contents and contexts of Palaeolithic art by assuming that modern knowledge about Palaeolithic behaviour and interests is sufficient to make similar ethnographically attested activities irrelevant to the study of Palaeolithic activities. To reject the variety of human experience in different conditions, past and present, for the assumption that at any given time in history one can (in whatever age one lives) be sure about the intentions of other peoples' activities is to go from the frying pan straight into the fire!

This leads immediately to the consideration whether ethnographic parallels are any more rewarding than any others. It should

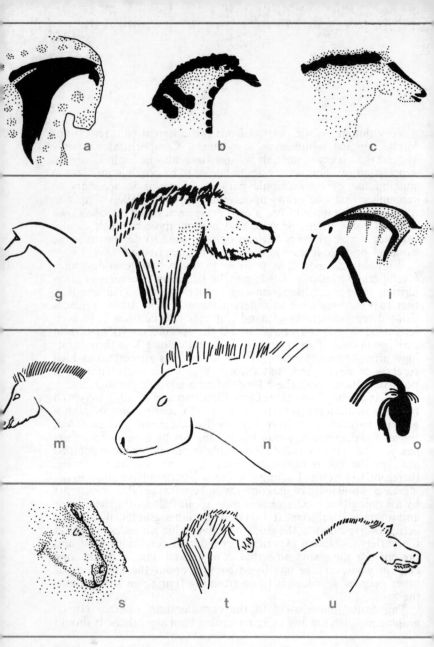

72 The variety of styles used by Palaeolithic artists for showing horses' heads: **a** Pech-Merle; **b** Lascaux; **c** Lascaux; **d** Le Gabillou; **e** Font de Gaume; **f** La Peña de los Hornos; **g** Pair non Pair; **h** Niaux; **i** Le Portel; **j** La Pasiega; **k** Gargas; **l** Lascaux; **m** Les Trois Frères; **n** Le Gabillou; **o** La Baume Latrone; **p** Gargas; **q** Labastide; **r** Altamira; **s** Commarque; **t** Le Gabillou; **u** Montespan; **v** Limeuil.

not be assumed that parallels between two groups of hunting and gathering peoples are *necessarily* the only ones to be meaningful. The situation revealed by ethnographic and anthropological documentation is much more complex than this. It is possible to find parallels in many aspects of culture between, for example, one hunting and gathering people and one agricultural people. It is not true to say that either the environment or the economy determines the rest of a particular people's activities. If one draws a parallel between a hunting artist's work and an agricultural artist's work it does not suffice to say simply that their different economies make the fact that they both paint, irrelevant. Each time a parallel is drawn or sought, it is necessary to analyse all the relevant social and economic activities practised by the people concerned before evaluating the significance of painting in the cultures concerned.

During the last two centuries argument was fierce[4] as to whether modern 'primitive' people should be assumed to have remained unchanged until this day from the 'Palaeolithic' or 'Neolithic' stage of their ancestors, or whether it should be assumed that they too had undergone as many, and as significant, changes as any people living today. In the light of the above discussion of the aim of the use of ethnographic parallels, such justification for comparisons between archaeological material and the practices of non-literate modern tribes are clearly irrelevant. In fact it is clear from almost all anthropological work that the customs and beliefs of 'primitive' peoples have undergone many changes in the past; all societies are continually changing. There is no reason, therefore, to assume that modern 'primitives' are any more like the Palaeolithic and Neolithic inhabitants of the world than modern Europeans, except in so far as their 'primitive' economies are associated with a tribal way of life in a way that modern industrialised economies make impossible.[5]

Since the use of ethnographic parallels is concerned with the documentation of the variety of possible factors involved in particular human activities any human activity which resembles, in its achievements, those which are being studied in an archaeological context is relevant and of interest. When 'industrial' features are such that they necessarily imply a quite different 'ethos' from that which can reasonably be inferred in prehistoric cultures, parallels are unlikely to be meaningful. Features such as these are few and far between; an industrial economy and the associated trading centres, ease of transport, money, a high evaluation on productivity, a low evaluation on leisure, for example, or specific techniques such as writing may be features which affect a particular culture in such a radical way that comparisons with a 'primitive' culture are unlikely to be very helpful. On the other hand it cannot be simply said (as has, however, often been maintained in archaeological literature) that once a culture has acquired the knowledge and skill of writing it has inevitably changed its character and has become 'civilised' and therefore qualitatively different from a 'primitive' non-literate society. This depends entirely on the use made of writing in any particular society. Many cases are known where writing has only a restricted role, for keeping accounts or sending messages (for instance, the Arab scribes in the non-literate Ashanti state), and there is no reason to suppose, in such a case, that the religious, artistic, or general 'ethos' of such a culture is necessarily any different from one which makes no use at all of writing. When, however, a culture uses writing for the recording of myths and dogma, it may well be presumed that the preservation of forms of ritual and dogma will be far greater than in a non-literate society. Again it follows from this that comparisons between the activities of 'peasant' groups which are themselves part of a larger literate culture but which are not themselves literate, may be useful as comparisons with non-literate 'primitive' groups. There is no reason, therefore, to confine the use of ethnographic parallels to modern Africa or Australia while ignoring Spanish or Cretan peasants.

In summary, the more varied and the more numerous the analogies that can be adduced, the more likely one is to find a convincing interpretation for an archaeological fact. The more numerous and the more detailed the parallels, the more likely one is to be able to assess the likelihood of a particular parallel being a significant one, and the greater the possibility of checking against the content and context of the archaeological material. In this connection it is important to stress another of the weaknesses of the use made of ethnographic parallels by the 'classic' workers on Palaeolithic art. Almost invariably the parallel which is chosen by the archaeologist as the most meaningful one has some esoteric or ritual association. There is no justification for this tendency unless the content and the context of the archaeological material itself warrants such a preference over a profane parallel. For example, as has been seen in chapter 3, numerous ethnographic parallels have been adduced to help in the interpretation of the Palaeolithic representations of hands. These parallels have mainly been concerned with the supplication of spirits to placate or avoid misfortune. No use has been made of the very common ethnographic practice of representing the hand simply 'for "amusement only" ' or as 'the artist's signature'.[6] To assume that a religious, ritual or esoteric meaning lies behind all, or some, Palaeolithic art is to negate at least some of the potential benefits of the use of ethnographic parallels.

The many occasions[7] when the systematic use of ethnographic parallels has in fact added a deeper understanding to the bare archaeological facts or offered the archaeologist a possible means of interpreting his material are, perhaps, more convincing than any of the theoretical justifications.

Ethnographic parietal art

Artisitic activity is not the prerogative of any one people, group of people or area of the world. 'Primitive' and 'peasant' groups perform an enormous variety of decorative and representational practices, varying from the striking sand paintings of the North American Navaho Indians to the crudest small figure of unbaked clay among, for example, many African tribes as well as Spanish peasants. Painting also (but less so engraving and relief-work) has a very wide distribution in the 'primitive' world, an activity which, as previously mentioned, is the response to many different situations. Paintings on house walls are very frequent in many areas of the world and the motifs employed for this purpose are usually abstract designs or representational items (such as hands) chosen for their visual effect, although in some cases a symbolic content has been presumed for ceremonial house-wall and door decorations. Equally frequent is the use of painting and engraving for the decoration of functional utensils or for the further embellishment of a modelled figure or carving. Except in terms of the generalised ethnographic parallel (see the above discussion) these practices are too diverse and the activities too general to have much relevance to the parietal art of Palaeolithic man, except for the parietal art in association with habitations (and possibly for mobile art).

To find closer parallels it is necessary to restrict examples to artistic activity on rocks or in caves, preferably artistic activity which is found in areas where there was no normal habitation. Unfortunately, although examples are by no means absent, the ethnographic information available about such works is in most cases lamentably poor. Painting and engraving on rocks are, curiously enough, extremely widespread and common forms of artistic activity (see chapter 1, p. 37), both archaeologically and ethnographically (e.g. figures 96 and 99). For present purposes there is little point in considering the archaeological examples (e.g. Tassili, Val Camonica, Negev Desert, North America) for in no case is there sufficient information about them to answer the sorts of questions which are of interest in the interpretation of Palaeolithic parietal art. In almost no case, in fact, is anyone yet clear why it was rocks which were used for painting and engraving, and archaeological interest has been mainly aimed at deciphering the motifs represented and assigning the works to a particular group of people. Much of the difficulty in referring to other examples of rock art is that their date is obscure (see chapter 1). In many parts of India, Australia, Africa and New Guinea, for example, there are paintings and engraving on rocks situated within areas now inhabited by particular tribes who either deny all knowledge of these works or presume them to be of great antiquity, often the work of mythical beings. In no such case, quite clearly, is there available any of the evidence required for the present discussion. There is little doubt that many groups of people are still today painting and carving on rocks but, although the evidence shows that this must long have been the case, detailed information about such activities is limited to one or two reports from Africa and much detailed work from Australia. Search for a variety of possible reasons behind Palaeolithic parietal art on the basis of ethnographic parallels must therefore, unfortunately (as it has been since the time of the discovery of Palaeolithic art) be based almost entirely on the Australian aboriginal material.

Contrary to the usual archaeological assumption, totemism and artistic representation do not necessarily go together[8], in fact their association among some Australian aborigines is most probably fortuitous. There are many totemic groups all over the world (including Australia) who carry out no art work and many non-totemic peoples who paint or engrave.

Australian aboriginal art is similar to the rock art in various different areas of the world (such as those in East Spain and those made by the Bushmen) in that human representations are frequent as are also vivacious narrative scenes usually connected with economic activities, and on both these counts it differs from Palaeolithic parietal art with its apparent absence of narration and its paucity of anthropomorphs. Australian art is not, however, the solitary response to totemic practices which it is so frequently accepted as being. Australians paint and engrave on rock walls for many different purposes. According to many statements by Mountford and McCarthy[9] Australian aboriginal art is often carried out purely for pleasure (Art for Art's Sake), to illustrate statements and stories, to record historical events of both economic and mythical/ceremonial importance (Totemic) and to act as teaching aids during initiation. Aboriginal rock art has also, sometimes, a (Sympathetic) magic importance both in the context of sorcery (e.g. figure 96) and increase rites (see below). The information regarding sympathetic hunting magic is, however, less clear for although many authors believe that some Australian art has this significance 'no direct proof of this assertion has yet been obtained from native informants'[10]. Some of the difficulties involved in interpreting the significance of Australian rock art are neatly summed up in an experience recorded by Mountford[11] who 'found a cave painting which pictures the chase, the capture, and the cooking of an emu, a painting which should have contained all the elements of hunting magic. On questioning the aborigines about the meaning of the painting, [he] was told that it had no magical significance whatever; it was simply the record of a successful hunt. If, [his] informants explained, they wanted to catch an emu, they chanted a magical song which made the bird so stupid and sleepy that they could approach and spear it without difficulty'. In many cases the problem whether the pictures were concerned with hunting magic or were records of a successful hunt is largely a 'question whether a painting was made before or after the incident portrayed took place'[12] and this information is largely lacking for Australia. The information available from a few areas in Africa clearly shows that some representations were made for hunting magic, some were 'doodles' and some were executed as part of initiation ceremonies (e.g. figure 99).

In all these forms of Australian aboriginal art animals, humans, weapons and vegetation feature predominantly. How far this should be taken as indicative of a significant difference from Palaeolithic parietal art is not easy to decide for interpretations by the aboriginal artists themselves make it very evident that what appears 'naturalistic' to the modern observer is very far from being the same for the aboriginal artist and it is not inconceivable that Palaeolithic 'signs' might in fact have clearly represented vegetation or humans to the Palaeolithic artists. What does seem certain is that the obvious 'pictorial compositions of everyday life'[13] in Australian art are absent in Palaeolithic art. There are more differences between Palaeolithic art of categories 2 and 3 (at least) (see pp. 110–15) and ethnographic rock art, for all the latter are normally on rock shelters and not deep down inside caves far from daylight. Only in some rare cases do Australian parietal representations extend out of the region of daylight. Again, how far this difference of context is to be taken as ruling out the relevance of the ethnographic parallels is a matter of personal opinion, but for Palaeolithic parietal art in category 1 (and probably category 2 also) the parallel holds good.

When it comes to more specific points about the ethnographic representations (such as their orientation, their localities within particular shelters, or their superpositioning) they share many features with the Palaeolithic parietal representations and it may, therefore, be instructive to note what is known about these aspects of living peoples' artistic works. The evidence regarding superpositioning reflects the variety of practices which exist in different parts of the world where rock art is carried out. In Australia alone it is possible to find some shelters in which representations are few and far between and others in which 'it is difficult to find a space

entirely devoid of any [representations] . . . and the work of hours must have run into the labour of years, yea, of generations, because . . . one design has been carved over the top of another, time after time, until eventually the ground appear[s] as though it were covered with an elaborate carpet. . . .'.[14] In some cases it appears that the Australian aborigines painted or engraved over older representations without any regard for them and without caring that they were obliterating them; indeed there are examples known where red ochre has been applied to obliterate previous works and to provide the canvas for new representations (see page 49). In some cases it is suggested that 'newer paintings derive some merit or value from being painted over . . . older paintings'[15] while it is also the case that superpositioning in other cases (but by no means always) indicated meaningful associations to the aboriginal artist. It is interesting to note that in the many cases where Australian aboriginal rock art is 'archaeological' material because no aboriginal artists survive to explain their works[16] interpretations have followed much the same lines as those adopted for Palaeolithic parietal art. Thus Professor Elkin has argued[17] that the fact that 'drawings overlay one another . . . suggests that satisfaction lies not

73 Painted ass, from Lascaux, recognisable by its long ears and tail.

163

so much in admiring the finished picture, as in the act of painting it or in some practical desire it expresses and in some result it will effect ... [the aboriginal] believes that this "ritual" act will bring about the desired result'. From Africa all that is known is that among the Marghi of Northern Nigeria 'there is no attempt to keep from covering the older faded paintings though the more recent or distinct paintings are not covered'[18] (figure 99).

Although in most cases known the rock art of 'primitive' peoples is placed on the most suitably available vertical faces of rock outcrops, often shelters beneath which they camped or worked, there are some instances from Australia where the localities chosen for artistic representation as well as the orientation of the pictures recall some of the peculiarities of Palaeolithic parietal localities. Thus in some Australian rock shelters paintings are placed high on the shelter ceilings while others are hidden under recesses and in narrow cavities so that in each respective case the artists must have clambered up the rock walls or squeezed through narrow passages and lain on their backs to carry out their art works. Unfortunately there is very little certain information about Australian parietal localities; it has been tentatively suggested that in one particular cave a decorated recess itself signified the female womb and that the representations within this recess were chosen with this symbolism in mind, while in other cases it seems probable that the particular totemic or historical myths with which the artistic representations are connected themselves influenced or dictated the choice of locality. There are occasions where the associated myth appears to have influenced the orientation of representations and many other occasions where it is the available rock surface which has conditioned orientation (figure 96).

Only for the Australian art works on rocks which are connected with totemic 'maintenance' rites (see chapter 3) is there evidence of regular retouching of paintings, for the addition or improvement of representations for critical reasons of inaccuracy or technical incompetence must be an occasional and irregular occurrence. In certain parts of Australia where rock art was used for totemic ceremonies the act of retouching or renovating a painting or engraving was the mechanical means of ensuring the reactivation of the totemic 'magic' so that, for example, the retouching of certain

paintings causes the rain to fall and the plentiful supply of food animals and plants.

In Australia and Africa the available information suggests that anyone (at least any male) can be an artist although, everywhere, some people are well known as more skillful than others and their paintings and engravings are easily recognised and are fully appreciated. There seems very little standardisation in Australia regarding who is allowed to see rock wall representations; in many cases it has been claimed that shelters which contain totemic paintings and engravings are sacred spots into which few are allowed, but examples are frequent where there is no such selectivity and anyone is free to admire the representations. The variety of Australian artistic practice is again seen in the situation where some shelters are 'owned' by a particular person to whom payments are made before anyone is allowed to paint or engrave in his shelter, while other shelters contain not only totemic representations but also (sometimes superimposed on the totemic example) 'casual' representations whose aim is no more than to give aesthetic pleasure, to indicate that a particular person had been there, or to illustrate a particular domestic episode.

Rock paintings and engravings undoubtedly play an important part in initiation ceremonies in both Australia and Africa (e.g.

74 Painted bichrome cow, from Lascaux;
the black head, brown body and pale
stripe alongs its back probably indicate
the real colouring of wild cows;
compare with figure 56 which shows
the much darker colouring of wild bulls.

figure 99). In Australia there are places where engravings were shown to initiates as aids and explanations for the teaching of tribal myths and beliefs. In one example these engravings were laid out in galleries along which the initiates were led but here, too, it is interesting to note that intermingled with these didactic engravings were many examples of 'casual' art. In Africa there is some reason to think that some 'archaeological' examples of rock art may have been used during the initiation ceremonies of 'secret societies', while among the Marghi of Northern Nigeria the paintings of animals and humans on a rock face is surrounded by no secrecy or mystique, rather 'an analogy to a collection of signatures seems apt'[19] (figure 99).

Finally it is not surprising to find that among the Australian aborigines where artistic activity fulfils so many functions for adults, children also enjoy this form of self expression and there is evidence for their skill and success in modelling and engraving on clay floors.

The remainder of this chapter is concerned with a critical assessment of the various interpretations reviewed in previous pages. Although some of these past theories were based on the then incomplete evidence, they must now be reviewed in the light of modern knowledge of the content and context of Palaeolithic art (chapter 2 above), and in the light of 'primitive' artistic practices. It is necessary to stress again that this book is concerned solely with Palaeolithic *parietal* art (see Introduction) so that any suggestions made about this art cannot necessarily be assumed to apply also to mobile works. Parietal art has remained in its original position since Palaeolithic times so that useful discussion based on both content and locality can be attempted and the relevance of different modern ethnographic practices can be assessed.

Art for Art's Sake

The idea that Palaeolithic men were artists simply because they appreciated beautiful things, and that therefore their artistic work had no special functional aim, was rejected very early on, mainly on the basis of one simple argument. As pointed out by Reinach (see chapter 3), the context of Palaeolithic art precluded any such interpretation for no one would go deep down into caves which were not used as living places in order to decorate walls which would not often be looked at, unless they had a very special reason for so doing. The important reason could not be simply that they were 'artistic' for they would then have carried out their artistic works in places where they could at least see the results.

Assumptions about the necessarily simple nature of Palaeolithic man and his inability to evolve religious concepts were disproved by the ethnographic practices of the very hunters and foragers which supporters of the Art for Art's Sake theory had themselves originally drawn upon. The reasons for the Australian aboriginal paintings were not at all 'primitive', nor were they the simple expression of man's innate artistic nature, but some at least were acts of specific intent. Supporters of the Art for Art's Sake theory of Palaeolithic art also conjured up a luxurious Palaeolithic environment to explain artistic activity. In a sense such an environment may have existed (see chapter 1), but it was also shown by the Australian aboriginal parallel not to be a prerequisite for painting. The Australian aborigines were not living in luxury. Of course no one will paint if they have no time to do so; but studies of modern hunting and gathering peoples have shown that, despite relatively inhospitable environments, these people generally still have time for leisure activities (and even exercise considerable selective choice as to the particular animals and berries that they will or will not eat[20]). The idea of a particularly rich environment is, therefore, largely irrelevant for the Art for Art's Sake interpretation.

The existence of two very different contexts of Palaeolithic art as stressed by Laming, already made the situation considerably more complex than that assumed by Reinach and others, while the threefold classification of parietal art followed in this book (see chapter 2): – 1 associated with a living site; 2 starting within or near the living area of the cave, but also penetrating beyond this into the darker regions of the cave; and 3 in no way associated with habitation debris, complicates the picture even further. The existence of the first category of Palaeolithic parietal art, which includes Laming's 'open-air' sites, has removed the ground from the argument that some very important, non-materialistic, driving force must necessarily be the basis for all of Palaeolithic man's art. For the category of parietal art associated with habitations, therefore, there is no reason to reject out-of-hand an Art for Art's Sake interpretation. On the basis both of generalised ethnographic parallels for painting, engraving and sculpting in a domestic context, as well as the evidence of the Palaeolithic art itself, this category of parietal work may have had either a profane or a religious/ ritual/sacred meaning.[21]

Although she accepts this in theory, Laming is at pains at various points in her work to suggest that ceremonies of some sort were carried out around the parietal works found on or surrounding living sites, and she stresses their 'inspirational unity' with other parietal works deep down in caves.[22] There is very little positive evidence of any kind to support the assumption that ceremonies were associated with these works. Laming herself finds no definite evidence of usage on any of the examples of parietal art which she considers, and accepts that they were placed in positions that suggest that they were looked at.[23] Nevertheless, she suggests that an esoteric interpretation of open-air parietal art may well apply, and assumes the same symbolism for open-air and cave art. This view is based on the content of the art, for although she finds specific differences between the contents of the two art groups, she also attributes an overall unity of symbolism between the two (see chapter 3). The actual symbolism deduced by Laming will be considered below. It is important, at this stage, to emphasise that irrespective of whether the artistic repertoire of both groups of the art is in fact similar, it cannot be allowed that an esoteric meaning for the representations of particular objects necessarily implies that every representation of the same object is therefore also bound to be esoteric. Thus, we know that in churches the representation of woman and child represents the Virgin Mary and her son Jesus, but this does not mean that the representation of a mother and child in a particular private dwelling house also represents the Virgin Mary and Jesus, rather than Mrs Smith with her son Albert.

It must be accepted, therefore, that there is no *a priori* reason to assume either from the evidence of the content of this category 1 art (animals and humans), or from its context (associated with habitation debris) that the aim in making these representations was esoteric.

This leads one straight on to a consideration of the Art for Art's Sake interpretation in the context of the second two categories of parietal art, inside caves. It is a remarkable fact that the original supporters of this interpretation have almost entirely ignored the reasons why the Palaeolithic artists should have chosen such contexts for their works; indeed, this is the reason why the adverse arguments of Reinach etc. were almost immediately accepted. Only Piette[24] offered a specific reason for this context of parietal art. According to him, the Palaeolithic artist first carried out his parietal works near to the openings of caves where he lived. However, the frost destroyed this work and the artist was forced to go deeper and deeper into the cave to find spots where his art could safely remain. It is, of course, impossible to accept this view for all the Palaeolithic representations, for although in several caves works of art begin at or near the entrance and continue far into the dark passages (category 2), there are also caves in which works of art are found only far inside the cave (category 3). Although it may sometimes be argued that works of art near the entrances have been destroyed, there are many cases in which this appears very unlikely (see chapter 2 for a discussion of the original entrances).

Even in some of the category 2 caves, where Piette's suggestion might at first sight seem plausible, difficulties arise in the interpretation of these works as purely Art for Art's Sake. It would have to be assumed that the dark cave passages which were not inhabited were kept scrupulously clean and perhaps even lit as some sort of art gallery, or were decorated places used for sleeping or other leisure activities only. A more serious objection to Piette's thesis lies in the distribution of paintings and engravings within these galleries. Representations do not follow each other in some ordered way down the passages, and many apparently suitable wall or ceiling areas were not decorated, whereas on other areas representations were superimposed. Assuming that representations in the blank spaces had not perished (and there is no reason to assume that they have; indeed Piette's argument presupposes that the Palaeolithic artist had chosen a spot where this would not happen) it would follow that superpositioning was intentional, as suggested by Laming and Leroi-Gourhan, and that there were certain places (possibly defined by cavern features and relationship to other

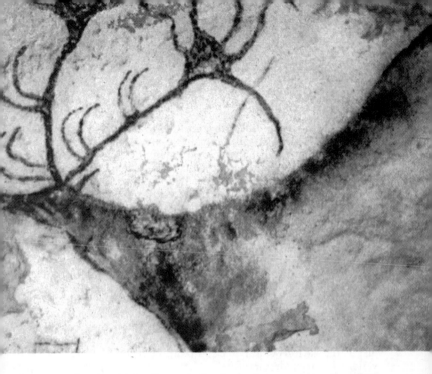

representations) which dictated the irregular spacing of artistic works in these passages; a sort of 'art gallery' with rigorously observed codes of 'hanging'. Furthermore it is difficult to imagine, among primitive or peasant societies of today, a comparable situation where artistic works are placed in a 'room' kept strictly separate from other day-to-day activities unless their function is ritual or religious, although it has already been seen that among the Australian aborigines there is occasionally one particular individual who can control the artistic activities within a particular cave whose contents are not only 'magico-religious' but sometimes 'casual'.

It would seem, therefore, on the basis of these arguments, that this second category of parietal art should, in the main, probably be grouped with the third category of representations not associated with habitation. It is necessary to stress the words 'in the main', however, for it is not at all impossible, or even improbable, that from time to time a Palaeolithic man moved a little way away from the strict area in which he worked and ate, and painted or engraved an animal, sign, or anthropomorph.[25] As Reinach said so long ago (although in a very different context, see chapter 3), there is no reason to assume that all Palaeolithic art results from one single cause, and that even if there is one major reason for Palaeolithic art, this does not exclude occasional works by individuals, adult and child, who were not concerned with the general painting complex. Painting, engraving and sculpting is not, after all, a necessary response to one particular situation only. In fact, people paint all over the world sometimes for specific ulterior reasons and sometimes simply for enjoyment, and there is no evidence to show that this situation has not always applied, whatever the period of man's history. The grouping of categories 2 and 3 together is, perhaps, supported by the total absence of signs, tectiforms, etc. in category 1 and their characteristic profusion inside caves.[26]

The technically most difficult works, the bas-relief sculptures, are almost exclusively found in daylight shelters with habitation debris but, as in the case of Commarque (figure 95), they occasionally extend beyond the entrance shelter into the dark regions of the cave just as the various engraving and painting techniques do. It cannot validly be argued, therefore[27], that the most difficult techniques could only be worked in daylight so that inside caves, where lighting had to be provided by oil/fat lamps or resinous torches, the artists had to restrict themselves to painting and engraving. Such an argument also assumes that lighting for any length of time presented an insuperable problem to Palaeolithic man, whereas the profusion of works of art found, sometimes at great depth, belies this assumption, as do also the few hearths from inside some caves (see chapter 2). On the basis of technique, therefore, art in categories 1 and 2 appear distinct from art of category 3.

Although, where the limestone rock is hard, there are no bas-reliefs even in shelters and shallow caves, it is clear that use of sculpturing techniques is not simply a matter of technology or lithology for in areas with bas-reliefs there are also paintings and engravings and these are more or less contemporary with the bas-reliefs, and certainly overlap the span of time during which such low reliefs were made. There may, however, be a chrono-logical difference between the use of shelters and shallow caves and the use of deep caves for art work, as suggested by Leroi-Gourhan[28]. Since the art in deep caves is difficult to date by direct archaeological means, such a chronological difference cannot at present be definitely established. Clearly a chronological study of parietal art based on reliable archaeological evidence rather than theories of stylistic evolution could be valuable in assessing the relationship between works of art in deep caves and category 1 caves.

Thus any interpretation of Palaeolithic art must recognise that the most difficult technique was used to carry out detailed representations of animals and humans for works which were placed in association with, or near to, habitation. Deep outline engraving, light engraving and painting were also used in these contexts. How far it is possible on this basis to carry inferences about the relative importance of the representations is very difficult to assess. It may be argued that as the most difficult techniques were used where they were either close by or in full view of everyone, such works were considered more important than the less accessible ones on which less energy and skill were expended. It could also be argued that whereas category 1 and 2 works were so important that a difficult technique was used for them, the art of deep caves was equally important but that, for definite reasons, other techniques were preferred. This might imply that the significance of these category 3 works lay primarily in the act of representation as opposed to the visual effect, so that a quicker technique would be preferable to a laborious one. This implication accepted by so many workers (see chapter 3), is denied by several important considerations. Thus, one of the basic arguments of supporters of the sympathetic magic interpretation of Palaeolithic art that the aim of Palaeolithic representations was expressed in the magical act of representation itself as opposed to its visual effect is contradicted by representations found in all three contexts of Palaeolithic art in which more than one technique is employed. Thus where two techniques, painting and engraving (figures 16 and 89) or bas-reliefs and painting (figure 60), were employed for a single representation it is strong evidence that the visual effect of the work was the overriding interest of the artist concerned. Similarly the occasional instance of Palaeolithic representations which were subsequently 'improved' or 'corrected' at a later Palaeolithic date (e.g. figure 21) seems proof that the visual impact of that particular representation was

76 Engraved reindeer, from Le Gabillou.

considered important by the Palaeolithic artists. Only one piece of evidence might argue against the conclusion that Palaeolithic artists were concerned with the visual effects of their (and their forebears') artistic works. In decorated habitation sites it is not uncommon to find that habitation debris gradually accumulated in such a way that it obscured many representations. As far as can be seen no attempt was made in many cases to prevent refuse and soil from covering Palaeolithic representations made at some previous time (see section on Dated works of parietal art, chapter 2). The significance of superpositioning is crucial to this argument; if superpositioning means that previous, but more or less contemporary, representations were disregarded then it seems plausible that in some cases the act of painting and engraving was more important than the final visual result; if, on the other hand, superpositioning is a means of indicating composition the final effect was clearly significant, and it remains difficult to explain why sculpturing techniques were not normally used on suitable rock. Again it may be significant that some Australian superimposed representations may sometimes indicate meaningful association in the same cave as representations superimposed for no artistic purpose.

The existence of bas-relief sculptures around or near to habitations can be viewed either as evidence that Palaeolithic man placed a high premium on domestic surroundings (implicit in Breuil's interpretation of the function of the Magdelaine Venusses, see chapter 3), or that these works were too greatly valued to have been simply designed to brighten up domestic activities. The interpretation of the significance of category 1 art (at least) depends largely on which of these two explanations is preferred, and it may be important to note that bas-reliefs are associated with habitation sites which show signs of having been used on many different occasions and were not simply camp sites used once and never again. It is possible, therefore, to imagine that such more or less permanent sites were considered worthwhile 'decorating' while purely temporary camping grounds were not.

Before it can be accepted that category 3 representations are only Art for Art's Sake one or all of the following conditions would have to be assumed: a strict Palaeolithic convention regarding the spacing of parietal representations; differential destruction of some

representations in the same part of caves; superpositioning as a conscious act of producing composite pictures; category 1 (and 2?) art as the work of different people from those who created category 3 art.

Where enough of these conditions can be seen to have applied to caves of category 3 it is possible to envisage situations where the art acted as 'prestige' representations not directly connected with magical rites, religious ceremony or symbolic expression.[29] Assuming no differential destruction, much of category 3 art might have been placed inside caves in passages and niches just because these locations were difficult to reach. This would not, in itself, imply that the reasons for so doing were magical or mystical for the aim in some cases could have been to impress anyone who saw the artistic work by its very inaccessibility. If this was the aim it does not necessarily imply magic or ceremony for an important 'visitor' to an artistic treasure house would equally well fit the bill. It is possible to imagine that once the 'visitor' had been taken to a particular decorated wall in a cave the panel of superpositioning would impress; possibly as the visible expression of the energies of the particular group who 'owned' or 'used' the cave (see the 'ownership' and control of certain caves among the Australian aborigines, above). On analogy with some of the Australian aboriginal parietal art it is also possible that such 'difficult' localities were chosen because they especially suited a particular narrative myth or his-

toric episode. It is even conceivable that the maze of superpositioned representations might present an exercise in identification. Perhaps, if the imagination is allowed to wander a little, it was the pride of one group of Palaeolithic men that more cows or horses, for example, were hidden away somewhere on a particular wall than on any cave wall 'owned' by another group. Perhaps, on the other hand, it was just the impression of animality which was desired; numerous possibilities can be envisaged!

Totemism, sympathetic hunting and fertility magic

As was stressed in chapter 3 the totemic and sympathetic magic interpretations of Palaeolithic art were originally one and the same. Although acceptance of totemism as the *raison d'être* of Palaeolithic art was short lived and found few supporters the grounds for originally accepting it were much the same as those for accepting sympathetic magic. The fertility magic and hunting magic interpretations are usually combined together as one Sympathetic Magic interpretation. In themselves, however, the totemic and fertility magic interpretations are the most closely related.

There are many features of these interpretations of Palaeolithic art which do not stand up to close analysis and scrutiny and in this critique, which deals with the logical implications of the interpretations themselves, these three interpretations are considered together as far as possible. Many of the following criticisms have been made possible because of the work of factual re-analysis of the content of Palaeolithic art by Professor Leroi-Gourhan.

The argument that Palaeolithic art was hidden away deep inside caves, while delivering the death blow to the Art for Art's Sake interpretation, proved at the same time to be the corner stone of the totemic and magical interpretations (see chapter 3). Previous

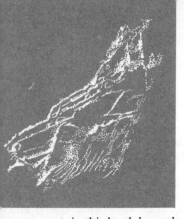

77 *Far left* Engraved glutton, from Los Casares; this is the only certain example of this animal in Palaeolithic parietal art.

78 *Left* Engraved wolf's head, from Les Combarelles; one of the very rare representations of this animal.

arguments in this book have shown that all Palaeolithic art is not of necessity to be found in the most inaccessible parts of caves for much is in open-air sites, much in galleries leading off from inhabited cave entrances, and only little completely separated from habitation areas. To explain these contexts, some supporters of the sympathetic magic and totemic interpretations (notably Breuil) postulated different functions for the hidden and the daylight art (daylight sites for totemism (or Art for Art's Sake) and hidden sites for initiation). It is a strange fact that the ethnographic parallels on which both the totemic and the sympathetic magic interpretations relied do not, in fact, suggest that these activities, which may or may not be associated with artistic expression, need necessarily be hidden away from the general public. Only when it comes to considering Australian totemism in connection with initiation ceremonies (see above) is 'discreetness' a vital feature; and even so the point is not necessarily to hide away the initiation region but only to delimit it and to forbid the presence of the uninitiated in the delimited area. Thus the fact that Palaeolithic art is found frequently in or near to habitation does not rule out a secret or non-profane significance. Equally, of course, there is nothing about the locality of category 1 representations to suggest that the function was not profane. Similarly, it can also be argued that the locality of category 2 representations does not rule out a profane function (see previous discussion in Art for Art's Sake section). Only if category 3 representations really do exist in localities far removed from normal habitation areas may there be some positive indication that the motivations for this category of Palaeolithic parietal art were not profane. A true appreciation of the facts must wait until modern excavations and explorations attempt to fill the lamentable gaps in knowledge of caves with artistic works apparently confined to dark passages far from habitation areas.

The second feature of Palaeolithic parietal art which was isolated by the protagonists of the sympathetic hunting or fertility magic interpretations was that the representations were not primarily intended to be looked at and that the artists were not primarily concerned with aesthetic appeal. At a later date these features were used as strong arguments against a totemic interpretation; since in Australia, for example, totemic localities were often visited and totemic representations often viewed. Similarly, the absence of evidence for frequent visits to regions where parietal art was situated conformed well to the hypothesis inherent in the magical interpretations, namely that it was the act of representation itself which had meaning – on the occasion of its performance only – and much less well with the totemic view of initiation ceremonies carried out in regions of especial mythological or ritual importance.

The evidence regarding all these points is anything but clear (see pp. 105–6). How frequently Palaeolithic man visited the parietal representations inside caves rests on the evidence of footprints in the localities concerned and the evidence of representations of different dates in these localities. The dates assigned to various representations by different archaeologists do not really help very much for they are largely based on subjective stylistic considerations (see chapter 2) and are concerned with activities spread over many thousands of years. They reveal, in some cases, the fact that certain Palaeolithic artists living thousands of years after some of their forebears painted or engraved in the same regions of caves but they give little information about the frequency of visits to these regions of a cave during one or two consecutive generations. The evidence of footprints, also, is far from satisfactory. In the first place footprints will only survive in a cave passage under certain exceptional conditions of preservation where the original clay floor has not been disturbed by the action of water or by collapse, etc. In the second place, Palaeolithic footprints will only survive where they have not been later destroyed by the activities of animals inhabiting the cave or of later human explorers of the caves. Unfortunately there are numerous examples[30] both of vandals destroying the evidence of Palaeolithic activity inside caves and of explorers inadvertently treading on valuable evidence which they failed to notice at the time by the light of their dim lamps. The little evidence that still remains to be analysed appears contradictory. In many caves footprints are few, and the conclusion is therefore that Palaeolithic man rarely visited decorated regions of caves, whereas in a few caves the ground is covered with footprints (see chapter 2). How far it would be correct to assume that the former situation be due to exploration and conditions of preservation is impossible to say. It is, however, an unwarranted assumption to say, on the basis of the evidence of footprints alone as have done many supporters of the magical interpretations of Palaeolithic parietal art, that decorated regions of caves were never revisited after their initial use except by other artists living many thousands of years later. Whatever the true situation, the evidence suggests (see chapter 2, Contexts) that in the majority of caves, e.g. Lascaux, Altamira, etc., Palaeolithic activity inside the decorated regions of caves was not concerned with knapping flints and eating animal flesh as in normal habitation areas (but see the evidence of caves such as Labastide, chapter 2).

The main evidence in favour of initiation ceremonies, usually discussed in the context of the totemic interpretation, comes from the cave of Le Tuc d'Audoubert. In several caves (see chapter 2) footprints have been said to be those of children but only in Le Tuc d'Audoubert has the evidence been taken as demonstrating that the children were definitely in these regions of the cave for the specific purpose of their initiation. At Le Tuc d'Audoubert there are many clear heel prints in the small chamber with a very low roof (less than one and half metres high in all places) which contained the so-called 'phalli' (figure 39) (see chapter 2). The heel prints have been interpreted[31] as belonging to children, of between eleven and fifteen years old, who had intentionally walked on their heels with their toes in the air in five or six files. This information has been hailed as conclusive evidence either of the magical or the initiation function of Palaeolithic activities inside caves: – Charet [32], for example, has taken this evidence to mean that 'having magically wounded the bison [in the nearby chamber] (figure 36) . . . the adolescents wearing their clay penis sheaths left the room on their heels. At the exit of the chamber [where, incidentally, the original report mentions the presence of an adult footprint] they then threw away the clay sausages which they no longer needed', while many authors[33] have taken the footprints as evidence of an 'initiation dance'. How little support for either interpretation this evidence really gives, and how fanciful any such interpretation must be, is clear when it is remembered that no connection with the bison has been established, that the 'phalli' may well have been intended for the modelling of animals (see chapter 2), that the correlation of age and heelprint size is a very doubtful matter especially when the relationship of body size and foot size of Palaeolithic man is quite unknown (chapter 2), and that, in the sane view of Luquet and Patte,[34] the number of heelprints would imply something more in the nature of a march than a dance and that such heelprints could well be the result simply of attempts to lessen the contact of the foot with wet mud when walking with a stoop in a low chamber.

What is clear from the evidence of footprints in several caves is that both adults and children penetrated into the dark regions of caves, both into areas where parietal representations existed and into areas where there was no parietal art. To try to see in this evidence the after-effects of initiation ceremonies or of children wandering away from the 'beaten tracks'[35] is to read much too much into the partial information available.

In the Art for Art's Sake section of this chapter, much of the evidence which supports the view that Palaeolithic art *was* intended to have a visual effect has been reviewed: the combination of more than one technique in one representation, the retouching and alteration of various representations, the breakage of stalagmites and stalagtites in a large area around representations, etc. Insofar as these features are accepted to be evidence that Palaeolithic representations were intended to be viewed they argue against the assumption of followers of the sympathetic hunting and fertility magic interpretations that it was the act of representation itself and not the visual effect that was important; they can, however, be seen as meaningful within a totemic interpretation which assumes the religious importance of the representations which would be often revisited and admired.

There are several supporters of sympathetic magic interpretations who attempted to include the notion that Palaeolithic man was at one and the same time interested in the act of representation itself and also in the final artistic result (notably Breuil and Bégouen, see chapter 3). As has already been seen in chapter 3, they led to some self contradictory expositions about unfinished, partially finished and completed representations (see the theories of Bégouen in chapter 3). Throughout the works of supporters of the sympathetic hunting and fertility magic interpretations run the two themes, first that Palaeolithic art was created for a specific reason and with a particular aim in mind and, second, that Palaeolithic art is nevertheless beautiful to look at. These workers never managed satisfactorily to reconcile these two points of view although Breuil[36] attempted to do so when he wrote that 'these aims are not opposed and do not exclude each other, being merely complementary'.

As has been seen in the above section (and chapters 2 and 3) it is the meaning of superpositioning which remains fundamental to any interpretation of the significance of the locality and relationships of individual Palaeolithic parietal representations, for it is this frequent and characteristic superpositioning in Palaeolithic parietal art which would appear to support the contention that it was the act of representation itself, and not the final visual result, which was important to the Palaeolithic 'artists'.[37] It is natural that discussion at this point turns to the work of Leroi-Gourhan and Laming for it is they who have made it possible to look again with an open mind at the possible significance of superpositioning: whether it be evidence of later work placed on top of much earlier work, or whether it be a Palaeolithic artistic convention to denote association. It is significant that neither of these authors pose the question in this way. To both of them superpositioning of Palaeolithic parietal art may reflect either of these two alternatives; to distinguish them is only possible when dealing with works of clearly different styles and techniques. In other words, unless the style or technique of two superimposed works is different both authors assume that superpositioning was a conscious act of association by the Palaeolithic artists.

The basis of Laming's argument lies in her observation that, with all the blank spaces available on cave walls or nearby blocks of stone, Palaeolithic man superimposed representations without first removing or covering earlier representations, while Leroi-Gourhan simply states that Palaeolithic man only superimposed representations when he desired association or when no available blank spaces existed within a cave. These two sets of reasoning are not exactly equivalent, but both clearly rely on the evidence of the modern investigator being able to isolate correctly the various different styles and techniques employed at different times by many different Palaeolithic artists. As previously shown in chapter 2 this is by no means as easy as it might theoretically seem for, when dealing with the Palaeolithic period (see chapter 1) one is dealing with many thousands of years when styles and techniques can be assumed to have changed many times and old techniques and styles are likely to have come back frequently into vogue. In addition conditions of preservation in different caves are likely to have further complicated matters; in some caves existing engravings or paintings may well have been almost invisible to later artists who may have thought the walls which they were using free from earlier representations, while in other caves previously engraved walls may either have become naturally covered with a layer of clay or have been intentionally covered with a layer of clay to make them suitable for further engraving so that the impression of extensive superpositioning would only result from the subsequent peeling off of the clay layer (see footnote 2, chapter 2).

Even if the extensive claims of Laming and Leroi-Gourhan regarding superpositioning in Palaeolithic parietal art are not all fully accepted, Laming has certainly managed to establish certain very important points about the intentions behind superpositioning. That some superpositioning by Palaeolithic artists was indeed conscious is made quite clear by representations such as the two bison at Lascaux (figure 100), the two horses at Pech-Merle (figure 31) and several others where the artistic balance and careful positioning of the limbs and/or details of the representations can leave no doubts regarding the intentional use of the space available. As Laming has correctly shown there are many examples of Palaeolithic parietal art where representations of seemingly similar techniques and styles appear intentionally superimposed[38] and various combinations of animals often repeated in various different regions of the same cave as well as in different caves, although sometimes only by superimposed silhouettes[39] (see figure 12), support the view that certain animals were often associated together. There are, therefore, some powerful indications from the art itself that much superpositioning of Palaeolithic parietal representations was intimately concerned with the visual effect of the art.

From all that has been said above it would seem, therefore, that facts revealed by the art itself suggest that many Palaeolithic representations were intended to have a visual effect, despite their situation in regions of caves where normal domestic activities were not carried out. This evidence does not necessarily conflict with the view that Palaeolithic parietal art was associated with totemic beliefs and actions, but does appear to conflict with the classic view that it was the act of representation itself, and not the aesthetic result, which was the concern of the Palaeolithic 'artists' who were involved in sympathetic or fertility magic rites. It must be emphasised that, (as already stated in the section on Art for Art's Sake above), the visual effect of superpositioning even if it was not in the main a question of demonstrating associations between various representations, could well have had the specific aim of creating an impression of 'animalness' or 'vitality' which need not have been due to repeated and unconnected acts of magical representation.

As shown in the historical review of interpretations of Palaeolithic art (in chapter 3) one of its essential features which was isolated very early on and became the starting point both for magical and totemic interpretations was that the majority of representations were of animals. It was the particular range of animals chosen for representation by Palaeolithic artists which supported a magical as opposed to a non-functional artistic interpretation of the art and also argued against a totemic interpretation.

That Palaeolithic man was not just decorating habitation areas and caves with 'scenery' was proved for supporters of the hunting magic, totemic and fertility magic interpretations by the absence of natural objects, such as trees, plants, rivers, etc. from the repertoire of Palaeolithic parietal art and they stressed that all the animals represented could be divided between those which were potential food and those which were dangerous. The facts about the content of Palaeolithic parietal art are, however, more complex than envisaged by most supporters of the magical interpretation (see

chapter 2, Content) and frequently appear to argue against many of their assumptions. Taking first the 'food animals' it is the essential assumption of the magical interpretations that they were represented to ensure either their capture or their increase. If this were a correct interpretation it could be expected that the animals represented in Palaeolithic parietal art would reflect a close relationship with the actual environmental conditions surrounding Palaeolithic man. It is known from actual animal bones that throughout much of the Magdalenian period at least (see chapter 1) the reindeer was staple food throughout western Europe but it is extremely rare in Palaeolithic parietal art.[40] Throughout the cold periods of the Palaeolithic the saiga antelope was eaten, yet no sure parietal representation of this animal is known. Also in a cave such as Rouffignac where the mammoth is, very exceptionally, a common subject it cannot be concluded that there was specialist mammoth hunting for this animal was extremely rare in western Europe throughout the Palaeolithic period.

Only one explanation for the facts about the food animals represented in parietal art is offered by supporters of the magical interpretations. It has been suggested that it was only worth Palaeolithic man's effort to represent an animal for the purposes of sympathetic hunting magic if that animal was particularly difficult to catch. In this way it could be thought that the reindeer was an easy catch and for this reason not commonly represented in parietal art, but this argument will not bear scrutiny in the case of the mammoth. This animal was certainly a difficult animal to hunt and this could conceivably explain its frequency on the walls of Rouffignac despite its rarity throughout the Palaeolithic period in western Europe. But if this were the correct explanation there is no reason to find the mammoth shown commonly only at Rouffignac for it must have been equally difficult to hunt at other sites in western Europe.

A further embarrassment to supporters of the magical interpretations is caused by the occasional parietal representations of birds (see chapter 2, Content). Quite clearly these birds cannot be classified as dangerous so that they must have been represented either to ensure their capture as food or to increased their number as a source of food. It is known from bone debris in habitations that

79 Engraved bear, from Les Combarelles, with a drawing of it.

Palaeolithic man did in fact eat birds and it is therefore difficult to explain satisfactorily their extreme rarity in parietal representations. Simonnet[41] has attempted to explain this by resorting to an interpretation which is the direct contrary of that adopted for the mammoth and reindeer. He regards the rarity of birds in Palaeolithic art both as 'normal' and as further support for the magical interpretation for birds are difficult to catch and not as worthwhile as quadrupeds (even those of about the same size). In this explanation Palaeolithic man only represented the animals which he enjoyed eating; an explanation contradicted by the case of the reindeer.

In the case of the dangerous animals also, supporters of the sympathetic magic interpretation have failed to explain satisfactorily the choice of animals represented in Palaeolithic parietal art. Cave lion and cave bear are known to have been common and widespread during the Palaeolithic period. They are both dangerous animals and difficult to catch but representations of them are very few (see chapter 2, Content). Even more peculiar is the fact that there is no single parietal representation which can surely be interpreted as a hyaena although this dangerous animal is known to have existed in Palaeolithic times in western Europe.

Clearly the sympathetic fertility magic interpretation is normally taken to apply only to the representations of food animals. As has been seen, however, in chapter 3, (Fertility magic), this has been extended by some to apply also to parietal representations of humans. It is instructive to note several facts about the contents of parietal art in this connection. If fertility magic was the aim of many parietal representations it is extraordinary that there is no sure example within Palaeolithic parietal art which certainly represents a copulation scene. The one possible example of human coitus often quoted, from Laussel (figure 59), has recently been shown in a brilliant analysis by Leroi-Gourhan[42] to be either the result of reworking a previously sculpted piece of rock or an unfinished piece of sculpture. The assumption made frequently by supporters of the fertility magic interpretation that when two animals are shown closely following each other they are animals of opposite sex about to copulate is purely speculative. Furthermore it is a striking fact of Palaeolithic art that primary sexual organs are very rarely indicated on representations of animals or humans. The absence of overt sexual interest in Palaeolithic parietal art can be interpreted in two ways: either that it was not concerned with sexual matters or that it was concerned with sex but that the Palaeolithic artists were so 'discreet'[43] that they omitted to show the sexual organs (see the discussion of Leroi-Gourhan's views, chapter 3 above, and below).

A final detail taken as support of the fertility magic interpretation needs mention. Several parietal representations have been taken to represent pregnant animals (e.g. figures 9 and 52). In all the cases referred to in the literature this interpretation has been based on the (slightly) swollen stomachs of the animals concerned. Whether this interpretation is accepted or not depends ultimately on the view taken regarding the likelihood of a modern observer being able to recognise, identify and correctly interpret the significance of a stylistic convention of artists living thousands of years ago, and many Australian aboriginal examples show how impossible this is likely to be[44] (figure 96). In this particular case the question boils down to the simple one of deciding whether a particular Palaeolithic representation of a horse, for example, with slightly swollen stomach can be assumed to have been intended to represent a pregnant mare, or whether it should rather be assumed that the Palaeolithic artist conceived the horse to have a more rounded stomach than is commonly assumed by modern western artists and commentators. How important it is for the modern commentator to recognise the fact that he may not only look at a representation with quite different eyes from the artist responsible for the representation but also react in a totally different way from that intended by the original artist has often been discussed[45] and stressed but all too often is forgotten in the interpretation of Palaeolithic art. One of the most ingenious articles written about

Palaeolithic parietal art, by Leason,[46] looked at the representations with the eyes of a modern game-hunter. He correctly stressed that on many of the animals shown on cave walls could be seen more of the underside of the belly than would be possible if the standing animal had been observed from the side. Leason also drew attention to the fact that many animals were shown on tip-toe or hoof-tip, that very few of the animals gave an impression of body tension, that some of the animals were shown with the feet nearest to the observer at a higher level than the other feet, that some of the animals were shown with raised tail and projecting tongue and that many of the animals were shown with prominent lower jaw.

All these features, according to Leason, were explicable if the Palaeolithic artists' models had been dead animals lying on their sides on the ground (compare figure 102). Some of the features, such as the raised tails and perspective of the feet, need not necessarily be accepted as features visible only on dead animals[47] but this does not detract from the ingenuity of Leason's argument. What has to be decided in this case, as also with the rounded stomachs of some representations of animals, is whether to attempt to correlate such representational feature with the accurate copying of models or whether they should be attributed to artistic licence. In the case of the 'pregnant' animals, at least, which are few in number and have relatively little swelling of the stomach it is more satisfactory to assume that Palaeolithic man thought of, and saw, the animals with more protruding stomachs than is done today, rather than to postulate that he intended to represent pregnant animals. Had he really been interested in showing a horse, for example, as a mother it could be expected that the Palaeolithic artist would have occasionally shown the birth of a foal, the mare with her foal, copulation between a stallion and mare, or an advanced stage of pregnancy.

Similarly with the suggestions of Leason, it is foolhardy to accept the conclusions derived from a twentieth century visual impression without fully taking into account the technical achievements and stylistic conventions of the artists concerned for these may offer a much more likely explanation for features such as the perspective of the legs and feet. As for the slightly swollen stomachs of some horses, so also with the expanse of underside of the belly shown on some representations, for Palaeolithic man may well have conceived of his animal in this way (perhaps a concept indeed originally derived from seeing dead animals) without implying that he intended to represent dead animals. Finally it is a striking fact about many secondary supporters of both these theories that although only very few animals are shown with slightly swollen stomachs and only a few are shown with the features isolated by Leason, they see the conclusions regarding pregnancy and death as applying to all Palaeolithic parietal art.

Several other detailed features of the content of Palaeolithic parietal art have been taken as support for the magical and/or totemic interpretations. As shown in chapter 3 many anthropomorphic representations have been interpreted as sorcerers (often disguised) officiating at the magical or totemic rites. Quite apart from the difficulty of correctly identifying many of the features of these 'anthropomorphs' (see chapters 2 and 3) the question arises whether their acceptance as sorcerers makes logical sense within the totemic and magical interpretations. As Laming[48] has cogently argued, 'Why should the sorcerer, who was probably also the artist of the tribe, portray his own image? A ritual ceremony is efficacious in itself, and there would appear to be no valid reason why it should be recorded on the rock surface'. An alternative view of these anthropomorphs often suggested by supporters of the magical hunting interpretation sees them as disguised hunters creeping up on their quarries. But again it can be argued that since the hunters themselves were present at the magical ceremonies there was no reason to represent them on the walls. Furthermore this explanation fails to account for the rarity of such anthropomorphs, their 'schematic' nature as opposed to the animal representations (see chapter 2) and their positions on the cave walls, as frequently isolated as in any obvious relationship to animals.

As has already been seen in chapter 3 much support for the sympathetic hunting magic interpretation was gained from the interpretation of various details of the animal representations and the identification of the 'signs' (see chapter 2) as implements for catching food or killing dangerous animals. For all attempts at identification of the various parietal signs in the context of sympathetic magic, the same argument holds true, namely that the authors concerned have all started with the assumption that the signs must represent either the means for achieving capture or increase, or the actual objects that Palaeolithic man desired to catch or increase in number. Without a rigorous investigation of these signs (see chapter 3 and below, for the work of reanalysis by Leroi-Gourhan) all that can be done is to assess on the basis of their realism and their localities how likely these identifications are to be true. To reject an identification on the basis of criteria of 'naturalism' is extremely dangerous (see above) but it must be noted that the interpretation of circles as stacked fruit (see the views of Astre, chapter 3), for example, ignores the fact that Palaeolithic parietal art contains no example which convincingly represents any kind of vegetation whereas all animal representations are clearly recognisable to the modern observer. The situation of many painted circles in isolated corners and galleries of caves, far from any representation of animals, also argues against their identification as projectile stones. Bégouen (see chapter 3) also interpreted some holes in the wall in a gallery at Montespan as projectile stones to drive horses towards a pallisade (figure 101). Breuil[49] and others have doubted that Bégouen's interpretation of this scene was correct. The identifications which have had perhaps the profoundest effect on the dismissal of the totemic interpretation and the acceptance of the sympathetic hunting magic interpretation are those of arrows and traps. According to the classic view, animals are commonly shown either wounded (sometimes with blood dripping from their mouth) or caught in traps. How difficult it is to identify any particular type of arrow from the parietal representations has already been stated in chapter 2, (Content, Signs) but two more reasons argue against the acceptance of this identification.

First, there are many representations where the 'arrows' are about to, or have already just, 'missed' an animal (e.g. figure 52). There is no conceivable reason why Palaeolithic man should have wanted to shoot an arrow past a food or dangerous animal or, as it would appear from many representations, wound such an animal just above the ankle! Second, as has been stressed by Leroi-Gourhan,[50] less than ten per cent of animals shown in parietal art are wounded in any way (and less than two and a half per cent of bison, one of the most frequently represented animals in parietal art) so that, following the sympathetic magic interpretation, for the vast

188

80 *Right* Red painted dolphins, from Nerja;
the only known Palaeolithic
representations of this animal.
81 *Far right* Engraved goose, from Labastide.
82 *Bottom right* Engraved bird, from Le Roc de Sers;
sometimes identified as a bustard.

majority of parietal animal representations it would have to be
assumed that Palaeolithic man had given up any hope of wounding
the animal, had resigned himself to some other form of capture, or
was concerned with the increase of that species and not its capture
(but what about the dangerous animals?).

No less troubling is the question of traps in parietal art for even if
all the signs which have been claimed to represent different traps
are accepted as such, the number of animals represented neither
with wounds nor caught in traps is enormous. Furthermore, Breuil
pointed out at a very early date (see chapter 3) that the number of
times when a tectiform or other sign can be certainly said to be
associated with an animal representation, and not to be either a
later superpositioning or an earlier representation, is extremely
small. There seems little doubt, therefore, that the real significance
of many of these signs still remains obscure and it is understandable
that authors have recently preferred to seek some symbolic, rather
than representational, meaning for them (see chapter 3, Recent
work, and below).

If any one group of Palaeolithic representations can be said to
epitomise the sympathetic hunting magical practices of Palaeolithic
man it is those in the cave of Montespan: clay horses, a 'lion' and
clay model of a bear (figures 97 and 101; see chapter 3). Until very
recently these representations, and especially the small clay bear's
body with bear's skull lying at its feet, remained unexplained by those
who wished to criticise the classic interpretations of Palaeolithic
art.[51] Unfortunately no photographs were published of these
fascinating and significant representations at the time of their
discovery and since that time their state of preservation has deteriorated very badly. It is impossible, therefore, to carry out any
systematic reanalysis of the evidence at Montespan. It is interesting
to note, however, that a reliable and firm follower of the classic
interpretations of Palaeolithic art, Graziosi,[52] had to admit that
when he later looked at the bear model he 'could see no trace of
some of the details described by Bégouen and Casteret. The section
of the neck did not appear to be polished at all: on the contrary, it
was rather rough. The hole that is presumed to have contained a
peg to support the head does not exist – at least, it is not large
enough for its alleged purpose. There are several little holes here

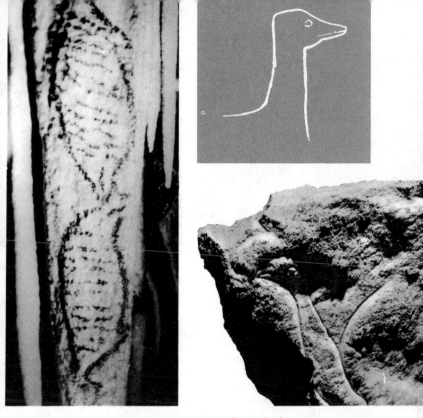

and there on the neck and chest, many of which, however, appear to be due to natural causes – the sort of small cavities in the clay that can be seen all over the cave'. It may be significant that when Breuil[53] attempted to refute this statement of Graziosi's he produced no evidence but simply reiterated that the young bear's head had been attached to the clay body and that the holes in the clay body were artificial and not natural. Only one further point can be made about the evidence from Montespan. As Leroi-Gourhan has correctly pointed out[54] the height of the cave roof is very low in the galleries which contained both the 'hunting scene' and some of the clay models. It is incorrect, therefore, to imagine that any Palaeolithic rite could have taken place there during which men stood and threw their spears or javelins at the parietal representations. If anyone really stuck their weapons into these representations they must have crept up to them and then pierced them with an implement held in the hand.

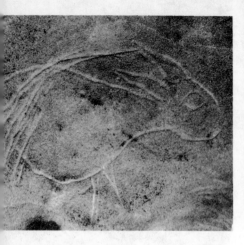

Representations of food animals as such offered no difficulties to those who favoured a totemic interpretation of Palaeolithic parietal art and even the existence of the second group of animals, the dangerous ones, was incorporated into the totemic interpretation (see the early views ,of Breuil, chapter 3). Two of the features incorporated into the sympathetic hunting magic interpretation, however, did appear to rule out a totemic interpretation. First, that animals were wounded or caught in traps in Palaeolithic art, for the Australian evidence, according to those who attacked the totemic interpretation, made it clear that one's totem was never eaten or killed. Second, that caves contained representations of several different species of animals whereas, in a totemic system, each group would have its own distinctive totem.

As has already been seen in the discussion of the Sympathetic Magic interpretations the situation is not as simple as was made out by followers of the hunting or fertility magic interpretations. First, it is no longer at all clear that the animals represented in caves were really wounded or caught in traps. Second, although it is correct to say that caves do contain representations of more than one species of animal, it is also true (see chapter 2) that certain passages of certain caves house predominantly one species of animal (e.g. Le Portel) and that certain caves, for example Rouffignac, appear to 'specialise' in certain species of animal which predominate numerically over several other species of animals represented. On neither of these counts, therefore, does the totemic interpretation deserve to be rejected out of hand.

83 *Far left* Engraved hare, from Le Gabillou; one of the very few Palaeolithic parietal representations of this animal.
84 *Left* Engraved rhinoceros on the ceiling at Rouffignac; originally identified as a bird when viewed upside down.

Furthermore, as was stated in chapter 3, the early reports of totemic beliefs and practices from Australia in fact presented a much more flexible and heterogeneous scheme than that usually assumed by the archaeologists who referred to these reports. Thus, for example, the stress that Frazer and many others (see chapter 3) laid on the taboo against eating ones own totem is not a universal principle of Australian totemism but only applies in certain specific groups of Australian aborigines and to only some of the totemic practices of these particular groups of Australians. Equally, it is not accurate to state that each group of Australian aborigines has only one totem, for any person in Australian society may belong to several totemic groups by virtue of his kinship, his membership of a local group and his acquired social status (e.g. a medicine man). For each of these memberships he will have a particular totemic relationship to an animal species or natural object. On the evidence of Australian totemism also, therefore, the totemic explanation of Palaeolithic parietal art cannot be rejected out of hand. In addition, modern anthropological analysis has devoted much further thought to the subject of totemism, analysis which has largely escaped the notice of archaeologists.

Totemism is a word applied to concepts relating to many different social activities and institutions and one of the difficulties in using this term is to find a common denominator for the various phenomena which have been included within this categorisation. 'When social anthropologists speak of a totemic society, they usually refer to a society which is divided into a number of named

85 Black painted imaginary creature, from Lascaux; the first animal of a long painted frieze of bulls, horses and deer, etc.; shown with a sagging stomach exceptional in Palaeolithic representations.

groups, the members of which believe themselves to be descended unilineally from a common ancestor, and stand in a special relationship, usually involving respect and avoidance, to some object . . . but in some North American Indian tribes people may have individual totems . . . Totemic groups are very often exogamous. But they are not always so . . . There may be a mythical belief that members of each totemic clan are descended from the totemic species associated with it: this is common in Australia and Melanesia, rare in Africa. It is not even the case that there is always an attitude of reverence or respect towards the totem . . . The increase ritual of [a] totemic group . . . is now recognised to be a particular type, probably limited to Australia . . .'.[55] 'So the term totemism covers a multitude of phenomena. As it is generally used, however, it refers to situations where each one of a number of discrete social groups into which a society is divided maintains a particular regard – though not necessarily one of worship or reverence – for a particular object in the natural or cultural environment'.[56] It is quite obvious from this refreshingly clear and accurate statement about modern views of totemism that few of the criteria isolated by the social anthropologists are directly relevant to the archaeologists. It is impossible, for example, to speak about the principles of social organisation which operated in Palaeolithic times, and it is these very principles which serve to define a totemic organisation.[57] What is important for archaeological studies, however, is the realisation that an intimate relationship between human and animal or natural phenomenon (as postulated for Palaeolithic art by such authors as Klingender and Giedion, see chapter 3) need not necessarily imply the strict rules of observance (regarding killing and eating) nor the unitary identification which was presumed by the archaeologists who attacked the totemic interpretation of Palaeolithic art.

Anthropological analysis of totemism in fact provides much more information relevant to those seeking to interpret Palaeolithic parietal art in the light of intimate relationships between man and animals in 'primitive' societies. Despite many theoretical statements to the contrary,[58] 'in many parts of the world where totemism is found, the totems are not national objects of importance to the totemists . . . Thus the totems of the Tallensi of

Northern Ghana ... are mostly animals of little or no practical importance to human beings ... the choice of totemic objects is [often] alleged to be due to some historic event linking the forebears of the totemic group with the totem ... In other cases the choice seems to have been based on whimsy or private predilection. It should be remembered ... that in a simple, small-scale society where there are scores, perhaps hundreds, of named totemic groups, the environment must be combed pretty thoroughly if the totemic emblems are not to overlap confusingly'.[59] It is perhaps even more instructive to take one particular example of a totemic society, the Dinka, amongst whom clans have more than one totem but of different rankings. Amongst the Dinka of the Sudan the totemic animals are often not important items of diet, indeed one particular Dinka clan has the giraffe amongst its totems and its members therefore have 'a special relationship with all giraffes, and will not spear them ... [but] in many parts of Dinkaland giraffes have not been seen for many years, and there are members of this clan ... who have never seen a giraffe. This is also the case ... with clan-divinity Elephant in a country where elephants have not been seen for many years'.[60]

What has been established, therefore, is that an intimate relationship between man and animals in primitive societies often exists irrespective of the role of these animals in the actual environment.

The discrepancies noted between the animal content of Palaeolithic parietal art and the animal bones found in actual habitation debris would not therefore be inconsistent with a totemic interpretation. Amongst the Dinka, also, 'respect for the clan-divinity [totem] requires that its emblem should not be killed or injured, and in principle that it should not be eaten. But ... few are of dietic importance, and where they are the respect paid to them may yet permit them to be eaten'.[61]

It has been seen in this discussion that both the fertility and hunting magic interpretations of Palaeolithic parietal art include many unwarranted assumptions, several contradictory premises and a considerable number of obscurities. In addition they fail to account for many of the subjects of parietal art. They offer no interpretation for the numerous undeniable cases of representations of files of animals (see chapter 2), many of which are not, in nature, found associating together. They offer no explanation for the repeated associations of different animals in different caves and on different walls of the same cave (see above and chapter 3, Recent work). They fail to explain the instances of intentional superpositioning and care for artistic balance (for example the Lascaux bison, figure 100) unless some theory is advanced to combine the magical act of representation itself with an inherent human desire to express himself artistically. Finally, they ignore the undeniable representations of imaginary creatures or 'monsters' (e.g. figures 87, 88 and 89) for there was clearly no purpose in either killing off these animals or increasing their numbers.

Many of these criticisms of the sympathetic magic interpretations cannot be levelled at the totemic interpretation of Palaeolithic parietal art but it is quite another matter to assess whether there are any features positively in favour of a totemic interpretation. Totemism as an aspect of social organisation is not particularly relevant to the interpretation of Palaeolithic parietal art for it cannot be shown that a totemic social organisation existed in Palaeolithic times; there is no evidence available either to support or to deny such a presumption. It is not sufficient to presume such a principle of social organisation simply on the basis of inferences from the parietal art of a close relationship between Palaeolithic man and animals. Such an intimate relationship, in any case, is not exclusive to totemism for it can be found amongst many 'primitive' people, utterly devoid from any totemic beliefs or practices. There is no reason to single out totemism on this basis in favour of cattle cults or sacrificial ancestor cults, etc. Finally, as has been shown at some length above, even among the totemic Australian aborigines totemism is far from being the only incentive to paint or engrave on rocks.

Leroi-Gourhan

There is no doubt at all that Leroi-Gourhan's book, *Préhistoire de l'Art Occidental*, is a work of outstanding ingenuity. It may appear ungrateful, therefore, that in this section many points of his work are isolated specifically for criticism. Part of the importance of Leroi-Gourhan's work lies in his acute reanalysis of long accepted 'characteristics' of Palaeolithic art and it should be clear from previous pages how immensely valuable his reanalyses really are. A second feature of his work is its vitality, and most important of all is the shock with which Leroi-Gourhan has revolutionised the whole study of Palaeolithic art. No criticisms of his work can detract from any of these points. References in this section to Leroi-Gourhan's work will, whenever possible, be to his most recent large book except where previous publications shed extra light on his views or differ significantly from his major book.

From the resumé of Leroi-Gourhan's views presented in chapter 3 it is important to recognise the two stages of analysis implicit in his work; first, that from a numerical analysis of the topography of decorated caves and the subjects shown in Palaeolithic parietal art it is possible to show that caves were regularly organised with certain animals and signs regularly placed together as meaningful groups. Secondly, that from this evidence it is possible to induce that certain animals and certain signs symbolised the female principle and others the male principle and that these are arranged in certain groups of pairs of the same or opposite sexual significance this he describes in terms of 'complementarity' and 'opposition'.

Whenever re-analyses of caves were attempted in this work several difficulties had to be overcome. Detailed and full publications had

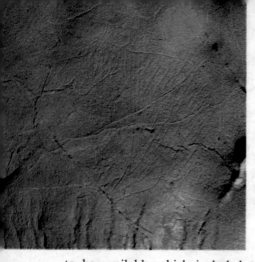

to be available which included a cave plan and an account of the position and content of the art. This imposed serious limitations, for many caves, particularly the smaller ones, have been published inadequately from this point of view since in earlier interpretations the exact positions of the representations were not particularly relevant. Some of the early discoveries, however, are admirably published as are also a few recently discovered caves. Furthermore, the caves had to be sufficiently well preserved that most of the original parietal representations still exist and the original entrance(s) of the cave had to be known. Lastly, to make re-analyses as uncontroversial as possible caves chosen for comparison had to contain art generally agreed to belong to one period only, or very largely so. With these difficulties in mind, three caves were chosen for comparative purposes: Les Combarelles, one of the first caves for which Leroi-Gourhan recognised 'sanctuary organisation', Font de Gaume and Le Gabillou[62] (figures 104, 105 and 106).

There is no doubt that the first step in any analysis such as that of Leroi-Gourhan's must be the clear definition of the regions of a cave for on this foundation is built his construction of panels, associations and groupings. The most detailed of Leroi-Gourhan's exposé of his topographical division of caves has been given in chapter 3 (pp. 140–1), and is the basis for his less detailed statement in his latest book.

Any description of natural cave regions must recognise that no cave follows a rigid scheme. In many caves a passage widens gradually into a main chamber while in others the junction between a passage and a main chamber is clearly defined. Similarly, the bends

86 Lightly engraved imaginary
creature in a narrow passage at
Le Tuc d'Audoubert, with a
drawing of it.

197

and rock projections in a long passage vary from minor changes in
the rock shapes to abrupt bends, corners and constrictions. In
many cases, therefore, it is not at all easy to delimit the regions used
by Leroi-Gourhan. Furthermore there is always the question of
recognising the original cave entrance (see detailed discussion in
chapter 2). In much of his work when the first representations
encountered do not conflict with his 'ideal' scheme (see chapter 3)
Leroi-Gourhan does not question that the existing entrance was
also used in Palaeolithic times. In a cave such as Villars,[63] where
the present cave entrance is artificial he points to the presence of
red-painted dots in one of the passages as a possible indication that
this was the original approach to the main panels. When as at La
Pasiega,[64] none of the known entrances contains 'entrance' representations, he suggests that either these have been destroyed or, as
at Aldène and La Baume Latrone, that the Palaeolithic entrance
may not yet have been found. For category 1 caves many of his
criteria for defining regions of a cave are inapplicable. Even for
caves of categories 2 and 3 the recognition of the entrance region,
where the first representations begin (often at the last point of
daylight, and always in a niche or bend) is anything but easy to
determine, for in caves such as Les Combarelles and Font de
Gaume the entrance region is accepted by Leroi-Gourhan to be
where the first representations are found today, irrespective of the
fact that they are well out of daylight far from the cave entrance.

In practice, even where clear topographical features of a cave do
exist and the original entrance is known, it is difficult to draw a line
between groups of representations for they may follow the gentle
curve of a bend without any distinct break, as also do those on the
floors or ceilings (no distinction is made by Leroi-Gourhan
between representations on floors, walls, or ceilings). In practice
Leroi-Gourhan has no rigid rules and defines some regions in some
caves both in terms of natural features and of contents. At Pair non
Pair, for example, he divides the representations on the basis of
topographical features despite the fact that the representations
appear to have overlapped the rock projections. At Le Gabillou, on
the other hand, his divisions of the representations must be largely
on the basis of their contents, for the full publication states that the
division of Le Gabillou into various sections by natural features is

not possible, since the cave is remarkably uniform in width with only very minor narrowings and bends (of which there are so many that any selection must be arbitrary) (figure 106).[65]

In some cases it is difficult to apply Leroi-Gourhan's topographical criteria (as has been discussed above) while in others his cavern areas are explicitly based on content and not topography. Thus, the distinction between the central theme and marginal areas of a central decorated panel is based solely on the content of the representations placed in the same topographical area of a principal chamber or cave section.

The Palaeolithic artist unfortunately did not always make it as clear as the modern observer would like where one composition ended and the other began. Leroi-Gourhan admits that in some cases[66] it is difficult to tell whether a particular representation belongs to a marginal or central area, or whether it belongs to the end of a central area or the terminal area.

Just as it was essential to define each cave region clearly for a topographical analysis, so it is essential for the recognition of groups of representations to define unambiguously an 'association'. Leroi-Gourhan's clearest statement on associations is in an early work[67] which recognises associations only if they are immediately adjacent to each other and are also sufficiently isolated from other representations to be recognisable as groups. In his most recent work[68] Leroi-Gourhan repeats that in difficult cases the 'association' of representations which are taken to constitute a group is that of animals or signs which are 'strictly next to each other' and he adds that associations are also shown by superpositioning. In the rock shelter of La Magdelaine, however, an association has been postulated between the female figure on the left hand wall and the adjacent engraved bison, as well as between another low relief female figure on the right hand wall and an engraved horse about two metres further along the wall (figures 90 and 91). To Leroi-Gourhan the representations on each wall are equally significantly associated, despite the striking spatial differences between the two groups.

At first glance it appears crucial to be able to recognise works of different dates (but see chapter 2, Chronology and styles) before considering that closely-spaced or superimposed representations were consciously associated by the artists. But this is not so to Leroi-Gourhan for, as has been seen in previous chapters, he considers most superpositions to be contemporaneous attempts to group representations together, unless there was no available free space in which later to place separate subjects. Furthermore even when superpositioning was forced on the artist by lack of space, Leroi-Gourhan considers that the same localities were generally chosen at different times for the same purpose. In his view, respect for previous work encouraged the later Palaeolithic artist who was forced to superimpose his work on earlier representations (for lack of other space) to place equivalent works in that particular locality. For practical purposes, therefore, Leroi-Gourhan takes all, or at least the vast majority, of superimposed representations as significantly associated.

Before examining other criteria for the recognition of groupings it is as well to remember that the evidence from the Australian aborigines and African Marghi suggests that in some primitive art rules of superpositioning and association are not anywhere near as consistent as suggested by Leroi-Gourhan for Palaeolithic art; in some cases later superimposed work is conscious of the earlier work which it is covering, while in other cases no notice is taken of the work partially covered at a later date; in some cases association is shown by superpositioning, while in other cases associated representations are widely separated from each other.

In order to define a significant association several other characteristics of Palaeolithic parietal art (see chapter 2) should have been taken into account; for example, the degree of completion of a representation, the number of representations concerned, the size of the representations and colour. For Leroi-Gourhan both colour and finish are irrelevant, for association is defined by spacing and superpositioning. Throughout his work Leroi-Gourhan ignores the number of individuals of a particular species of animal, for he takes association as concerned with themes. Thus, for example, he sees no difficulty in considering one bison as significantly associated with twelve horses represented nearby. Throughout his numerical analyses, therefore, Leroi-Gourhan has rated twelve bison 'associated' with one horse, just as if it were one bison 'associated' with one horse (as will be seen below this leads to considerable difficulty

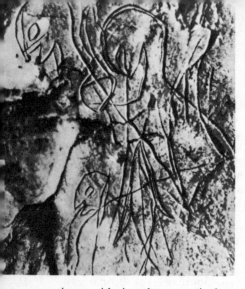

87 *Left* Engraved anthropomorphs, from Los Casares; said by Abbé Breuil to resemble something like frogs or fish. 88 *Right* Black painted imaginary creatures, from Pech-Merle; three minute heads appear to belong to four swollen bodies.

in considering the numerical results of his analysis). Although it is difficult to see why Leroi-Gourhan has chosen to ignore criteria such as colour and numbers of individuals in his definition of association it is possible to follow his analytical processes for he has consistently held to them. When it comes to criteria of size and position, however, the situation becomes more complex. Theoretically Leroi-Gourhan does not consider the relative sizes of representations as significant but, when specific cases are examined, there are several instances where size is referred to. The topographical position within a cave is the same for the central and the marginal representations in a main panel, so that a criterion other than topography must be used to separate them; Leroi-Gourhan has here often used size. At Niaux, for example, marginal animals are recognised by their small size, whereas at Les Trois Frères and Lascaux (figure 14) small horses are considered to be significantly associated with large bison and bovids[69] in the central panels.

At Font de Gaume (figure 105) Leroi-Gourhan states that the principal theme is one of bison-horse-mammoth with the addition of reindeer. From even a cursory examination of this cave it is clear that the most prominent animals of the distinct panels, both in size, number and position within the panel are bison and mammoth. Next in prominence, size and finish are reindeer, whereas horses are all small, few in number and generally placed in somewhat peripheral positions. Leroi-Gourhan's analysis of Font de Gaume shows it to consist of three main panels, an entrance and a terminal

zone and at least two lateral passages. The intermediate zones are not easily isolated, either topographically or spatially, unless some of the main panel sections be taken to fall into this category, but such a solution would mean a rather arbitrary division of the main panel section, and Leroi-Gourhan does not mention these inter-panel groups in Font de Gaume. The distinction between the central panel and the marginal area is not much easier to make, though a certain number of figures spaced at some distance above and below the main concentration of figures could be taken as marginal.

Throughout his work Leroi-Gourhan stresses both the fluidity of the Palaeolithic artistic scheme (as he envisages it) and the possibility of error by the modern observer; he allows a twenty to thirty per cent error for his numerical analyses and such caution is laudable. It must be recognised, however, that if too much latitude is allowed in such an analysis it becomes difficult to estimate how far apparent 'groupings' are really significant and how far they are due to chance. Both on the basis of Leroi-Gourhan's scheme and the variety of artistic practices among the Australian aborigines it is legitimate to ask, first whether association defined in terms of numbers of individuals represented, size of representations, colour used and degree of finish of representations would reveal the same significant groups as those isolated by Leroi-Gourhan (see re-analysis of Les Combarelles, below) and second whether it can be legitimate to leave the definition of association so vague that groups cannot always be recognised on the basis of cave topo-

graphy and can often only be distinguished on the basis of a
dividing line drawn on apparently arbitrary grounds. Leroi-
Gourhan is very free in his handling of spatial separation of representations and this fluidity may well be connected with his view (see
chapter 3 and especially note 66 of that chapter) that 'coupling' is
fundamental to Palaeolithic parietal art although juxtaposition,
completion and framing also play a part in Palaeolithic artistic
organisation. It is perhaps not unreasonable to ask at this point
whether the variety of intentions and conventions of organisation
postulated by Leroi-Gourhan for Palaeolithic artists may not be so
wide that as many 'significant' schemes would be found as investi-
gators at work.

The numerical distribution of animals and signs in the various
cave regions (see chapter 3) does, of course, depend on the manner
in which these regions have been determined. However, even
allowing a wide margin of error for difficulties Leroi-Gourhan
concludes that different species of animals and signs still show
different distributions.

Leroi-Gourhan has counted the number of individual representations of each animal species and finds that the two most commonly
represented are horse and bison. Next in order of frequency are
mammoths (mainly from the cave of Rouffignac), ibex, wild ox and
male and female deer. Reindeer, bear, lion and rhinoceros are much
rarer, and imaginary creatures, megaloceros, fish, birds, some
carnivores, boars, chamoix and saiga antelope are limited to a few
representations. Although Leroi-Gourhan says that the rare
animals – lion, bear and rhinoceros – are either found singly or are
absent from caves,[70] he recognises apparent exceptions such as
Rouffignac which contains many rhinoceros and Les Trois Frères
and Aldène which contain several lions. As already shown,
Leroi-Gourhan in fact does not rely in his numerical analyses on
numbers of individual representations, but on what he identifies as
'themes' and 'compositions'. The frequency of any 'theme' in
Palaeolithic parietal art refers to the number of caves or shelters
in which any particular species is represented, irrespective of
the number of individuals represented within the cave. The
frequency of 'compositions' on the other hand, refers to the
numbers of distinct panels in which any particular species occurs,

again irrespective of the number of individuals within such a panel.

Assuming that Leroi-Gourhan is right to deal with the contents of panels rather than with the number of individuals represented (but see above), it is clear from the calculation of frequencies of animal contents that Palaeolithic parietal art does not accurately reflect the Palaeolithic environmental situation (see above for the importance of this with regard to a sympathetic magic interpretation).

Within any composition Leroi-Gourhan has identified associated animals, and calculated which of the animals are most frequently found together: thirty eight per cent of mammoths are associated with bison, fifty four per cent of horses are associated with bison, thirty three per cent of stags are associated with horse ('rarely'), forty nine per cent of oxen are found with horse ('often'), sixty four per cent of bison are found with horse ('usually'), and forty per cent of ibex are found with horse.[71] How far this numerical evidence for 'associations' really indicates conscious grouping and not a haphazard distribution is not easy to assess. What they imply is that, for example, in panels which feature the horse there is an even chance of finding also a bison, and less chance of finding virtually any other animal. These figures in themselves do not appear surprising in view of the overall frequencies of the animal species represented.[72] Nor is it surprising that for the relatively common representations of ibex and ox about half of them are found in panels with horse. Strong evidence that the 'associations' may not be haphazard is provided by the fact that less than thirty per cent of these two animals are found in panels with bison which is almost as frequent as horse, although it must be remembered that the distribution of oxen is geographically limited.

The numerical data presented refer to associations between pairs of species of animals only. It is not clear how panels with more than two species have been rated when calculating the frequencies of animal associations. For instance, in the Font de Gaume example where bison are found in groups superimposed with mammoth, reindeer and horse it is not clear whether all possible combinations, bison-horse, bison-mammoth, bison-reindeer, etc., have all been taken into account when calculating the percentages of associations, for in the cave analysis Leroi-Gourhan considers that some

89 *Right* Engraved and painted 'sorcerer' which is situated in a recess above the maze of engravings in a small chamber of Les Trois Frères known as the 'sanctuary'.
Overleaf left Drawing of the sorcerer by Breuil.
Overleaf right Drawing of the same representation after recent photographs. Many of the details shown in Breuil's drawings are not visible. Some, such as the second antler, may either have been damaged since Breuil's study or be his interpretation of faint scratches on the rock. Damage by visitors is unlikely as the sorcerer is difficult of access. Other details, such as the facial features, tufted ears, shoulders and legs, also differ from Breuil's reconstruction.

of these animals are marginal (see above). Similarly at Altamira[73] where the ceiling of the main chamber in the cave is covered with both single and superimposed animals and signs, the recognition of panels, and therefore the establishing of numerical 'associations' can only be attempted on a subjective basis. This is clear from Leroi-Gourhan's own analysis of this ceiling. One of the largest bison has been isolated to represent the main theme of the panel, and this is found to be associated with the one horse of the composition which is on the other side of the panel. The deer superimposed on the horse is taken as complementary to the horse, whereas the other two deer (one of which is lost among the bison) are taken as marginal animals, together with the two boars. The rating of this composition from the point of view of associations remains obscure.

Finally the question of associations of animals is further complicated by Leroi-Gourhan's occasional distinction between the male and female of a species, for he conceives of the ideal Palaeolithic parietal composition as consisting of associated couples of opposite sex of each species of animal. As has been shown, the sexing of animal representations, on which the primary sexual organs are normally not shown, is extremely hazardous. Leroi-Gourhan takes some features of representations, such as the spots on several reindeer, as stylistic or chronological criteria whereas they could conceivably be correlated with evidence of the sex or age of the animals depicted. Although he admits that some representations, such as the Lascaux 'imaginary creature' (figure 85) which might conceivably be an inaccurate representation of a panther, are difficult to identify he interprets some cases of size differentiation, when two animals are shown close together, as evidence of sexual dimorphism. Although in some cases, such as the ibex at Cougnac (figure 103), such an identification does seem convincing, in most cases size differences[74] are part of the Palaeolithic stylistic convention which does not designate species or sex (see chapter 2). Throughout his numerical tables Leroi-Gourhan distinguishes between stags and does; on this basis alone he himself shows that only thirty per cent of these animals are shown together. In fact, however, stags can only be distinguished from does by their antlers and are therefore indistinguishable for some time after the rutting season.

Some regions of France and Spain contain very few decorated caves (see chapter 1) and for this reason, in several of his analyses, Leroi-Gourhan[75] excludes south and central Spain as well as the Mediterranean region. The Perigord region of France includes the largest number of caves with Palaeolithic parietal art (twenty-two) and throughout his latest work, Leroi-Gourhan has related the results from different regions by expressing them in terms of the Perigord results – i.e. as 'per – Perigord – ages' rather than as percentages.[76]

Leroi-Gourhan proceeds in his analyses to group together the representations in the central panel, as against all the representations in the entrance, marginal and terminal areas of caves. To follow such a procedure is hazardous unless topographical areas can be definitely distinguished. Thus at Font de Gaume (figure 105) if the animals slightly apart from the main concentration of representations in the central panels are considered they are seen to contain bison and certain signs (of Leroi-Gourhan's 'female' group) as well as several other animals and signs (of Leroi-Gourhan's 'male' groups). To isolate these representations causes anomalies of cave sanctuary organisation as envisaged by Leroi-Gourhan. To include these representations with the main panel compositions, however, complicates the theme of bison-mammoth with reindeer and horse by introducing some deer and ibex as well as various unidentifiable representations. Even if marginal areas of a central panel can be reliably distinguished from the main area it is still questionable whether such a twofold grouping is legitimate (see above). There is no objective reason why central surrounds should not be included together with central panel within one group, especially as third, fourth and fifth animals may on Leroi-Gourhan's own evidence numerically dominate a central group. Examination of the different works by Leroi-Gourhan shows that he has not always grouped together the contents of the same topographical regions of a cave;[77] in his later works, the entrance, marginal and terminal areas were grouped together and distinguished from the central areas. This is not only a point of academic interest, but also one which radically affects Leroi-Gourhan's numerical findings.

On the basis of his latest numerical results Leroi-Gourhan claims

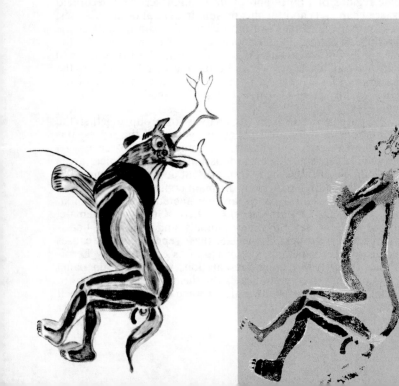

to have shown that central panels of a cave are almost exclusively concerned with compositions of bison, ox, horse and less frequently, mammoth; less than ten per cent of each other species are shown in central panels. If, on the other hand, central marginal areas are counted together with central panels different results emerge: the rhinoceros becomes equally frequent in the centre as in other areas, and the ibex becomes a central (i.e. marginal) animal as well as belonging to other areas. In other words unless the marginal area is exclusively distinguished from the central area (and that this is not based on topographical considerations has already been shown) only the carnivores, horse, bison and ox are clearly distinct from other species which are found both in central and other areas of a cave.

Leroi-Gourhan claims that almost all animals are found significantly in either central or other regions of a cave. He does admit that does are characteristic both of the central panels and of other cave regions depending on the geographical area concerned;[78] his figures show that lions are only central animals in the caves of the Ardèche such as Bayol and La Baume Latrone; mammoths may be found in any area of a cave depending on the geographical region;[79] as has already been noted the distribution of ibex appears haphazardly distributed throughout the entrance, central and terminal areas of caves unless, following Leroi-Gourhan, the 'marginal areas' of central panels are classified apart from central panels and together with entrance and terminal regions. But it is the horse which is the most important of animals for it is fundamental to Leroi-Gourhan's interpretation of the symbolism of Palaeolithic parietal art. He claims that the horse, although largely a central animal, is also found in relatively large numbers in other regions of a cave, and for this reason is different in kind from the bison and ox which are largely confined to central regions. In Leroi-Gourhan's latest book ninety-one per cent and ninety-two per cent of bison and ox 'themes' respectively are found in central panels, as opposed to eighty-three per cent of horse 'themes'. The fact that twelve per cent of horse 'themes'[80] are found in other cave areas is taken by Leroi-Gourhan to show that the horse belongs to a signficantly different group of animals from the bison and ox. However, although Leroi-Gourhan has claimed throughout his published works that he has attempted a statistical analysis of Palaeolithic parietal representations (and this claim has been reiterated in several subsequent works which have used his results), in no place has he published any statistical test of numerical data. A simple chi square (χ^2) test[81] shows that there is no statistically significant difference between the cave distribution of compositions with bison, compositions with ox and compositions with horse. Were it true that the distribution of horse in a cave was different from the distribution of ox and bison, then it would appear logical to group the horse in a separate category from these 'central' animals and from the 'lateral' animals. Certainly Leroi-Gourhan has not shown statistically that the distribution of horse does not differ from that of animals such as ibex, lions, bears, etc.

Leroi-Gourhan's numerical analysis of the distribution of signs within caves is much more straightforward (but see chapter 2 for the differences in geographical distribution of sign – 'types'). If it is accepted both that the central area of a cave should be split into central panels and central surrounds, that the central surrounds should be grouped with lateral areas of a cave, and that Leroi-Gourhan's typological division of signs into different groups is legitimate and reasonably exclusive (but see below), then it is clear that lines, barbed signs and dots are found significantly more often in lateral areas of a cave (about sixty per cent) than are all other signs (about twenty per cent). Even if central marginal areas are classified together with central panels (and then Leroi-Gourhan's 'male' signs are found more frequently in central areas than in lateral areas) it still remains true that entrance, passage and terminal areas of a cave very rarely have detailed 'female' signs in them. Leroi-Gourhan admits that the distribution of hand representations is very difficult to analyse[82] and that their symbolism is 'obscure'.[83]

In chapter 3 the features of an 'ideal' sanctuary in Leroi-Gourhan's scheme were described. However, Leroi-Gourhan is the first to appreciate that his numerical analyses may contain several errors, so that it is not in itself surprising that the 'ideal' is not often met in actual cave analyses. It is surprising however, to note how frequent are the cases where Leroi-Gourhan's expectations, on the basis of his numerical analyses, are not fulfilled. At Font de

Gaume, for example, (see figure 105) the entrance region contains bison and signs of his 'female' group as well as the expected 'male' animals (unless Breuil was correct in his contention that the entrance representations have perished). The lateral passages at Font de Gaume contain representations which more or less repeat those of the main panels (although with fewer numbers of animals, especially mammoth). Only in the terminal area of Font de Gaume are all expectations fulfilled (rhinoceros, horses and lion) although a short series of animals (ox, bison and horse) situated just before the 'terminal area' is taken by Leroi-Gourhan to represent the remnants of an earlier phase of the sanctuary. Many of the caves which feature in Leroi-Gourhan's section on documentation in his latest book[84] contain, on the basis of his own analysis, similar unexpected combinations of animals and signs (e.g. Pair non Pair, Gargas, Cougnac, Commarque, Pergousset, Aldène).

To summarise the various critical comments of this section a re-analysis of the cave of Les Combarelles is presented (figure 104). Immediately such an analysis is attempted, there is the problem of unidentifiable figures. These are by no means all concentrated into what Leroi-Gourhan identifies as 'panels of unfinished contours'[85] but occur sometimes in central panels, sometimes in central marginal areas and sometimes in isolation in other cave areas. In several of Leroi-Gourhan's analyses these appear to have been ignored or called 'unidentifiable lines' for which he has cautiously offered no interpretation or classification.

Les Combarelles is one of the first caves on which Leroi-Gourhan based his theories of Palaeolithic parietal art. The decorations in the cave start some hundred metres from the entrance and then cover much of both walls of a long narrow tunnel with several right angled turns which provide reasonably sharp topographical limits for the various sanctuary sections. In his analysis[86] Leroi-Gourhan only makes use of these topographical features as rough guides for subdividing the representations of the sanctuary; for example, the three longer stretches of straight passage are 'main' or 'principal' sections separated by shorter intermediate sections at the bends but these intermediate sections overlap the main sections to various degrees and the actual position of Leroi-Gourhan's divisions is governed to a large extent by contents.

90 *Below* Low-relief sculpture of a reclining woman on the right hand wall of the cave of La Magdelaine; the actual position of the head is difficult to distinguish.
91 *Right* Low-relief sculpture of a reclining woman on the left hand wall of La Magdelaine with an engraved bison on the rock ledge at her feet; the bison is curled up to fit into the curve of the rock.

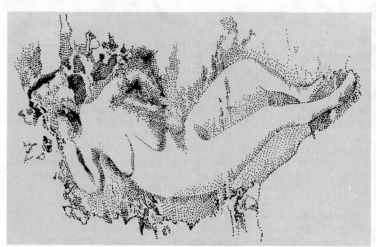

In order to simplify the diagrams and to bring out the salient principal themes at Les Combarelles, Leroi-Gourhan has omitted a large number of representations from his analysis and cave plan. The representations which he has retained are not necessarily either the largest, the most complete or the most prominent in any panel, nor are the species selected for discussion those which are represented in most detail or shown with most care. Leroi-Gourhan gives no detailed reasons for his omission of some representations and his retention of others but, to a certain extent, the omissions are covered by his analytical method of equal rating for every species in a composition whatever the number of individuals shown.

In figure 104 the representations omitted from Leroi-Gourhan's published plan have been inserted, on the basis of the very detailed original publication of Les Combarelles. In nearly every case, therefore, it can be securely established whether 'adjacent' groups of representations, as defined by the authors of the original report, are separated from each other by any distance or overlap each other. In general Leroi-Gourhan appears to have taken as a panel a group of overlapping or closely adjacent representations and to have indicated on his plan most of the species represented in any such panel. In some cases, however, he has omitted certain

representations from such panels, for example the mammoths in the entrance panels and some of the very doubtful anthropomorphs (which he is certainly correct in considering undecipherable). The position of figure 78 is indicated by Leroi-Gourhan although he does not show that it represents an ibex and he considers it as part of the entrance composition; yet from the original publication it is situated so close to a horse (77) and so clearly forms part of a long frieze of horses (78-72) that it does not seem logical to isolate it from the group of representations which Leroi-Gourhan considers constitutes the first main theme of horse-bison, man(=face), 'male' and 'female' symbols. Similarly, 'female' symbol (53) is placed by Leroi-Gourhan into the main panel whereas the original publication showed it as part of an overlapping group of representations (51-53) which Leroi-Gourhan considers to belong to the second intermediate zone. This ascription by Leroi-Gourhan can certainly not be defended on any grounds of topography or spatial organisation.

A count of all the representations of animals identified by Breuil in the original publication (but excluding those which both Breuil and Leroi-Gourhan considered doubtful) shows that when panels are distinguished as suggested by Leroi-Gourhan, horses are by far the most frequent of species represented (116), with at least 67 in

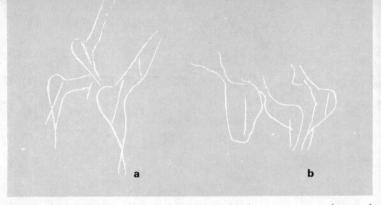

a   b

main panels, 27 in intermediate zones, 7 in the entrance region and 3 in the terminal area (the remaining 24 representations of horses are either so doubtful or so hidden within a maze of representations that their correct identification as well as their correct numbers are difficult to ascertain). Clearly, therefore, horses are numerically predominant in central panels (about two-thirds). Most of these representations of horses are found in long friezes whereas, in the intermediate areas, which are shorter, they occur in smaller groups. When each horse frieze is rated as one, as is done by Leroi-Gourhan, the horse appears to be distributed fairly equally throughout the cave (14 in main panels, 12 in intermediate zones).

14 bison representations feature in the main panels, 11 in inter-mediate zones and 7 in the terminal area; the bison is, therefore, found fairly evenly distributed throughout the cave. 8 of those in the intermediate zones are found in one long frieze while two others in this cave region are well drawn and are close to smaller horses. The bison in the main panels include many which are incomplete, some which are very sketchily indicated and others which are very small; they are on the periphery of friezes of horses. When the numerical system followed by Leroi-Gourhan is adopted, so that each 'composition' is rated equally irrespective of the number of individual representations concerned, bison no longer appear evenly distributed throughout the cave but are concentrated in the main zones of the cave. If other criteria, such as completeness, size and prominence of bison within a panel, are considered bison are found to be typical of intermediate and terminal zones.

Other animal species are found in comparatively small numbers in Les Combarelles and are fairly evenly distributed throughout the cave in main (and intermediate) zones: 5 (4) mammoth individuals, 6 (5) bear individuals, 6 (6) reindeer individuals, whereas deer and ibex show some tendency to concentration in the zones of the cave classified by Leroi-Gourhan as intermediate, 2 (8) deer individuals

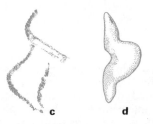

c   d

92 Representations usually interpreted as stylised females:
a Engraving from La Roche.
b Engravings from Les Combarelles.
c Red paintings from Pech-Merle; some of which closely resemble representations of bison.
d Figurine from Peterfels.

and 2 (5) ibex individuals.

From Leroi-Gourhan's new approach to Palaeolithic parietal art several important facts emerge. Certain species of animals are represented markedly more frequently than are others. Within a cave, bison and horse (and possibly ox and mammoth) 'themes' are more frequently shown on the walls of large chambers and passages whereas many 'themes' of other animals are found virtually anywhere and certain other animals (e.g. bear and lion) are usually shown isolated from major concentrations of other animals in a cave. How far this evidence can be taken to show that the compositions within a cave were regularly planned is still difficult to assess, for it is a fact that the two most commonly represented animals are also those which Palaeolithic man is likely to have seen on numerous occasions in large herds. Leroi-Gourhan has shown on a numerical basis that some caves contain certain galleries in which one animal species or sign is numerically predominant, and other caves in which the most frequent representation is of one animal species only. He has shown also that different 'signs' are shown in caves depending on the geographical area concerned and that some types of these signs are more commonly found in certain cave areas than other types. Leroi-Gourhan's numerical analysis has revealed that certain types of representations are not generally found close together; there are very few examples of male and female human representations in the same regions of a cave or shelter and where the bison, for example, is predominant in a central area of a cave it is unusual to find wild oxen in the same region (or vice versa).

The second stage of Leroi-Gourhan's analysis is concerned with the symbolism behind the postulated division of the animal and sign representations into two major groups. In his most recent work[87] Leroi-Gourhan makes the cautious statement that 'the hypothesis of male and female entities, regents of the male and female domain, is certainly simplistic and partial, that of the bison and the horse as symbolic animals within the same sphere is surely equally deficient and we are probably dealing with a system (which was perhaps not rationally formulated) of correspondence, equivalence, interchangeability and complementarity between all the representations'. However, on other occasions he is so sure of the correctness of his interpretation that he assumes the original existence of representations, long since perished, which must have been placed in certain positions to complement or juxtapose other representations. The different distribution of animal representations in a cave is basic to his interpretation of the symbolism behind these representations. As has been seen, the different frequencies of animal species represented, and in particular the predominance of bison and horse over other animals seems adequately to explain why 'themes' of these animals feature more prominently in main panels of a cave than do others, without resorting to any symbolic interpretation. Actual environmental conditions in the Palaeolithic period might also explain why it should be bison and horse which are the most numerous species represented in parietal art without recourse to any special symbolic significance in the choice of these two species. Since there is no topographical basis on which to distinguish the horse from the bison (or wild ox) the classification of these two species into opposed categories cannot be accepted.

From his topographical division of the artistic contents of a cave into two entities, in the lateral and central areas, Leroi-Gourhan infers two symbolic equivalences, the male and the female respectively. This inference is based primarily on the supposed equivalence of central animals (excepting, of course, the horse) and central female human representations. It must be noted, however, that female representations with recognisable sex indicated are extremely rare in Palaeolithic parietal art. Moreover, there is no obvious reason that, just because a certain species of animal and a human representation are found together in the same panel of cave, the two representations concerned should be assumed to have the same symbolic equivalence. After all, in Leroi-Gourhan's own system of equivalences, the horse which is found predominantly in the same panels as bison, is assumed to belong to the opposite sexual group from the bison.

Leroi-Gourhan's interpretation of the symbolism of signs is

again partially based on their topographical positions within caves and also on their assumed typological derivation from male and female sexual organs or whole figures. As has been seen above it is undoubtedly true that some signs are predominantly found in areas of caves where other signs are largely absent. It is, however, quite another matter to infer from this distribution that the signs commonly found in central panels have the same symbolic equivalence as the animals and occasional female representations also found in these central panels, or that the signs in lateral areas signify the same thing as the animals and rare male representations found in these areas.

If they could be accepted, the strongest evidence in favour of a sexual interpretation of these signs would be the typological derivations postulated by Leroi-Gourhan. According to Leroi-Gourhan[88] there are five major groups of 'female' signs (e.g. figures 93d, e, f, h); most of which are typologically derived from the naturalistic rendering of the vulva (see figure 34), and one of which is derived from the representation of the whole female body (see figure 17). According to Leroi-Gourhan not only are the most ancient representations of these signs naturalistic (e.g. figure 34) but the significance of even the later stylised ovals, triangles and rectangles 'leaps to ones eyes'. Unfortunately the situation is not really so simple; it cannot be assumed that just because triangles (with base either at top or bottom and with a vertical line within it) appear to some modern eyes to resemble vulvas that they did also to Palaeolithic man. Furthermore many of the 'stylised' signs classed by Leroi-Gourhan as derivations from the 'naturalistic' representations of vulvas or female bodies are extremely difficult to accept. It is admitted by Leroi-Gourhan that many of the derivatives of the five principal groups of 'female' signs are extremely complex and differ radically according to the geographical area concerned. It is also admitted by Leroi-Gourhan that different typological variations on the same basic sign-'type' can be found within the same cave. Some of the difficulty in accepting Leroi-Gourhan's typological derivations can be seen from the fact that he sees the 'tectiform' as derived both from triangular signs and from complete human figures. Bracket-like signs are also classed by Leroi-Gourhan as 'female' but their typological derivation and evolution

93 *Signs:* **a** Red painted band of dots and divided 'rectangles', from El Castillo.
b Red painted bell-shaped signs and black painted 'barbed' sign, from El Castillo.
c Engraved 'barbed' or 'hooked' sign, from Le Gabillou.
d Black painted 'bracket' sign, from Cougnac.
e Red painted 'bracket' sign, from Le Portel.
f Engraved 'tectiform', from Font de Gaume.

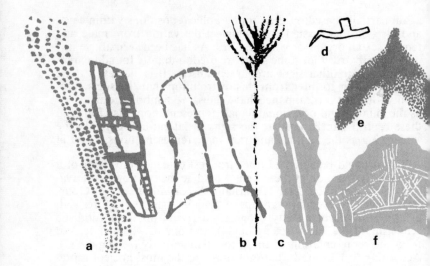

is obscure.[89] Basically what Leroi-Gourhan is assuming is that
Palaeolithic artists made use of several very different symbols to
express the 'female', symbols derived either from the vulva or from
the whole female figure; it is interesting to note that he derives no
symbol from breasts (although several of the supposed derivations
from triangles and from the whole figure could as well be derived
from breasts as from anything else) although several figurines and
low relief sculptures have breasts clearly and prominently marked
(e.g. figures 3, 58 and 60) and at Le Combel there is a small
chamber which contains rounded stalagtites which may indicate
Palaeolithic interest in breasts. In general, many of the signs isolated by Leroi-Gourhan as 'normal' forms closely resemble those
isolated (but not defined) as 'type' signs. Many of the 'derived' and
'reduced' signs, however, are much less convincing; for example,
many of the signs derived or reduced from the triangle with vertical
slit are no longer triangular (one is a circle) and contain no vertical
lines so that they retain none of the elements which served to define
this group.

According to Leroi-Gourhan there are three major groups of

g Red painted 'claviform' and dots, from Les Trois Frères.
h Red painted detailed 'rectangular' signs, from El Castillo.
i Painted and engraved bichrome 'rectangular' or 'lattice' sign, from Lascaux.
j Red painted 'barbed' sign, from Marsoulas.
k Red painted 'boat' sign, from La Pasiega.
l Yellow painted 'feather' sign, from Lascaux.

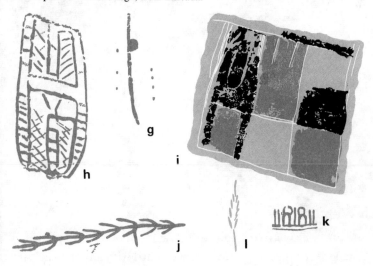

'male' signs (e.g. figures 93c, j, l). Although his works include tables showing their typological derivations he has admitted[90] that they are really only classifiable on the basis of their different topographical cave positions from 'female' signs. Only the hooked or 'spear' signs have been traced by Leroi-Gourhan to the male sexual organ, a unique representation in mobile art. The other signs classified as male are various combinations and variations of simple lines and dots which Leroi-Gourhan considers are originally evidently male sexual symbols which become very stylised and their typological development unclear. Obscurely, Leroi-Gourhan suspects[91] that the dots and lines may have different meanings. Very few of the 'reduced' and 'derived' male signs can be related to those considered 'normal' or 'type' signs. Many of the 'male' signs are found in isolation in 'lateral' areas of caves so that, as has been seen in previous chapters, some authors have suggested that they might mark topographical features such as narrow passages, dangerous areas and suchlike (e.g. figure 98). Leroi-Gourhan has gone a stage further for he has suggested that the isolation of these 'male' signs shows that the cave itself must have been considered

'female'[92] for these signs are not associated with any 'female' signs or animals. Although such an attitude to some cave regions has been claimed for some 'primitive' peoples, it would be more convincing in the context of Palaeolithic parietal art if the 'male' character of the signs was clearer and if isolated 'male' animal representations were also found 'in association' with the female cave.

Confirmations of Leroi-Gourhan's interpretation is claimed in the associations between male and female representations. However, the fact that Leroi-Gourhan considers that representations may be 'associated' for opposing reasons of 'complementarity' or of 'juxtaposition' makes it virtually impossible to establish whether 'association' corroborates the symbolic division of Palaeolithic parietal art into a world in which 'spear and wound, taken as symbols of sexual union and death, are integrated into a life cycle . . . of man-horse-spear and woman-bison-wound representations'.[93]

The last piece of evidence in support of Leroi-Gourhan's postulates about Palaeolithic parietal symbolism concerns the representation of male and female humans. It was important in the context of hunting magic to realise, as Leroi-Gourhan pointed out,

94 *Left* Engraved anthropomorph and tectiforms, from Le Gabillou; the anthropomorph has the horns and tail of a bovid; the most convincing of the Palaeolithic 'bison-men'.

95 *Right* Low-relief sculpture of the head of a horse, from Commarque; one of the few caves which contain low-relief sculptures in darkness.

that anthropomorphs were very 'stylised' and for the same reason it is impossible to accept much of Leroi-Gourhan's male sexing. For female and bison representations Leroi-Gourhan suggests a common stylistic parenthood[94] but this suggestion is weakened by a convincing illustration in his latest book[95] which shows the similarities in outline between a female at Pech-Merle (figure 17) and a horse at Le Combel. The linking of animals with human sex therefore relies on the topographical considerations already discussed above.

Perhaps the most worrying feature of Leroi-Gourhan's whole symbolic interpretation concerns the absence of primary sexual organs and the absence of any definite representations of copulation. He is well aware of this for in some of his works he talks about the 'prudishness' and 'discretion' of Palaeolithic parietal art.[96] Leroi-Gourhan is suggesting that the 'female', for example, was symbolised in Palaeolithic art equally by the representation of a female human being, by several different 'signs' (some of which are 'recognisably' representations of the vulva, others derived from it or the whole human figure), by certain animals, by wounds, by the caves themselves, by hands, etc. It is striking that he sees no incongruity in the fact that some of these symbols, such as the female human being and the signs, are by definition female in sex while others, such as male bison and male mammoth, are not. That fertility should be expressed in many different ways according to the context concerned is not in itself difficult to accept; that a complex system of symbolism should be difficult for the modern observer to unravel is very likely. What is much less easy to envisage is a situation whereby people who distinguish the female from the male sex (as proven by the primary sexual organs on many human figurines and some low-relief sculptures (e.g. figures 3 and 33) and possibly also from the signs in parietal art) should ignore the male and female sex of animals and regard them as equivalent to the male or female human (for a male bison is as much the symbol of the female element as is the female bison). To postulate that the Palaeolithic artists were prudes (and this is the reason, according to Leroi-Gourhan, why sexual signs so quickly became geometrical in form) cannot be reconciled with the fact that some examples of humans and animals are shown with primary sexual organs and that (according to Leroi-Gourhan) both isolated female vulva (figure 34) and isolated male phalli (figure 39) were shown by the Palaeolithic artists.

How difficult it is to accept Leroi-Gourhan's symbolic interpretation of Palaeolithic parietal art is reflected in his statements about the rites. These have virtually nothing to do with his symbolic interpretation and, in fact, are sometimes very similar to sympathetic magic interpretations. Although convinced of the religious nature of decorated caves he cautiously states[97] that almost anything could have happened in these caves (except art for art's sake!) but that the evidence is not good enough to tell exactly what. He sees the evidence of cave usage as conflicting, sometimes suggesting that caves had been rarely visited and sometimes that they had been often frequented, and accepts that children, as well as adults, went into the caves and were allowed to wander away from the main passages. He takes the panels of unfinished compositions and meanders as evidence for novices having attempted to copy the subjects on main cave panels (but see their actual positions, above) and points to evidence for retouching, replacement and improvement of old representations. Beyond this he accepts that wounding rituals (or rather theatrical ceremonies) may have taken place inside the caves. Little of this appears to be directly connected with the fertility symbolism which Leroi-Gourhan has induced from Palaeolithic parietal art.

Laming

Annette Laming infers the same inspirational basis for Palaeolithic parietal art in daylight and in darkness because in both cases large herbivores (and particularly horse, bison and wild ox) are the most commonly represented animals. Despite this, Laming also notes some differences between the two groups: the use of bas-relief in open-air shelters (she includes Commarque in the open-air shelters, but notes that it is somewhat anomalous [see below]); the 'characteristic realism' of the open-air sites (in which only two imaginary creatures are shown: the boar-headed bison and one, rather doubtful, goat-headed bison, both from Le Roc de Sers[98] (figure 10b); and the absence of 'signs' (tectiforms, etc.), many dangerous animals and mammoths from the daylight works.

In fact, however, Laming interprets the 'signs' from La Ferrassie, Laussel, Abri Cellier, etc. (figure 34) as female representations so that references only to the realism of whole human figures (e.g. figures 3, 58 and 60) is rather a distortion of the true state of affairs. Furthermore Laming admits that some open-air shelters do not conform to her generalised picture.[99] At Pair non Pair, for example, there are five bears, six mammoths and three felines; at Les Bernous there are possible examples of a bear, and a rhinoceros, and a definite lion; La Croze à Gontran has a mammoth; and Commarque a bear and a tectiform. Although Laming does not discuss these anomalies in any detail it could be said that Pair non Pair, Commarque and La Croze à Gontran really belong to category 2 caves (as defined in chapter 2) for decoration continues a little way into darkness, although in the first and last of these caves the decorations can all just be seen at certain times without artificial lighting. Les Bernous is without any doubt a category 1 cave.

If daylight caves which contain a mammoth or carnivore are really exceptional in this category, then it must be noted that several others, not isolated by Laming, must also be counted anomalous: Angles sur l'Anglin (one lion), Isturitz (one bear and one

96 Australian aboriginal rock painting from Bull Creek (Normanby River). The male figure is the most recent painting in this gallery and its upper part is drawn across the cave ceiling while its legs extend down the wall. According to an informant this is a 'curse' drawing whereby the artist inflicts on an enemy the deformities shown in the painting (e.g. absence of hands, three-pronged penis). To the left of this male representation is a white pipe-clay headless female figure about which there is no information. It is interesting to note that in this gallery there is no obvious reason, nor apparent significance, to explain why one representation should be vertical and the other horizontal.

97 *Below left* Front view of a modelled clay bear, from Montespan; the skull of a young bear was found at its feet and it has been suggested that this was originally attached to a hole in the neck and that the whole model was covered with real bear's skin.
98 *Below right* Red and black painted lines and dots on the 'signpost' panel at Niaux.

mammoth), Lalinde (a solitary mammoth), and possibly La Ferrassie (one doubtful lion, one doubtful mammoth and a very doubtful rhinoceros) whose animal contents cannot possibly be rated realistic.

Several shelters and open-air sites have not been included in Laming's inventory of contents. These include several mammoths which cannot, therefore, be accepted as exceptional in this category of caves (e.g. Chabot and Le Figuier).

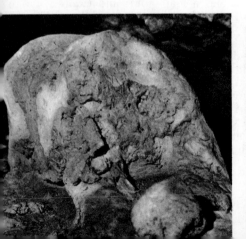

The inventory of open-air sites (excluding those, such as Teyjat, which Laming considers to be of much later date than the others) shows the relative scarcity of animals such as rhinoceros, lion and bear. However, in view of the extreme paucity of open-air sites considered by Laming (especially when compared to the number of caves considered by Leroi-Gourhan) the differences in frequencies of animals in the open-air and in darkness are likely to be due to chances of discovery and sampling (a view also accepted by Leroi-Gourhan).[100]

What does seem a possibly significant difference between representations in open-air sites and those in darkness is the abundance and variety of 'signs' in the latter. Laming's suggestion that their place is taken in open-air sites by 'cupules' (shallow hollows pecked out of the rock) and rings cut through thin rock projections seems to have little to support it. In chapter 2, however, reasons were given why it is more meaningful to group together caves on the basis of the relationship between habitation areas and decoration rather than on a criterion such as daylight. Laming's open-air sites include all those caves classed in this work as category 1 and some rare examples in category 2. She does not include those representations which start in daylight and continue into dark regions (many of those in category 2). If caves of categories 1 and 2 are combined together their contents are not distinguished from those of category 3 caves by the absence of signs; furthermore the preponderance of human representations over those in category 3 caves (especially since the discovery of Le Gabillou, see chapter 2) is greatly reduced.

5 Conclusions and problems

Anyone who has persevered through the preceding pages may well be asking whether, after all this, anything at all is definitely known about Palaeolithic man's reasons for painting, engraving and sculpting on rock walls. The truthful answer is: very little indeed; but on consideration this is less surprising than might at first appear.

After all not only is the amount of work carried out on Australian aboriginal art vast but there also exist some aboriginal artists to explain their works, and yet there are still enormous gaps in our understanding of aboriginal art. In many cases it even appears that there is some doubt as to which are meaningful questions to ask about Australian aboriginal rock art. When comparing the situations of aboriginal and Palaeolithic studies it has to be remembered that not only are there no Palaeolithic informants to explain their artistic conventions or why they decorated their rock walls, but virtually nothing at all is known about Palaeolithic social organisation.

It must be admitted that the historical development of French studies on Palaeolithic art has not been very helpful. Although his work was in many ways outstanding, and his accumulation of data invaluable, the Abbé H. Breuil exercised a virtual monopoly of studies on Palaeolithic art and this monopoly, together with the lamentable abscence of detailed and scientific excavation and exploration of decorated Palaeolithic caves, inevitably led to some stagnation. In this context the revitalisation and challenge of Professor A. Leroi-Gourhan's recent work can only be welcome.

Perhaps the most important single barrier to an understanding of the significance of Palaeolithic parietal art (and equally to any clear-cut conclusions to a book such as this) is the ignorance which still surrounds the use of caves by Palaeolithic man. Until it is known what exactly Palaeolithic man was doing inside caves, apart from painting and engraving on their walls, all interpretations of parietal art can only be tentative hypotheses. To what extent did Palaeolithic man live inside caves? Did he use caves as storage places (perhaps for sacred objects which have long since perished)? Did he fear to go inside caves unless for a special purpose, or did he nonchalantly and confidently explore their passages? It is, of course, fantastic that such vital evidence is still not available for it is surely context which one hopes will one day, together with the systematic study of content, reveal the best clues to the meaning of Palaeolithic art and it is, after all, the context which distinguishes parietal from mobile art and makes it potentially the most suitable Palaeolithic art form for interpretative studies.

It is possible to guess (but not to prove) that in reality there was considerably more Palaeolithic activity inside caves than is usually thought or admitted in the literature for, from some caves, there is data (largely chance finds) of considerable activity by a considerable number of people (e.g. Montespan – footprints, flints, animal bones; Labastide – hearths, flints, animal bones, engraved plaquettes; and many others). But it is impossible as yet to answer the vital question whether Palaeolithic man went into caves primarily in order to paint or engrave, or whether he went there for some quite different reason, and, while there anyway, took the opportunity to decorate the cavern walls.[1] Footprints have been found in several caves where no parietal art exists (and in several large galleries within decorated caves) and this might support the idea that Palaeolithic man had some other reasons beyond artistic representation, to penetrate caves.

Footprints also appear to prove that both adults and children went into caves. It is, however, again impossible, without knowing more about Palaeolithic uses of, and attitudes towards, caves to choose between the two possible alternative interpretations. Either the children went into caves for a particular purpose, such as initiation, which concerned them as children or they went there just as they would have gone elsewhere with, perhaps, the added appeal of exploration. There is, possibly, a little evidence from the footprints that children did wander quite freely inside parts of the caves and there is a report[2] from the cave of Le Tuc d'Audoubert that children had, presumably for fun, stuck their fingers vertically into the gooey mud. In this connection it is interesting to note that for amusement children among the Australian aborigines have developed considerable skill in the arts, especially engravings on clay floors.

It is definitely established that Palaeolithic man lived both in open sites and in rock shelters and cave entrances and that he sometimes decorated these areas with paintings, engravings and

99 *Below* Rock paintings and engravings by the Marghi of Northern Nigeria made in connection with initiation ceremonies. Superpositioning reflects a general disregard for previous work, although some of the most recent works are generally left uncovered; the attitude towards these representations is one of autographs (for example, the most recent representations are simply written signatures).

low-reliefs. It is also known that he penetrated deeper into some of the passages leading off from inhabited cave entrances and decorated these galleries also. On the available evidence there is also a third category of caves in which he did not live but into which he went, sometimes for considerable distances and with considerable difficulty (marks where he slipped on the wet clay are still to be seen in many caves), apparently with the express purpose of decorating walls, ceilings and floors despite the darkness in these regions. If these category 3 caves really do exist then they must be considered strong evidence in favour of there being some esoteric meaning behind these category 3 examples of Palaeolithic parietal art. But until it is finally determined not only whether Palaeolithic man ever lived inside the caves but also where the original entrances were, this problem will not be finally resolved. If they do exist they have no clear parallel in the practices of living 'primitive' peoples. Perhaps some support for an esoteric interpretation of art in this third category is, rather ironically, provided by the unlikely attempts to explain why the Palaeolithic artist should have penetrated so deep. Neither an explanation based on the destructive action of frost (Piette) nor one based on respect for previous work (Leroi-

100 *Top* Two painted bichrome bison, from Lascaux; their hind quarters
overlap in such a way that they form a balanced composition.
101 *Bottom* Deep outline engraving of a horse in clay, from Montespan,
covered with holes; part of a larger 'scene' which includes
other animals; lines and holes.

102 A dead wart hog
lying on its side
(for comparison with
Palaeolithic representations).

Gourhan) can convincingly explain art in category 3 caves.

Because of the paucity of definite contextual evidence about Palaeolithic parietal art, interpretations must be largely based on the contents of the art. There is, however, one other source of clues towards correct interpretation and this is the locality of representations. There are two striking features about much Palaeolithic parietal art: 1 that representations are often superimposed, 2 that some representations are placed in inaccessible places. There is a small range of possible explanations for these two characteristics; if the art was a response to explanatory myths or traditions which dictated where representations should be placed this would explain both superpositioning and hidden localities (an explanation which applies to some Australian art); the art might have been intended to impress a visitor either by its abundance (superpositioning) or by its ingenuity (placed in localities which were difficult of access); the art might have been concerned with associated subjects shown by superpositioning (a stylistic convention found also among some Australian aborigines); the art might have been the work of people living at different times who had no feeling or respect for earlier artistic representations (an attitude reported both from Australian aborigines and other 'primitive' peoples); the art might have been placed in localities which were considered especially sacred, thus explaining both superpositioning and localities which were difficult of access (an explanation which most probably applies to some Australian aboriginal art). On the evidence of context from some caves and content of some representations, some of these explanations appear more likely than others, but the significant feature may well be, as it is among the Australian aborigines, that more than one criterion was operative at any one time; thus it may well be that association was sometimes indicated by superpositioning (as it was undoubtedly for some Palaeolithic parietal representations) but that at other times, or in other places, superpositioning had no especial significance, indicating only disregard for previous works.

The contents of Palaeolithic art should provide some of the strongest evidence for its correct interpretation. It is a fact that in Palaeolithic art are represented only very few human beings and there are no certain representations of scenery (no vegetation nor

natural features such as rivers or mountains). Again, there are several very different possible explanations of these facts; either animals were the predominant concern of Palaeolithic artists for something like fertility or hunting magic for food-animals, or possibly the predominance of parietal representations of animals was bound up with their role as 'background' for actual human participation (as 'actors') during which 'props' may have been brought into the caves for any given occasion (for example, actual vegetation). It is possible also to explain the paucity of human representations and the absence of scenery and vegetation in terms of representational taboos on these subjects, but it is difficult to imagine an explanation which might, in this way, connect humans, vegetation and natural features such as rivers. It is unlikely that the art was exclusively concerned with increase or hunting magic directed at certain animals for this does not adequately explain either the different proportions of animals represented nor the representations of humans and part-humans. The relative frequencies of animals, the absence of representations of vegetation and also the evidence reviewed in previous pages, which shows that many representations were intended to be viewed, suggest that 'theatre' may well be behind some of the parietal representations.

The proportions of animal species represented in Palaeolithic art show conclusively that the Palaeolithic artist was selective in his choice of subjects; how his selection should be interpreted is debatable. At Lascaux virtually only stags and no does were shown on the cave walls; at Covalanas, on the other hand, virtually only does were represented. Obviously this selection did not reflect the actual environmental situation of Palaeolithic times; at Lascaux, perhaps, the choice was based on the impressive antler spread of male deer but at Covalanas it has to be presumed either that the deer represented were males in rutt (without antlers despite their sex), that the artists at Covalanas had some special reason for

103 Two red painted ibexes, from Cougnac; they may be sexed by the length of their horns, which are longer in the males.

showing only female deer or that for the artists concerned the female of the deer species had some special attraction (as did the male deer for the artists at Lascaux).

Such selectivity of animal species, as well as the distribution of animals within caves (as documented by Leroi-Gourhan), is not adequately explained by any sympathetic magic interpretation. It is necessary, however, to wait for much more numerical evidence (based upon criteria such as size and numbers of representations and tested by adequate statistical methods) before it is possible to determine whether the distribution of animals and signs within caves are the result of intentional selection, or of haphazard localisation of the animals most commonly encountered by the Palaeolithic artists. At the present time the distribution of human, bison and ibex representations at least, appear to indicate the likelihood of a certain degree of selection and planning by the Palaeolithic artists.

On the basis of the contextual evidence, of the practices of certain 'primitive' peoples and of the content of Palaeolithic art there seems little evidence against the assumption that much of the parietal art which surrounds Palaeolithic habitation (category 1) was intended to enliven and brighten domestic activities. In most art of this category there is little superpositioning, few enigmatic signs and no particular paucity of human representations.

If this inference about category 1 art should be true it is important to recognise the support that this gives to the assumption that the signs so often interpreted as sexual symbols (figure 34) need not necessarily be concerned with increase ceremonies but may be simply connected with eroticism.[3] That this may indeed be likely and that fertility magic interpretations of Palaeolithic art need considerable rethinking is supported by the fact that several modern hunting and gathering tribes are known to avoid, as opposed to increase, the possibility of having large families. It is a fact that the Bushmen regularly practice infanticide because, they maintain, a hunting and gathering life is too hard to be able to support many children. Among several tribes of Australian aborigines, also, there is evidence that increase ceremonies are a foreign concept, for the usual level of life is, for them, a normal and natural order of life and 'the need to increase their food supply was not felt

deeply enough to appear in their spiritual expressions, let alone in practice'.[4] Indeed it is as likely that Palaeolithic man was not interested in the fertility of the human species as that he was concerned with producing large families.

Although in the literature totemic and sympathetic magic interpretations are usually kept apart, in reality sympathetic fertility magic and totemic interpretations have much in common while sympathetic hunting magic interpretations are based on slightly different evidence. Although totemic practices and beliefs of living 'primitives' suggest that any animal, whatever its prominence or role in a society, may be selected as the subject of totemic practice it does not follow that just because the Australian aborigines are totemic so, therefore, were Palaeolithic men.

Perhaps the most striking feature which argues against a fertility interpretation, outside a symbolic totemic increase function, is that some of the content of Palaeolithic parietal art does not reflect the actual environment and eating habits of Palaeolithic man. This is also a feature which argues against a sympathetic hunting magic interpretation for there is no reason why Palaeolithic man should have been interested either in killing or increasing the number of 'imaginary beings' nor, on the other hand, why he should not have been interested either in killing or increasing the number of reindeer which, it is known, was staple food in one period of the Palaeolithic. Finally, in the context of increase and fertility, it would be strange to find that the Palaeolithic men who lived by hunting animals and gathering wild fruit and berries had no interest in the

104 Schematic plan of the cave of Les Combarelles (not to scale); details
of contents and topographic divisions as shown by Leroi-Gourhan (1965b, p291)
are indicated in black; those shown in brown are the additional data
given in the original publication (L. Capitan, H. Breuil, D. Peyrony, 1924).
Capital letters = relatively large representations; small letters = relatively

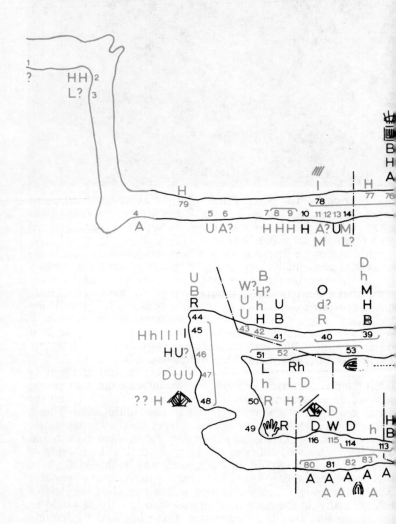

small representations: H = horse; B = bison; O = ox; M = mammoth;
I = ibex; U = bear; D = deer; R = reindeer; L = lion; Rh = rhinoceros;
W = wolf; A = anthropomorph; C = compound or imaginary creature.
'Signs' are indicated schematically. See detailed discussion in text (pp. 209–12).

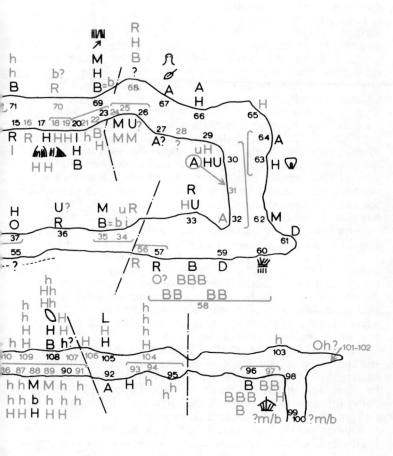

increase of vegetation. Even if the usual 'increase' interpretation is slightly adapted to fall more in line with the 'maintenance' rituals known from Australia it fails to account for the absence of representations of vegetation and for the not insignificant number of dangerous animals represented.

The choice of animals represented may either be due, in part at least, to actual environmental conditions throughout the vast number of years during which parietal art was made (e.g. the correlation between the actual and the parietal distribution of rhinoceros, bison, deer, etc.) or to the art being a record of myths or symbolism. A numerical analysis such as that attempted by Leroi-Gourhan reveals little to suggest that any underlying symbolism or myth was simple but rather, if it existed at all, that it was a complex system of inter-relationships. With time and more accurate recording of the contents of each decorated cave it may become possible to determine how likely it is that there was such an underlying 'philosophy'; there is little doubt that such analyses will have to take into account not only 'themes' represented (often only recognisable on the basis of rather arbitrary divisions of caves) but also the number, size and prominence of representations. Even on the basis of Leroi-Gourhan's suggestions it might be possible to attempt correlations between such features of the art and his suggested 'juxtapositioning', 'complementarity', 'completions', etc.

That one is still very far away from being able to solve the question of the significance of Palaeolithic parietal art is shown by the contents and contexts of several decorated caves which none of the interpretations reviewed in this book come anywhere near being able to explain. Although very damaged, the cave of Bédeilhac[5] affords a good example of the mysteries which still surround so much of Palaeolithic parietal art.

During the last war both the Germans and the French used the entrance of this cave for constructing aeroplanes. The damage incurred as well as the action of natural corrosion has been invoked by nearly all authors to explain the extraordinary distribution of Palaeolithic representations within this cave but, despite these ravages, this cave still challenges comprehension.

Walking into the huge 'aircraft factory' of the cave entrance, one is in an area in which excavations have revealed not only Palaeolithic, but also Neolithic, Bronze Age and Iron Age material. A narrow gallery leads off from the right-hand wall. This gallery (Vidal) is nowadays hidden behind an awkward wall of debris, but in Palaeolithic times it was probably reasonably accessible. In this side passage were many paintings, the vast majority of which have today totally vanished. Judging from the original documentation, the left-hand wall was covered with innumerable representations of bison and a single horse while the right-hand wall was already largely destroyed but did contain at least one representation of a horse.

Although the Vidal gallery started a good hundred and fifty metres from the cave entrance and daylight, it is only further on towards the interior of the main passage of Bédeilhac that a small gallery leads from the left wall of the cave.

To reach the parietal art in this (Jauze) gallery it is necessary (and it appears likely that it was necessary also in Palaeolithic times) to crawl on ones stomach through a very narrow and low passage for some considerable distance until one reaches a position where the ceiling rises slightly. At this point the Palaeolithic artist cut from the clay floor at least four low-relief bison (figure 46), and several signs. Behind these reliefs on the chamber wall he painted a large black-outline horse but did not complete its head or front legs.

Ignoring all the side-passages, one comes at length in the main gallery to a large black-brown painted outline bison (or possibly it is a horse) with red dots under its stomach between its legs. A little further on is a large stalagmite with positive hand impressions on it (it is not entirely clear whether these are really Palaeolithic or whether they were made recently by some of the people who have also scribbled on this stalagmite). Later the gallery becomes really vast and the floor is cut by a small meandering stream. Only very gradually does the ceiling become lower. As far as can be seen while walking through this gallery, there is absolutely no sign of Palaeolithic activity after the brown-outline bison until, where the ceiling is about seventy centimetres high, suddenly one comes across two small black-outline bison on the ceiling of this huge gallery. Further along in this vast chamber where the ceiling has become so low that it is about to meet the chamber floor the Palaeolithic artists have traced some clay floor engravings. In this corner of the gallery where the ceiling is only about twenty-five centimetres high are

105 Schematic plan of the cave of Font de Gaume. Details of contents and topographical divisions as shown by Leroi-Gourhan (1965b, p.293) are indicated in black; those in brown are additional data given in the original publication (L. Capitan, H. Breuil, D. Peyrony, 1910). Symbols and conventions are as for figure 104. Numbers indicate the number of individual representations of any species. The paintings at Font de Gaume are now very faded; from incomplete or badly preserved dorsal outlines of animals it is difficult to distinguish between bison and mammoths so that no real importance can be attached to the differences marked on

engraved on the floor a horse's head, some signs and a small bison. But it is not only the locality of these engravings which is striking, but also the fact that the small bison has been engraved with its feet pointing into the cavern corner so that the artist must have placed himself in a most uncomfortable and cramped position. Except for a floor engraving of a horse's leg and belly on the other side of this gallery, this huge chamber is devoid of Palaeolithic decoration.

It is very likely that in Palaeolithic times this cave contained much more parietal decoration (there are traces of paintings as well as red dots in many areas) but this would not detract from the amazing contexts of the parietal art which still survives. Although the Vidal gallery does not appear to have been exceptional (indeed Leroi-Gourhan claims it as an example of bison-horse theme), the locality of the small bison and signs is surprising. After their long

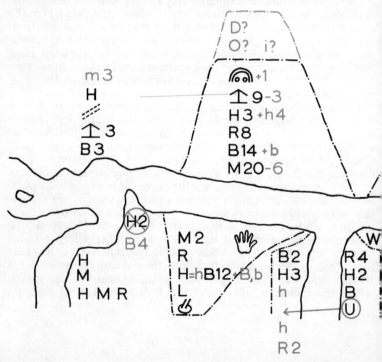

this figure between Leroi-Gourhan's identification of bison and mammoths and that of the original authors. The major discrepancy between Leroi-Gourhan and the original authors concerns the entrance to the 'sanctuary' in which Leroi-Gourhan has marked 2 horses while the original publication recorded 4 bison. Leroi-Gourhan has considered the one rhinoceros to form part of the terminal composition, which also includes horses and lion, although in fact this animal is situated amongst the bison-horse-ox group near to the terminal area of the cave; Leroi-Gourhan's justification for this is that he considers the bison-horse-ox group to be of earlier date.

crawl to the point where the ceiling was beginning to heighten the Palaeolithic artists were content to model these very small animals and to paint an incomplete horse outline. Although natural destruction has, most probably, been extensive at Bédeilhac there is no reason to think that it has had a differential effect within the depths of the large main chamber. It seems, therefore, that the Palaeolithic artists were content to leave this chamber bare but suddenly took it into their heads to place two small bison on the ceiling. Then, having left the rest of the chamber untouched, they engraved on the floor in a corner of this gallery with so much intensity of feeling that they were prepared to contort their bodies so that they could reach into the very extremity of the natural corner! There, as if to test the credulity of their modern survivors, they represented a bison upside down!

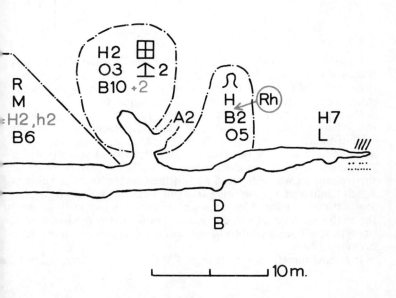

106 Schematic plan of the cave of Le Gabillou; the details of contents and topographical divisions as shown by Leroi-Gourhan (1965b, p.259) have been transferred on to the accurate plan in Gaussen (1964, pp. 26, 30, 33, 36) and are indicated in black; those in blue are the additional data in the Gaussen publication. Symbols and conventions are as for figure 104. Numbers indicate the number

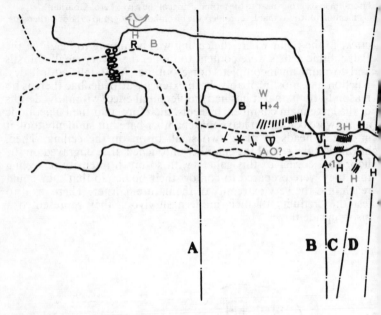

Clearly, even allowing for the fact that much Palaeolithic art in this cave has vanished, the localities of the Palaeolithic representations within the cave of Bédeilhac are not explained by any of the interpretations reviewed in the previous chapters.

Perhaps the main impression gained from visits to many decorated Palaeolithic caves is one of variety. Palaeolithic man was extraordinarily varied in his choice of where to camp, the use he appears to have made of caves, in the selectivity of subjects which he chose to represent, in the localities which he chose to decorate, in the techniques which he used and in the combinations of subjects which he favoured. With this variety in mind it is not at all surprising that none of the interpretations reviewed, adequately account for all the examples of Palaeolithic art known to the modern world; perhaps it is nonsensical to have expected that any one interpretation could be so.

It seems, therefore, that if any of the suggested interpretations

of individual representations of any species. The ibex shown by
Leroi-Gourhan dividing panel O from P is not indicated by Gaussen
who, however, does record an ibex in the centre of panel P. The
2 bison which form the centre of Leroi-Gourhan's panel P are shown
by Gaussen to be virtually on the line dividing panels O and P and
to be on opposite walls.

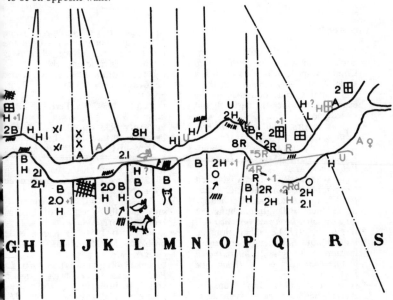

have any real validity, with regard to Palaeolithic parietal art each
of them is likely to apply to only certain works. There is nothing
against assuming that Palaeolithic art, as is also the art of many
living 'primitives' is the result of many different interests. Within
any one cave, therefore, it is possible to imagine that many of the
possibilities outlined in this book apply: that some representations
were the work of children (perhaps some of the floor engravings),
that some were used in acts of sympathetic magic (perhaps some of
the representations pierced with holes), that some were placed in
particular situations in order to please (perhaps some of the
open-air low-reliefs), and that some were illustrations of myths
and traditions (perhaps those which contain imaginary creatures,
anthropomorphs and unexpected combinations of animal species).
It is very possible, however, that some and perhaps many Palaeolithic representations were made for reasons which still totally
escape the modern observer.

5/13/72

Bibliography and notes

Chapter 1

1 In fact, however, the only early Peri-gordian burial known is that from Combe Capelle which contained a skeleton of *Homo sapiens*; but there still remains some doubt as to the exact level to which the burial should be assigned.

2 e.g. G. CLARK 1961. *World Pre-history*, London, p.23.

3 A. LEROI-GOURHAN (No Date). Ebauches de l'Art, in *L'art et l'Homme*, Paris.

4 e.g. L. VERTES 1960. Die Altsteinzeit der Südlichen Donaugebiete, *Quar-tär*, 12; M. GABORY 1960. Der heutige Stand der Paläolithforschung in Ungarn, *Archaeologia Austriaca*, 27.

5 H. BREUIL 1912. Les subdivisions du Paléolithique Supérieur et leur signi-fication, *Congrès International d'Anthropologie et d'Archéologie Préhistorique*.

6 D. PEYRONY 1933. Les Industries Aurignaciennes dans le basin de la Vézère. Aurignacien et Périgordien, *Bulletin de la Société Préhistorique Française*, 30.

7 PEYRONY 1933, ibid, p.544. Much of Peyrony's views found support in his discovery in the cave of Laugerie Haute of a Perigordian level, with abruptly blunted blades of a form intermediate between the early and the late Perigordian blades, which was beneath a late Aurignacian level.

8 Aurignacian is now used only to denote the cultures described ori-ginally as middle Aurignacian by Breuil. Early, middle and upper refer to substages of this culture (see below).

9 Retouch refers to the small flakes removed from the edge of a flint flake or blade, either to shape it or to blunt the edge. The retouch-flakes are commonly removed from the upper, ridged, surface of stone tools, but sometimes also from the lower, smooth, surface when it is known as 'inverse retouch'.

10 e.g. F. LACORRE 1960. La Gravette. *Le Gravétien et le Bayacien*, Paris, p.98 ff.

11 PEYRONY 1934. La Ferrassie, *Pré-histoire*, 3.

12 PEYRONY 1933, op. cit.

13 LEROI-GOURHAN 1961. Les Fouilles d'Arcy-sur-Cure, *Gallia. Préhistoire*, 4, p.10.

14 M. THORAL, R. RIQUET, J. COMBIER 1955. *Solutré*, Faculté des Sciences de Lyon, N.S.2.

15 P. E. L. SMITH 1961. Solutrean Ori-gins and the question of Eastern Diffusion, *Arctic Anthropology*, 1.

16 J. BOUCHUD 1954. Le Renne et le problème des Migrations, *l'Anthro-pologie*, 58.

17 D. de SONNEVILLE-BORDES 1960. *Le Paléolithique Supérieur en Périgord*, vols. I, II, Bordeaux.

18 See e.g. F. E. ZEUNER 1959. *The Pleistocene Period*, London, p.209.

19 Ibid, p.208 ff.

20 W. F. LIBBY 1955. *Radiocarbon Dat-ing*, Chicago.

21 BP = Before the Present, i.e. before 1950.

22 The Magdalenian III levels of the decorated caves at Altamira and Angles sur l'Anglin have been dated to 15,500 ± 700 BP and 13,920 ± 80 BP respectively.

23 E. HARLE 1881. La grotte d'Altamira, pres de Santander (Espagne), *Matériaux pour l'histoire primitive et naturelle de l'homme*, 12, p.280 ff.

24 These animals are in fact quite clearly bison.

25 L. CAPITAN, H. BREUIL 1902. La Grotte des Combarelles, *Revue de l'Ecole d'Anthropologie de Paris*, 12, p.34.

26 BREUIL 1952. *Quatre Cents siècles*

d'Art pariétal, Montignac, p.24.

[27] Ibid, p.25.

[28] O. N. BADER 1962. Otkrytie paleo-liticeskoi pescernoi jivopisi na Utale, *Istoriko arheologic sbornik*, pp. 14–23.

[29] e.g. J. MARINGER, H. BANDI 1953. *Art in the Ice Age*, London, p.114 ff.

[30] e.g. BREUIL 1952, op. cit., pp.40–1.

[31] e.g. P. GRAZIOSI 1960. *Palaeolithic Art*, London (English edition), p.30.

Chapter 2

[1] According to Leroi-Gourhan (1964, *Les Religions de la Préhistoire*, Paris, p.105) however, couplings of animals of the same species but of opposite sex are quite frequent (see chapter 3). In view of the difficulty of sexing animals represented in Palaeolithic art, see below, all that can be safely said is that animals of the same species with opposite primary sexual organs marked are not usually shown together.

[2] M. BOUILLON (Laboratoire Souter-rain, Moulis) has suggested to the authors that a maze of superimposed engravings, as at Les Trois Frères, results from the engraving at different times on a rock surface covered by a thin coat of clay. Before each new engraving, earlier ones would have been effaced by respreading the clay so that in Palaeolithic times the representations were not seen as an undecipherable maze; this only results from the flaking off of the clay cover leaving all the engraved lines which had penetrated into the rock surface. This is an ingenious suggestion but it does not, of course, explain superimposed paintings or finger tracings. See also p.49, chapter 2 and p.162, chapter 4 for a similar practice among some Australian Aborigines (A. P. ELKIN, 1952. Cave-Paintings in Southern Arnhem Land, *Oceania*, 224.

[3] e.g. GRAZIOSI, op. cit., pp.28, 32.

[4] MARINGER, BANDI, op. cit., p.120.

[5] L. CAPITAN, H. BREUIL, D. PEYRONY 1910. *La Caverne de Font de Gaume, aux Eyzies (Dordogne)*, Monaco, p.74.

[6] BREUIL 1952. Op. cit. pp.134–6; BREUIL 1957. En Lisant L'Arte dell'Antica Eta della Pietra de P. Graziosi, *Quaternaria*, 4, p.237.

[7] A. LAMING 1959. *Lascaux*, London, p.95.

[8] Ibid, pp.95–6.

[9] G. LECHLER 1951. The Interpretation of the 'Accident Scene' at Lascaux, *Man*, no. 283, pp.165–7.

[10] ZEUNER 1952, Lascaux, *Man*, no.153.

[11] F. de F. DANIEL 1950. Lascaux and the Sudan, *Man*, no.65.

[12] LECHLER 1951, op. cit., p.166.

[13] GRAZIOSI 1960. op. cit., pp.28, 163.

[14] LEROI-GOURHAN 1964. op. cit. p.148. In his most recent work (1965b. *Préhistoire de l'Art Occidental*, Paris, p.258) Leroi-Gourhan has further elaborated his interpretations. The rhinoceros he no longer considers to form part of the scene. He takes both the human and the dart (and perhaps the bird) as equivalent male symbols and the bison, its wound and its oval entrails as female symbols.

[15] GRAZIOSI 1960, op. cit., p.164.

[16] e.g. E. BOURDELLE 1938. Essai d'une étude morphologique des équidés préhistorique de France d'après les gravures rupestres, *Mammalia*, 2.

[17] P. A. LEASON 1939. A New View of the Western European Group of Quaternary Cave Art, *Proceedings of the Prehistoric Society*, 5.

[18] A. LEROI-GOURHAN 1963. *Art et Religion au Paléolithique Supérieur*, Paris, p.6.

[19] BREUIL 1952, op. cit., p.40.

[20] Ibid, p.45.

242

21 Ibid, p.39.

22 GRAZIOSI 1960, op. cit., p.136. It is interesting to note the similarities between this technique and that suggested by Bouillon, note 2, chapter 2.

23 Bégouen's statement (Comte Henri BEGOUEN 1912. Les Statues de bison en argile de la caverne du Tuc d'Audoubert, *L'Anthropologie*, p.664) that the foremost animal is female is based primarily on its slightly more slender build and slightly smaller size (2 cm) which are not sufficient criteria for sexing Palaeolithic representations (see below).

24 As suggested by G. H. LUQUET 1930. (English edition) *The Art and Religion of Fossil Man*, Paris, p.195.

25 Report in the *Illustrated London News*, 3 November 1923.

26 cf. J. CHARET 1948. Réflexions sur la magie de la chasse, II. Les bisons d'argile de Tuc d'Audoubert. *Bulletin de la Société Préhistorique Française*, 45, p.270, who has drawn attention to the similarity between the lines on the Niaux bison and the Tuc d'Audoubert bison.

27 LEROI-GOURHAN has correctly pointed out (1965b. Op. cit., p.79) that 'twisted perspective' is a technique employed in all periods of Palaeolithic art.

28 e.g. GRAZIOSI 1960, op. cit., pp.23, 26.

29 e.g. Ibid, p.2.

30 H. ALCALDE DEL RIO 1906. In E. CARTHAILLAC, H. BREUIL. *La Caverne d'Altamira à Santillane près Santander*, Monaco, pp.257 ff.

31 H. ALCALDE DEL RIO, H. BREUIL, L. SIERRA 1911. *Les Cavernes de la region Cantabrique*, Monaco, p.209.

32 PEYRONY 1934. Op. cit.

33 BREUIL 1952, op. cit., p.319. From an examination of the material from Pair non Pair Leroi-Gourhan (1965b,

op. cit., p.246) has concluded that most of the engravings really belong to the Gravettian. In fact the accurate dating of these representations is not clear.

34 PEYRONY 1932a. Les Abris Lartet et du Poisson à Gorge d'Enfer, *L'Anthropologie*, 42.

35 J. G. LALANNE, J. BOUYSSONIE 1941-6. Le Gisement Paléolithique de Laussel, *L'Anthropologie*, 50, p.156.

36 G. LALANNE 1911. Découverte d'un Bas-relief a Représentation Humaine dans les fouilles de Laussel, *L'Anthropologie*, 22.

37 BREUIL 1952, op. cit., p.277.

38 A. R. VERBRUGGE 1958. *Le Symbole de la Main dans la Préhistoire*, Milly-la-Foret, p.92.

39 S. de SAINT MARTHURIN, D. GARROD 1951. La Frize sculptée de l'Abri du Roc aux Sorciers à Angles sur l'Anglin (Vienne), *L'Anthropologie*, 55, pp.413–22.

40 LALANNE, BREUIL 1911. L'Abri sculpté de Cap Blanc a Laussel (Dordogne), *L'Anthropologie*, 22, p.385 ff.

41 CAPITAN, BREUIL, PEYRONY, 1924. *Les Combarelles aux Eyzies* (*Dordogne*), Monaco, op. cit., p.185.

42 BREUIL 1952, op. cit., p.239.

43 CAPITAN, BREUIL, PEYRONY, BOURRINET 1913. Les Gravures sur cascade stalagmique de la grotte de la Mairie à Teyjat (Dordogne), *Congrès International d'Anthropologie et d'Archéologie Préhistorique*, 14, p.500.

44 ALCALDE DEL RIO, BREUIL, SIERRA 1911, op. cit., p.205 ff.

45 BREUIL 1952, op. cit., p.38 ff.

46 Ibid, p.39.

47 Ibid, p.39.

48 LAMING 1959, op. cit., pp.47–8; A. LAMING-EMPERAIRE 1962. *La Signification de l'Art Rupestre Paléo-*

lithique, Paris, p.56.

[49] LEROI-GOURHAN 1965b, op. cit., p.156 ff.

[50] e.g. H. S. HARRISON 1954. Discovery, Invention, and Diffusion, in *A History of Technology*, vol. I, (Eds SINGER et al.), pp.60–2.

[51] e.g. BOURDELLE 1938, op. cit.; WINDELS 1949. *The Lascaux Cave Paintings*, London, p.111 ff.

[52] ZEUNER 1952, op. cit.

[53] ZEUNER 1963. *A History of Domesticated Animals*, London, p.309.

[54] BOURDELLE 1938, op. cit.

[55] WINDELS 1946, op. cit., pp.114–5.

[56] LAMING 1959, op. cit., p.128.

[57] H. STEHLIN, P. GRAZIOSI 1935. Ricerche sugli Asinidi Fossili d'Europa, *Mémoires de la Société de Paléontologie Suisse*, 56.

[58] We are grateful to Miss M. Howard (British Museum) for valuable advice on Pleistocene bison fossils.

[59] M. HILZHEIMER 1918. Dritte Beitrag zur Kenntnis der Fossilen Bisonten, *Archiv, der Naturgesellschaft*, 84.

[60] Personal Communication by the late Professor F. E. Zeuner.

[61] LAMING 1959, op. cit., p.138.

[62] BREUIL 1952, op. cit., p.144.

[63] F. KOBY 1954. Y a-t-il eu à Lascaux un Bos longifrons?, *Bulletin de la Société Préhistorique Française*, 51.

[64] e.g. BREUIL 1952, op. cit., pp.44, 210.

[65] e.g. S. REINACH 1913, *Répertoire de l'Art Quaternaire*, Paris, pp.137, 158.

[66] BREUIL 1952, op. cit., p.39.

[67] Ibid, Pl.377.

[68] GRAZIOSI 1960, op. cit., Pl.119a–b.

[69] A. LEROI-GOURHAN 1965a. *Le Geste et la Parole*, Paris, p.249; and for a suggestion that the tail hairs are part of the ox in front of it, see S. GIEDION 1962. *The Eternal Present. The Beginnings of Art*, London, p.189.

[70] H. BREUIL, H. OBERMAIER, Cl. WILLOUGHBY VERNER 1915. *La Pileta*, Monaco, Pl.XI.

[71] BREUIL 1952, op. cit., p.331.

[72] Ibid, pp.24, 391.

[73] J. GAUSSEN 1964. *La Grotte Ornée de Gabillou*, Bordeaux, Pl.35, 1.

[74] LALANNE 1911. op. cit.; LALANNE, BOUYSSONIE 1941–6, op. cit., p.132.

[75] e.g. BREUIL 1952, op. cit., p.307.

[76] e.g. A. LEROI-GOURHAN 1958. Le Symbolisme des Grands Signes dans l'Art Pariétal Paléolithique. *Bulletin de la Société Préhistorique Française*, 55, figs 3, 4.

[77] GAUSSEN 1964, op. cit., Pl.53.

[78] See for example the fascinating report by LÉON PALES (with M. TASSIN DE SAINT PEREUSE 1964). Une Scène Gravée Magdalénienne, Grotte de la Marche, Magdalénien III. *Objets et Mondes*, 4, 2. Which shows the result of reanalysis of some of the La Marche 'anthropomorphs' and the reanalysis by Leroi-Gourhan (1965b, op. cit., pp.90, 463) which explains the superpositioning of so-called anthropomorphs at Les Combarelles; it is interesting to note in this connection the recent rejection of the 'anthropomorph' at Cougnac by ETIENNE PATTE 1960, *Les Hommes Préhistoriques et la Religion*, Paris, pp.106–7, footnote 7.

[79] LEROI-GOURHAN 1964, op. cit., p.102.

[80] A. CARTAILHAC, H. BREUIL 1910. Les Peintures et Gravures Murales des Cavernes Pyrénénnes, Gargas, *L'Anthropologie*, 21, p.134.

[81] e.g. G. MALVESIN-FABRE, L. R. NOUGIER, R. ROBERT 1954. *Gargas*, Toulouse, p.12.

[82] P. A. JANSSENS 1957. Medical Views on Prehistoric Representations of Human Hands, *Medical History*, I, p.321.

[83] See LEROI-GOURHAN 1964, op. cit., p.102.

[84] GRAZIOSI 1960, op. cit., p.188.

[85] BREUIL 1952, op. cit., p.24.

244

86 A notable example of bas-relief in darkness is the magnificently sculpted horse in a narrow passage which leads off beyond the reach of daylight from the shelter of Commarque (figure 95).

87 LAMING-EMPERAIRE 1962, op. cit., p.291 ff.

88 LEROI-GOURHAN 1963, op. cit., pp.26, 27.

89 LEROI-GOURHAN 1965b, op. cit., p.260.

90 H. V. VALLOIS 1931. Les Empreintes de Pieds Humains des Grottes Préhistoriques du Midi de la France, *Palaeobiologica*, 4, p.84.

91 We are grateful to Dr M. Day (Department of Anatomy, Medical School, Middlesex Hospital, London) and Mr Jonathan Musgrave (Unit of Primatology and Human Evolution, Royal Free Hospital School of Medicine, London) for advice regarding the interpretation of footprints and handprints.

92 VALLOIS 1931, op. cit.

93 H. MARTIN 1932. Les Sculptures du Roc, *Préhistoire*, 1, pp.1–3.

94 PEYRONY 1932b. *Les Gisements Préhistoriques de Bourdeilles* (*Dordogne*). Archives de l'Institut de Paléontologie Humaine 10, Paris, pp.54–64, and p.24.

95 CAPITAN, BREUIL, PEYRONY 1910, op. cit., p.58.

96 BREUIL 1952, op. cit., p.179.

97 Personal Communication by Michel Bouillon (Laboratoire Souterrain, Moulis).

98 L. MEROC, J. MAZET 1956. *Cougnac, Grotte Peinte*, Stuttgart, p.72.

Chapter 3

1 M. BOUCHER de PERTHES 1846. *Antiquités celtiques et anté diluviennes*, vol. I, Paris; e.g. P. C. SCHMERLING 1833. *Recherches sur les ossements fossiles découverts dans les cavernes de la province de Liège*, vol. I, Liege.

2 SIR J. LUBBOCK 1863. *Prehistoric times, as illustrated by ancient remains, and the manners and customs of modern savages*, London, p.1 ff.

3 'One who studies . . . the scientific description of nations or races of men, their customs, habits and differences' (*The Shorter Oxford English Dictionary*, 1950). In this book ethnography is taken to refer especially to the study of living 'primitive' peoples.

4 Ed. LARTET, H. CHRISTY 1864. Figures d'animaux gravées ou sculptées, *Revue Archéologique*, 9.

5 G. de MORTILLET 1883. *Le préhistorique antiquité de l'homme*, Paris, p.415.

6 E. CARTHAILAC 1889. *La France préhistorique d'après les sépultures et les monuments*. Bibliographie scientifique internationale, 48, Paris, pp.7–8.

7 E. PIETTE 1907. *L'art pendant l'age du renne*, vol. I, Paris, p.68.

8 e.g. M. BOULE 1914. Review of Luquet, *l'Anthropologie*, 25, p.127.

9 GRAZIOSI 1960, op. cit., p.32.

10 H. BREUIL 1954. Bas reliefs feminins de La Magdeleine (Penne, Tarn près Montauban (Tarnet-Garonne), *Quaternaria*, 1.

11 G. H. LUQUET 1930. *The art and religion of fossil man*, New Haven and London (English edition), p.113.

12 W. H. RIDDELL 1940. Dead or alive?, *Antiquity*, 14, p.156.

13 M. van GENNEP 1925. A propos du totémisme préhistorique, *Actes du Congrès international d'histoire des religions*, 1923, vol. I.

14 S. GIEDION 1962. *The Eternal Present. The Beginnings of Art*, London, p.3.

15 SIR E. B. TYLOR 1873. *Primitive Culture*, vols. I, II, London.

16 SIR J. FRAZER 1890 (First edition).

The Golden Bough, vol. I, London.

[17] W. B. SPENCER, F. J. GILLEN 1899. The Native Tribes of Central Australia, London.

[18] TYLOR 1873, op. cit., vol. II, p.17

[19] SPENCER, GILLEN 1899, op. cit.

[20] FRAZER 1887 (First edition). Totemism, London; 1960 (abridged edition) The Golden Bough, London, p.902.

[21] E. DURKHEIM 1915. The Elementary Forms of the Religious Life, London (English edition), pp.95–6, 167.

[22] S. REINACH 1889. Antiquités Nationales. Description raisonnée du Musée Saint-Germain-en-Laye. i. Epoque des alluvions et des cavernes, Paris, pp.170–1.

[23] S. REINACH 1903a. L'art et la magie. A propos des peintures et des gravures de l'age de renne, l'Anthropologie, 14.

[24] SIR J. FRAZER 1911. (Third edition.) The Golden Bough, vol. I, London, p.52.

[25] REINACH 1903a, op. cit., p.263.

[26] S. REINACH 1903b. Review of Chauvet, Revue archéologique, 1, p.290.

[27] DR CAPITAN 1925. Les figurations des grottes quaternaires, Acte du Congrès International d'Histoire des Religions 1923, 1.

[28] See e.g. A. LAMING-EMPERAIRE 1962. La Signification de l'Art Rupestre Paléolithique, Paris.

[29] Ibid, p.117.

[30] e.g. TH. MAINAGE 1921. Les Religions de la Préhistoire. L'Age Paléolithique, Paris, p.253.

[31] REINACH 1889, op. cit.; 1903b, op. cit.

[32] S. REINACH 1902. Totémisme et exogamie, l'Anthropologie, 13.

[33] S. REINACH 1900. Phénomènes généraux du totémisme animal, Revue scientifique.

[34] L. CAPITAN, H. BREUIL, D. PEYRONY 1910. La Caverne de Font de Gaume, aux Eyzies, (Dordogne), Monaco.

[35] As reported ibid.

[36] CAPITAN 1925, op. cit., pp.319–20.

[37] CAPITAN, BREUIL, PEYRONY 1910, op. cit., p.13.

[38] H. BREUIL 1952. Quatre Certs Siècles d'Art Pariétal, Montignac, p.23.

[39] CAPITAN, BREUIL, PEYRONY 1910, op. cit., p.165.

[40] L. CAPITAN, H. BREUIL, AMPOULANGE 1904. Une nouvelle grotte préhistorique à parois gravées. La grotte de La Grèze, Académie des inscriptions et belles lettres. Comptes Rendus.

[41] e.g. GRAZIOSI 1960, op. cit., p.32.

[42] COUNT BEGOUEN 1929. The magic origin of prehistoric art, Antiquity, 3.

[43] Leroi-Gourhan (1965b, op. cit., p.313) has recently queried the identification of this damaged representation as a feline, preferring to see it as a horse.

[44] BREUIL 1952, op. cit., p.58.

[45] GRAZIOSI 1960, op. cit., p.33.

[46] E. RIVIERE 1897. La grotte de La Mouthe, Bulletin de la société d'anthropologie de Paris, 8, p.325.

[47] CAPITAN, BREUIL, PEYRONY 1910, op. cit., p.230.

[48] BREUIL 1952, op. cit., p.195.

[49] M. ASTRE 1926. Pourquoi les représentations pariétales des grottes et cavernes sont-elles presque absolument exclusives de l'iconographie humaine? Revue anthropologique.

[50] BREUIL 1952, op. cit., p.176.

[51] BEGOUEN 1929, op. cit., p.11.

[52] ASTRE 1926, op. cit., p.194.

[53] CAPITAN 1925, op. cit., p.319.

[54] G. H. LUQUET 1910. Sur les charactères des figures humaines dans l'art paléolithique, L'anthropologie, 21.

[55] COMTE H. BEGOUEN 1926. Quelques nouvelles figurations humaines préhistoriques dans les grottes de l'Ariège, Revue Anthropologique, p.188.

246

[56] BEGOUEN 1929, op. cit., p.17.

[57] See P. J. UCKO 1965, *Anthropomorphic figurines from Predynastic Egypt and Neolithic Crete*, London, part 5, chapters 1–2 for a discussion of the historical development of the Mother Goddess interpretation and its influence on the interpretation of human representations.

[58] BREUIL 1952, op. cit., p.234.

[59] GRAZIOSI 1960, op. cit., p.32.

[60] GIEDION 1962, op. cit., p.393.

[61] In his most recent work Leroi-Gourhan (1965b, *Préhistoire de l'Art Occidental*, Paris, pp.30–1) is less extreme in his condemnation of the use of ethnographic parallels.

[62] LAMING-EMPERAIRE 1962, op. cit., p.31.

[63] LEROI-GOURHAN 1965a, op. cit., p.218.

[64] A. LEROI-GOURHAN 1964. *Les Religions de la Préhistoire (Paléolithique)*, Paris, p.105.

[65] A. LEROI-GOURHAN 1963. *Art et Religion au Paléolithique Supérieur*, Paris, p.30; 1964, op. cit., pp.109–13.

[66] It is difficult to conclude anything from Leroi-Gourhan's use of these different words. They most likely reflect his cautious statement (1956b, Forward) that he is able only to guess at the vague outline of the main structure of Palaeolithic symbolism and that details of interpretation are bound to remain enigmatic. A typical statement (1964, op. cit., p.104; 1965b, op. cit., p.86) reads 'Another coupling appears constant, that of animals; . . an animal of group B (bison or aurochs) opposes an animal of group A which is practically always the horse . . . The principal theme is a bison-horse couple juxtaposed to the male-female theme'. Elsewhere (1963, op. cit., p.25) he writes that 'the central group of animals of group B . . . is framed, preceded and followed by animals of group A' and (1963, op. cit., p.27; 1965b, op. cit., p.87) that 'one or several animals of group A are associated with one or several animals of group B'. Most recently Leroi-Gourhan (1965b, op. cit., p.88) talks about 'associations of complementarity . . . associations of equivalent symbols', (1965b, op. cit., p.81) 'animals of group A frame or complete animals of group B'. (1965b, op. cit., p.105) 'female signs completed by the addition of animals . . . signs reinforced' by male representations and (1965b, op. cit., p.120) that 'the basis of the system depends on the alternation, the complementarity or the antagonism of the male and female essence'.

[67] In 1965b, op. cit., p.107, Leroi-Gourhan states that he has been unable to construct an evolutionary derivation for the male signs but has identified many of them as male simply because they are found in different positions from signs which he considers female.

[68] LEROI-GOURHAN 1964, op. cit., p.98.

[69] Ibid, p.104.

[70] Ibid, p.105.

[71] Ibid, p.103.

[72] A. LEROI-GOURHAN 1958. Le symbolisme des grands signes dans l'art pariétal paléolithique, *Bulletin de la Société Préhistorique Française*, 55, p.395.

[73] Ibid, p.395.

[74] LEROI-GOURHAN 1965b, op. cit., p.121.

[75] LEROI-GOURHAN 1964, op. cit., p.151.

[76] A. LAMING 1959. *Lascaux*, London; LAMING-EMPERAIRE 1962, op. cit.

[77] LAMING-EMPERAIRE 1962, op. cit., p.238.

[78] LAMING 1959, op. cit., p.186. LAMING-EMPERAIRE 1962, op. cit.,

p.282.

[79] LAMING-EMPERAIRE 1962, op. cit., pp.236–7.

[80] Ibid, p. 293.

[81] Ibid, p.294.

[82] Thus Leroi-Gourhan has suggested (1965b, op. cit., pp.126, 128) that panels of incomplete outlines and meanders may be the work of those attempting to recreate the themes of the main panels in a cave.

[83] LEROI-GOURHAN 1958, op. cit., pp.388–90.

[84] e.g. LAMING 1959, op. cit., p.96.

[85] GIEDION 1962, op. cit., p.100.

[86] From A. R. VERBRUGGE 1958. *Le Symbole de la Main dans la Préhistoire*, Milly-la-Foret, p.185, but not accepted by him.

[87] BREUIL 1952, op. cit., p.21.

[88] GRAZIOSI 1960, op. cit., p.33.

[89] C. ZERVOS 1959. *L'Art de l'Epoque de Renne en France*, Paris, p.81.

[90] LEROI-GOURHAN 1964, op. cit., pp.102–3.

Chapter 4

[1] We are grateful to Mr Peter Morton-Williams (Department of Anthropology, University College, London) for his comments on the section dealing with ethnographic material. We owe a deep debt of gratitude to Captain P. J. Trezise (Cairnes, Australia) for information about, as well as drawings and photographs of Australian rock art.

[2] BREUIL 1952. *Quatre Cents Siècles d'Art Pariétal*, Montignac, p.24.

[3] Ibid, figs 111, 112.

[4] As can be seen from the discussion of this problem in Th. MAINAGE 1921. *Les Religions de la Préhistoire. L'Age Paléolithique*, Paris, chapters 3, 5.

[5] See I. M. LEWIS forthcoming. Tribal

Society, *Encyclopaedia for Social Sciences*, for a discussion of terminology.

[6] S. F. NADEL 1954. *Nupe Religion*, London, p.29; Pl.3; N. W. G. MACINTOSH 1952. Paintings in Beswick Creek Cave, Northern Territory, *Oceania*, 22, 4, p.266.

[7] e.g. Analogies between the distribution of Australian and European Neolithic stone axes have illuminated the problem of the nature of trade in Neolithic Europe (e.g. G. CLARK 1965. Traffic in Stone Axe and Adze blades, *Economic History Review*, **18,** 1, pp.1–28); study of the worship of a divine king and cattle among 'primitive' people has enabled a higher degree of understanding than before of some aspects of historic (with writing) Egyptian religious beliefs and practices (e.g. H. FRANKFORT 1955. *Kingship and the Gods*, London, pp.162 passim, 198 passim); close examination of the uses, manufacture and disposal of small human figurines among both 'primitive' and 'peasant' societies has suggested very different, profane, interpretations for many of the archaeological human figurines which are usually interpreted as evidence of the worship of a Mother Goddess (e.g. UCKO 1965 op. cit., part 5); etc., etc. It is significant, therefore, that a recent book on Nigerian art (W. FAGG 1963, *Nigerian Images*, London, p.21) includes the following statement: 'the popular "hunting-magic" theory of prehistoric rock art satisfies only those who are exempt from any true understanding of the nature of tribal belief and who do not feel able to attribute any higher form of religion to the "primitive" peoples than the naive concept of homeopathic magic'.

[8] A point already made by M. VAN GENNEP 1925. A propos du Tote-

248

misme Préhistorique, *Actes du Congrès International d'Histoire des Religions*, 1923, I, p.335.

[9] e.g. C. P. MOUNTFORD 1961. The Artist and his Art in an Australian Aboriginal Society, in *The Artist in Tribal Society* (Ed.: M. W. Smith), London, pp. 7–8; F. D. MCCARTHY 1958. *Australian Aboriginal Rock Art*, Sydney, p.9; F. D. MCCARTHY 1960. The Cave Paintings of Groote Eylandt and Chasm Island, *Records of the American-Australian Scientific Expedition to Arnhem Land*, 2, p.299.

[10] F. D. MCCARTHY 1965. The Aboriginal Past: Archaeology and Material Equipment, in *Aboriginal Man in Australia* (Eds.: R. M. and C. H. Berndt), London, p.90.

[11] MOUNTFORD 1961, op. cit., p.13; a somewhat similar situation exists among the now sedentary East African Sandawe (TEN RAA, personal communication).

[12] MCCARTHY 1960, op. cit., p.389.

[13] MCCARTHY 1958, op. cit., p.12.

[14] H. BASEDOW 1925. *The Australian Aboriginal*, Adelaide, p.303.

[15] MACINTOSH 1952, op. cit., p.269.

[16] Unfortunately as stated by McCarthy in his Presidential Address to the Royal Society of New South Wales (1957, *Journal and Proceedings of the Royal Society of New South Wales*, 91, p.10) 'one of the main deficiencies in our knowledge of aboriginal art lies in the significance of many sites of rock engravings and cave paintings. Few aborigines have made comments worth recording about the engravings . . .'.

[17] A. P. ELKIN 1954. *The Australian Aborigines*, Sydney, p.232.

[18] J. H. VAUGHAN 1962. Rock Paintings and Rock Gongs among the Marghi of Nigeria, *Man*, 83, p.50.

[19] Ibid, p.51.

[20] e.g. F. D. MCCARTHY, M. MCARTHUR 1960. The Food Quest and the Time Factor in Aboriginal Economic Life, in *Records of the American-Australian Expedition to Arnhem Land* (Ed.: Mountford), London, pp.147, 190–2.

[21] A logical point made but largely ignored by G. H. LUQUET 1930 (English edition). *The Art and Religion of Fossil Man*, London, p.99.

[22] A. LAMING-EMPERAIRE 1962. *La Signification de l'Art Rupestre Paléolithique*, Paris, p.293.

[23] Ibid, p.206.

[24] E. PIETTE 1907. *L'Art Pendant l'Age du Renne*, Paris, p.106.

[25] In the same way it must be recognised that, even if all intentional representations inside a cave had some magical or ritual function, the occasional positive hand impression might have been accidental.

[26] It should be noted, however, that female 'sexual symbols' are common in open-air sites (see chapter 2, Content). If Leroi-Gourhan (see chapter 3 and below) is right in seeing the derivation of 'signs' from such sexual symbols this apparent differentiation of art in category 1 from art in categories 2 and 3 may be more misleading than real, a difference perhaps due to chronological development or archaeological sampling.

[27] e.g. A. LEROI-GOURHAN 1965b. *Préhistoire de l'Art Occidental*, Paris, p.41.

[28] Ibid, pp.114–6, 140.

[29] And these explanations must be included within the loosely defined archaeological use of the term 'Art for Art's Sake'.

[30] e.g. at Aldène, Le Tuc d'Audoubert, Montespan, Rouffignac, etc., etc.

[31] H. V. VALLOIS 1931. Les Empreintes de Pieds Humains des Préhistoriques du Midi de la France, *Palaeobiologica*,

4, pp.89–90.

32 J. CHARET 1948. Réflexions sur la Magie de la Chasse. II. Les Bisons d'argile du Tuc d'Audoubert *Bulletin de la Société Préhistorique Française*, 45, p.271.

33 e.g. S. GIEDION 1962. *The Eternal Present. The Beginnings of Art*, London, p.284.

34 E. PATTE 1960. *Les Hommes Préhistoriques et la Religion*, Paris, p.99; LUQUET 1930, op. cit., p.195.

35 LEROI-GOURHAN 1965b, op. cit., p.123, who admits that the footprints at Aldène conflict with this view.

36 BREUIL 1952, op. cit., p.23.

37 The fact that, as seen in the Art for Art's Sake section (see chapter 4, above) some category 1 art was allowed to become covered with habitation rubbish cannot in this connection be taken as strong evidence against a visual intention for Palaeolithic art, for many thousands of years may have elapsed between the original act of representation and the covering with habitation debris (see chapter 2, Dated Works of Parietal Art).

38 A. LAMING 1959. *Lascaux*, London, pp.105–11.

39 e.g. Ibid, p.184.

40 As has been stated in chapter 2, reindeer are frequently shown on mobile art. This has led Leroi-Gourhan (1965b, op. cit., p.73) to postulate a close relationship between mobile art and parietal art whereby the respective roles of these two art forms are interchangeable.

41 G. SIMONNET 1947. Une nouvelle plaquette de pierre gravée Magdalenienne de la grande grotte de Labastide. Commune de Labastide (Hautes-Pyrénées), *Bulletin de la Société Préhistorique Française*, 44, p.64.

42 LEROI-GOURHAN 1965b, op. cit., p.460, fig 794.

43 A. LEROI-GOURHAN 1964. *Les Réligions de la Préhistoire*, Paris, p.94; 1965a, *Le Geste et la Parole*, Paris, p.234.

44 e.g. in the cave reported by Macintosh (1952, op. cit., figs. 1, 2, pp.262–3) are 'two elongated paintings . . . completely infilled with red ochre . . . Without native interpretation they do not suggest any obvious diagnosis to a European, but to the native they are adequate naturalistic representations of long yams'. There is also a representation with 'some superficial resemblance to a female human figure . . . but it was a water lizard . . . a "devil-devil lizard, little weeny one go down waddy then go up trees".'

45 e.g. See the discussion and bibliography in UCKO 1965, op. cit., part 5.

46 P. A. LEASON 1939. A New View of the Western European Group of Quaternary Cave Art, *Proceedings of the Prehistoric Society*, 5.

47 See W. H. RIDDELL 1940. Dead or Alive?, *Antiquity*, 14, pp.158–62 for a refutation of some of the details of Leason's argument.

48 LAMING 1959, op. cit., p.160.

49 H. BREUIL 1957. En lisant 'L'Arte dell'Antica Età della Pietrà' de P. Graziosi, *Quaternia*, 4, p.237.

50 LEROI-GOURHAN 1965b, op. cit., p.119; 1958. Le Symbolisme des Grands Signes dans l'Art Periétal Paléolithique, *Bulletin de la Société Préhistorique Française*, 55, p.390; in 1964, op. cit., it is said to be less than three per cent of all animals.

51 It is significant in this context that the attack on the classic interpretation of Palaeolithic art by Laming (1959, op. cit., p.171) included only a footnoted reference to the Montespan bear.

250

[52] GRAZIOSI 1960, op. cit., p. 152.

[53] BREUIL 1957, op. cit., p.237.

[54] LEROI-GOURHAN 1964, op. cit., pp.138–9. Actually F. TROMBE and G. DUBUC (1947. Le Centre Préhistorique de Ganties-Montespan, *Archives de l'Institut de Paléontologie Humaine*, Memoire 22, Paris, p.69) report that in *some places* (our italics) in the room which contains the bear it was just possible to stand upright whereas in the chamber which contained the 'feline' the roof was relatively high. Leroi-Gourhan has also suggested (1965b, op. cit., p.313) that the holes in these clay representations must, on account of their regularity and disposition, have been made at the same time as, and as part of, the whole composition.

[55] J. BEATTIE 1964. *Other Cultures, Aims, Methods and Achievements in Social Anthropology*, London, pp. 219–20.

[56] Ibid, pp.223–4.

[57] This view was put most strongly by VAN GENNEP (1925, op. cit., p.333) who maintained that it was pointless even to talk about Palaeolithic totemism until it was known on what principles Palaeolithic *society* (our italics) had been organised.

[58] e.g. A. R. RADCLIFFE-BROWN 1952. The Sociological Theory of Totemism, in *Structure and Function in Primitive Society*, London, pp.126–7.

[59] BEATTIE 1964, op. cit., pp.222–3.

[60] G. LIENHARDT 1961. *Divinity and Experience. The Religion of the Dinka*, Oxford, p.107.

[61] Ibid, pp.114–5.

[62] e.g. Les Combarelles (L. CAPITAN, H. BREUIL, D. PEYRONY 1924. *Les Combarelles aux Eyzies*, Dordogne, Monaco); and Font de Gaume (L. CAPITAN, H. BREUIL, D. PEYRONY 1910. *La Caverne de Font Gaume aux Eyzies, Dordogne*, Monaco); and Le Gabillou (J. GAUSSEN 1964. *La Grotte Ornée du Gabillou, Bordeaux*).

[63] LEROI-GOURHAN 1965b, op. cit., p.260.

[64] A. LEROI-GOURHAN 1958. La Fonction des Signes dans les Sanctuaires Paléolith'iques, *Bulletin de la Société Préhistorique Française*, 55, p.310.

[65] Ibid, pp.246–7; ibid. p.259–60; GAUSSEN (1964, op. cit., GAUSSEN (1964, that the cave cannot be differentiated into chambers.

[66] LEROI-GOURHAN 1964, op. cit., p.97.

[67] LEROI-GOURHAN 1958, op. cit., p.310.

[68] LEROI-GOURHAN 1965b, op. cit., p.111.

[69] Leroi-Gourhan's views on this subject are scattered throughout his work; see especially 1958, op. cit., p.390; 1965b, op. cit., pp.78, 139–40.

[70] LEROI-GOURHAN 1965b, op. cit., p.82.

[71] LEROI-GOURHAN 1958, op. cit., p.517; 1965b, op. cit., pp.87–8.

[72] Unfortunately Leroi-Gourhan (1965b, op. cit.) has not published the numerical data (e.g. the total number of 'compositions') which would make it possible to test the statistical validity of these 'associations'.

[73] Ibid, p.271.

[74] See ibid, pp.51, 89, 150–1, 154, 254, 266 for example.

[75] Ibid, p.438.

[76] Eleven of the twenty-two Perigord caves ($\frac{1}{2}$) have compositions featuring stags, for example, against one of the three North caves ($\frac{1}{3}$). This difference is expressed as a 'stag-coefficient' for the North of $\frac{1}{3} \div \frac{1}{2} \times 100$. Such coefficients hardly seem an aid to understanding; indeed, they may give a spurious air of precision. Most people are chary of proportions based on small numbers, but 'coefficients' so based may inspire false confidence. If the 'true' expectation were 50 (as in the Perigord example)

one would in fact *not expect* exactly
$1\frac{1}{2}$ of the three North caves to
contain pictures of stags.

[77] LEROI-GOURHAN 1958, op. cit.,
pp.516–19.

[78] In 1965b, op. cit., p.82 he suggests
that in some areas the doe was
considered a large herbivore, while
in others it was accepted together
with the male deer and rare reindeer.

[79] Ibid, pp.82, 87.

[80] 18% according to Leroi-Gourhan,
1964, op. cit., p.98.

[81] $\chi^2 = 3.14$. This means that there is
a probability greater than 20% that
one would find at least as great a
difference in a sample of this size
even if there were no differences
between the distribution of oxen,
bison and horse (even adopting the
most generous test (not corrected for
continuity and pooling the results
for oxen and bison) the probability
is about 10%).

[82] LEROI-GOURHAN 1965b, op. cit.,
pp.109, 441; in 1964, op. cit., p.103
it is said that there are only 14
definable situations.

[83] Ibid, p.151.

[84] Ibid, pp.242–333.

[85] Ibid, pp.125–8.

[86] Ibid, pp.290–3.

[87] Ibid, p.121.

[88] Ibid, pp.104–7, 141, 453–5.

[89] LEROI-GOURHAN 1958, op. cit.,
p.388; 1965b, op. cit., p.107.

[90] LEROI-GOURHAN 1965b, op. cit.,
pp.104, 107–8, 453–5.

[91] Ibid, pp.108–9.

[92] Ibid, pp.117, 120; in 1964, op. cit.,
150, it is suggested that parts of caves
only were considered female.

[93] LEROI-GOURHAN 1965b, op. cit.,
pp.120–1, 147.

[94] Ibid, p.97.

[95] Ibid, p.461, fig 796.

[96] LEROI-GOURHAN 1965a, op. cit.,
p.234; 1965b, op. cit., p.120.

[97] LEROI-GOURHAN 1964, op. cit.,

pp.148–9.

[98] LAMING-EMPERAIRE 1962, op. cit.,
p.209.

[99] Ibid, p.211.

[100] LEROI-GOURHAN 1965b, op. cit.,
p.115.

Chapter 5

[1] An extremely important question
posed by G. H. LUQUET (1930, *The
Art and Religion of Fossil Man*,
London, p.29).

[2] COUNT BEGOUEN 1928. Empreintes
de doigts préhistoriques et de quelques dessins. *Institut International d'
Anthropologie.* IIIe Session Amster-
dam. 20–9 Septembre 1927, p.6.

[3] See LUQUET 1930, op. cit., pp.109–10.

[4] W. ARNDT 1962. The Nargorkun-
Narlinji Cult. *Oceania* 32, 3, pp.
316–7; see also M. J. MEGGITT 1962.
*A Study of the Walbiri Aborigines of
Central Australia*, Melbourne, p.221.

[5] The most important publications
on the parietal art in this cave are:
E. CARTAILHAC, H. BREUIL 1910.
Les Peintures et Gravures Murales
des Cavernes Pyrénéennes. *L'Anthropologie*, 21; COUNT BEGOUEN
1929. Les Peintures et Dessins de la
Grotte de Bédeilhac (Ariège). *Institut
fur Prähistorische und Ethngraphische
Kunst;* COUNT BEGOUEN 1931. Les
Modelages d'Argile de la Caverne de
Bédeilhac (Ariège), *Institut fur Prä-
historische und Ethnographische
Kunst*; Commandant OCTOBON 1939.
Grotte de Bédeilhac (Ariège), Pein-
tures et Gravures sur Parois ou Sol
de la Grotte, *Revue Anthropologique*
49; H. BREUIL, M. G. VIDAL 1949.
Les Fresques de la Galerie Vidal à
la caverne de Bédeilhac (Ariège),
*Bulletin de la Société Préhistorique
de l'Ariège*, 4; H. BREUIL 1952.
Quatre Cents Siècles d'Art Pariétal,
Montignac, pp.216–9.

Acknowledgments

We have the pleasure to record the kindness and trouble taken by a number of individuals in France who have helped us at various times to see the decorated caves and shelters which are not regularly open to the public. To Monsieur Max Bégouen, Monsieur M. Vézian, Madame Vesperini and Monsieur and Madame Soulié we acknowledge our gratitude. We owe to our friend Michel Bouillon (Laboratoire Souterrain, Moulis) many days of enjoyment, exploration, and discussion during visits to the caves of Le Tuc d'Audoubert and Les Trois Frères.

We should like to make it clear that we have enjoyed and benefited from our meeting and discussions with Professor André Leroi-Gourhan. We are convinced that his work on Palaeolithic art represents as important a contribution to this subject as those of Reinach and Breuil. That we do not always agree with his interpretations in no way implies that we are unaware of the brilliance of his analyses.

Since this book is aimed at the non-specialist as well as the specialist reader, we asked a number of colleagues and friends to read through and comment on sections of the manuscript of this work. Several of these are referred to in chapter notes but we would like to especially thank: Professor C. Daryll Forde (Department of Anthropology, University College London) for his comments on chapters 3 and 4; Mr Colin Groves (Unit of Primatology and Human Evolution, Royal Free Hospital School of Medicine, London) for his excellent comments and suggestions regarding our treatment of Pleistocene fauna; Dr J. P. Garlick (Department of Anthropology, University College London) for information about the stature and body proportions of Palaeolithic man, and advice on handling some of the numerical data in this book; Miss Mary-Jane Mountain (Department of Prehistoric Archaeology, University of Edinburgh) for her valuable comments on chapter 1.

Our gratitude is immense to several of our friends who allowed themselves to be used as guinea pigs and read through the entire book. We hope they know how much we have enjoyed and appreciated their help. They are: Mr Henry Hodges (Department of Conservation and Technology, Institute of Archaeology, London); Dr Ioan M. Lewis (Department of Anthropology, University College London); Dr Andrew Manasse (London); Mrs L. E. Ucko (Centre for the Study of Human Development, University of London); Mr John L. Williams (Departments of Prehistoric and Environmental Archaeology, Institute of Archaeology, London). We feel we must acknowledge separately our debt to Mr Michael Baxandall (The Warburg Institute, London) for many of the ideas in chapters 4 and 5 originate from his comments and discussion with him. Nevertheless we must take full responsibility for the opinions and conclusions in the book.

Messrs Martin Weaver and John Stengelhofen have provided us with most wonderful examples of their skill as artists, and we are deeply indebted to them. We are proud to be able to include in our book some of the superb photographs of M. Jean Vertut (Paris).

Acknowledgments are due to the following sources of illustrations. **Frontispiece** Photo: J. Vertut, courtesy Musée d'Aquitaine. **1a–c, e–k** After D. de Sonneville-Bordes, *Le Paléolithique Supérieur en Périgord*, 1960, Imprimerie Delmas, Bordeaux, 11, 4; 12, 6; 14, 10; 91, 10; 113, 3; 126, 2; 123, 19; 155, 1; 155, 12; 142, 7. **1d** After A. Leroi-Gourhan, *Préhistoire de l'Art Occidental*, 1965, Mazenod, Paris, 17. **2a–f** After D. de Sonneville-Bordes, op. cit., 186,15; 243, 18; 233, 3; 178, 4; 184,12; 190, 8. **2g** After A. Leroi-Gourhan, op. cit., 35. **3** Photo: J. Vertut, courtesy Musée d'Aquitaine; Leroi-Gourhan, op cit., 55. **4** Photo: J. Vertut. **5** After maps

253

in Leroi-Gourhan, op. cit., and P. Graziosi, *Palaeolithic Art*, 1960, London.
6a After Leroi-Gourhan, op. cit., 99; 486: and H. Breuil, *Quatre Cent* Siècles
d'Art Parietal, 1952, Montignac, 374. **6b, c, e** After authors' photos. **6d** After
Leroi-Gourhan, op. cit., 55; 271, and S. Giedion, *The Eternal Present: The Beginnings
of Art*, 1962, New York, 20; 107; 320; 321. **6f** After Graziosi, op. cit., 118c. **6g** After
Giedon, op. cit., 112. **7, 8** Photo: J. Vertut. **9** Photo: M. Farinha dos Santos
(*Vestígios de Pinturas Rupestres Descobertos na Gruta do Escoural*, 1964, Lisbon, 5).
10a, b Photo: Véronèse. **11** Photo: E. Ortega; S. Gimenez Reyna, *The Cave of La
Pileta*, 1965, Malaga, 5. **12** Photo: J. Vertut; Leroi-Gourhan, op. cit., 67. **13**
Photo: René. **14** Photo: Delvert. **15** and **16** Photo: M. Bouillon. **17** After Giedion,
op. cit., 51. **18** Photo: J. Vertut, courtesy M. Bégouen. **19** Photo: R. Laborie.
20 L. Capitan, H. Breuil, D. Peyrony, *La Caverne de Font de Gaume*, 1910, Monaco,
7. **21** Photo: M. Bouillon, courtesy M. Bégouen. **22** Photo: F. Windels; Caisse
Nationale des Monuments Historiques. **23** Photo: J. Vertut; Leroi-Gourhan,
op. cit., 323. **24** Photo: P. Graziosi (op. cit., 293). **25** Photo: F. Windels; Caisse
Nationale des Monuments Historiques. **26** After Photo: M. Bouillon. **27** Photo:
M. Bouillon, courtesy M. Bégouen. **28** Photo: Geb. **29** Photo: J. Vertut; Leroi-
Gourhan, op. cit., 313. **30** Photo: Authors. **31** Photo: Robert; Graziosi, op. cit.,
277. **32** Photo: M. Bouillon. **33** Photo: René. **34** Drawing: see **6f**. Photos: H. P.
Herdeg, courtesy A. B. Weider; Giedion, op. cit., 113; 116. **35** Photo: J. Vertut.
36 and **37** Photo: Authors, courtesy M. Bégouen. **38** Photo: H. Bégouen; H.
Bégouen, H. Breuil, *Les Cavernes du Volp*, 1958, Arts et Métiers Graphiques,
Paris, 39. **39** and **40** Photo: Authors, courtesy M. Bégouen. **41** Photo: Caisse
Nationale des Monuments Historiques; L. Capitan, H. Breuil, D. Peyrony, *Les
Combarelles aux Evzies (Dordogne)*, 1924, Paris, 15. **42** After Leroi-Gourhan,
op. cit., 392; Graziosi, op. cit., 164a. **43** Photo: Leroi-Gourhan (op. cit., 24).
44 Photo: Louis; Graziosi, op. cit., 287a. **45, 46** and **47** Photo: J. Vertut. **48** Photo:
J. Vertut; Leroi-Gourhan, op. cit., 66. **49** Photo: J. Vertut. **50** Photo: Authors.
51 Photo: P. Graziosi (op. cit., 221c). **52** Photo: Delvert. **53** Photo: Leroi-Gourhan
(op. cit., 722). **54** and **55** Photo: Authors. **56** Photo: Delvert. **57a** H. Breuil,
H. Obermaier, *The Cave of Altamira at Santillana del Mar, Spain*, 1935, Madrid,
58. **57b** H. Alcalde del Rio, H. Breuil, L. Sierra, *Les Cavernes de la Région Cantabrique*, 1911, Monaco, 169. **58** Photo: J. Vertut, courtesy Musée d'Aquitaine;
Leroi-Gourhan, op. cit., 273. **59** Leroi-Gourhan, op. cit., 794. **60** Photo: J. Vertut,
courtesy Musée d'Aquitaine; Leroi-Gourhan, op. cit., 272. **61** H. Breuil, Oeuvres
d'Art Paléolithiques inédites du Périgord et Art Oriental d'Espagne, *Revue Anthropologique*, 1927, 2. **62** H. Breuil, 1952, op. cit., 316. **63** Photo: J. Vertut. **64** Photo:
J. Vertut; Leroi-Gourhan, op. cit., 492. **65** After Breuil, op. cit., 334. **66** Photo:
J. Vertut; Leroi-Gourhan, op. cit., 494. **67** After Leroi-Gourhan, op. cit., 99; 486;
Breuil, op. cit., 374. **68** Photo: D. Garrod, Finding the earliest realistic portait in the
history of man, *Illustrated London News*, 1949. **69** Photo: René. **70** After Graziosi,
op. cit., 220b; Leroi-Gourhan, op. cit., 102. **71** After Photo: Geb. **72d–e, m–o, q, r–s,
u–v** After Leroi-Gourhan, op. cit., 352; 532; 77; 637; 339; 732; 79; 401; 13; 651; 85.
72f–g, j, p After Graziosi, op. cit., 126b; 119a; 228e; 129a. **72n, t** After J. Gaussen, *La
Grotte Ornée de Gabillou (près Mussidan, Dordogne)*, 1964, Imprimerie Delmas,
Bordeaux. 49; 54. **73** Photo: J. Vertut. **74** and **75** Photo: Delvert. **76** Photo: J. Gaussen
(op. cit., 65). **77** After Graziosi, op. cit., 127c. **78** After Capitan, Breuil, Peyrony, op.
cit., pl. XIIIb. **79** Photo: J. Vertut; Leroi-Gourhan, op. cit., 519. **80** Photo: E. Ortega;

S. Gimenez Reyna, *The Cave of Nerja*, 1965, Malaga, 22. **81** After Leroi-Gourhan, op. cit., 575. **82** Photo: J. Vertut; Leroi-Gourhan, op. cit., 310. **83** Photo: J. Vertut; Leroi-Gourhan, op. cit., 350. **84** Photo: L-R. Nougier, R. Robert, *The Cave of Rouffignac*, 1958, Newnes, London, 21. **85** Photo: Delvert. **86** Photo: Authors; Drawing: after authors' photo, courtesy M. Bégouen. **87** Photo: J. Cabré Aguiló, Figuras Antropomorfas de la Cueva de los Casares (Guadalajara), *Archivo Español de Arqueología*, 1940, 2, 9. **88** Photo: Authors. **89a** Photo: M. Bouillon, courtesy M. Bégouen. **89b** Bégouen, Breuil, op. cit., 20. **89c** After Leroi-Gourhan, op. cit., 57. **90** and **91** After authors' photos. **92a–c** After Leroi-Gourhan, op. cit., 56; 514; 368. **92d** After Giedion, op. cit., 82. **93f** After Giedion, op. cit., 179. **93i, k** After Graziosi, op. cit., 269; 266e. **94** Photo: J. Vertut. **95** Photo: H. P. Herdeg, courtesy A. B. Weider; Giedion, op. cit., 250. **96** Photo: P. Trezise. **97** Photo: P. Graziosi (op. cit., 168b). **98** Photo: J. Vertut; Leroi-Gourhan, op. cit., 9. **99** Photo: Delvert. **100** Photo: J. Vaughan, courtesy B. Fagg. **101** Photo: A. Leroi-Gourhan (op cit., 651). **102** Photo: V. Reynolds. **103** Photo: Geb. **104** After Leroi-Gourhan, op. cit., 291; Capitan, Breuil, Peyrony, 1924, op. cit. **105** After Leroi-Gourhan, op. cit., 293; Capitan, Breuil, Peyrony, 1910, op. cit. **106** After Leroi-Gourhan, op. cit., 259; Gaussen, op. cit.

Index

Sites, subjects and principal references to authors in the text (cave sites in italics)